7-8

POETIC DESIGN

James G. Hepburn

POETIC DESIGN

Handbook and Anthology

THE MACMILLAN COMPANY, *New York*

CHATTO AND WINDUS LTD. /*Wilfred Owen*/ "Has Your Soul Sipped?," "Shadwell Stair," "Insensibility," "Greater Love," "Anthem for Doomed Youth," "A Terre," from *Collected Poems of Wilfred Owen,* by permission of Mr. Harold Owen and the publishers.

J. M. DENT & SONS LTD. /*Dylan Thomas*/ "The force that through the green fuse drives the flower," "In my craft or sullen art," "A Refusal to Mourn the Death by Fire of a Child in London," from *Collected Poems of Dylan Thomas,* by permission of the Literary Executors of the Dylan Thomas Estate and the publishers.

DOUBLEDAY & COMPANY, INC. /*Rudyard Kipling*/ "Danny Deever," from *Barrack Room Ballads* by Rudyard Kipling. Reprinted by permission of Doubleday & Company, New York, The Macmillan Co. of Canada, Limited, and Mrs. George Bambridge. /*Robert Graves*/ "Hell," "The Philosopher," "The Thieves," from *Collected Poems* by Robert Graves. Reprinted by permission of Doubleday & Company, New York, and International Authors N. V.

E. P. DUTTON & CO., INC. /*Lawrence Durrell*/ "Nemea," from *Collected Poems— Lawrence Durrell.* Copyright, © 1956, 1960, by Lawrence Durrell. Reprinted by permission of E. P. Dutton & Co., Inc.

iv

ACKNOWLEDGMENTS

FABER AND FABER LTD. /*T. S. Eliot*/ "The Love Song of J. Alfred Prufrock," "Rhapsody on a Windy Night," "The Hollow Men," from *Collected Poems 1909–1962* by T. S. Eliot. /*Lawrence Durrell*/ "Nemea," from *Collected Poems—Lawrence Durrell*. /*Stephen Spender*/ "Weep, Girl, Weep," from *The Edge of Being* by Stephen Spender. /*Thom Gunn*/ "The Unsettled Motorcyclist's Vision of His Death," from *The Sense of Movement* by Thom Gunn.

FARRAR, STRAUS & GIROUX, INC. /*Robert Lowell*/ "Commander Lowell," reprinted from *Life Studies* by Robert Lowell, by permission of Farrar, Straus & Giroux, Inc. Copyright © 1959 by Robert Lowell.

HARCOURT, BRACE & WORLD, INC. /*e. e. cummings*/ "All in green went my love riding": Copyright, 1923, 1951, by E. E. Cummings. Reprinted from his volume *Poems 1923–1954* by permission of Harcourt, Brace & World, Inc. "Humanity i love you": Copyright, 1925, 1953, by E. E. Cummings. Reprinted from his volume *Poems 1923–1954* by permission of Harcourt, Brace & World, Inc. /*T. S. Eliot*/ "The Love Song of J. Alfred Prufrock," "The Hollow Men," and "Rhapsody on a Windy Night": From *Collected Poems 1909–1962* by T. S. Eliot, Copyright, 1936, by Harcourt, Brace & World, Inc; Copyright © 1963, 1964 by T. S. Eliot. Reprinted by permission of the publishers.

HARVARD UNIVERSITY PRESS /*Emily Dickinson*/ "Success is counted sweetest," "The soul selects her own society," "After great pain, a formal feeling comes," "Because I could not stop for death," "My life closed twice before its close." Reprinted by permission of the publishers from Thomas H. Johnson, Editor, *The Poems of Emily Dickinson*, Cambridge, Mass.: The Belknap Press of Harvard University Press, Copyright, 1951, 1955, by The President and Fellows of Harvard College.

HOLT, RINEHART AND WINSTON, INC. /*Robert Frost*/ "The Pasture," " 'Out, Out—,' " "Fire and Ice," "Dust of Snow," "Stopping by Woods on a Snowy Evening," "The Lockless Door," "Once by the Pacific," "Acquainted with the Night," "Canis Major," "A Drumlin Woodchuck," "Desert Places," "Neither Out Far Nor In Deep," "Provide, Provide," "Not All There," "In Divés' Dive,", "The Subverted Flower," "It Bids Pretty Fair," from *Complete Poems of Robert Frost*. Copyright 1916, 1921, 1923, 1928, 1930, 1939, 1947 by Holt, Rinehart and Winston, Inc. Copyright 1936, 1942, 1944, 1951, © 1956, 1958 by Robert Frost. Copyright © 1964 by Lesley Frost Ballantine. Reprinted by permission of Holt, Rinehart and Winston, Inc. /*A. E. Housman*/ "In the morning, in the morning," "They say my verse is sad: no wonder," "I did not lose my heart in summer's even," "Epitaph on an Army of Mercenaries," "The chestnut casts his flambeaux," from *The Collected Poems of A. E. Housman*. Copyright 1922 by Holt, Rinehart and Winston, Inc. Copyright 1936, 1950 by Barclays Bank Ltd. Copyright © 1964 by Robert E. Symons. Reprinted by permission of Holt, Rinehart and Winston, Inc. "Be Still, My Soul," " 'Is my team ploughing?,' " "1887," from "A Shropshire Lad"—Authorised Edition—from *The Collected Poems of A. E. Housman*. Copyright 1939, 1940, © 1959 by Holt, Rinehart and Winston, Inc. Reprinted by permission of Holt, Rinehart and Winston, Inc.

LITTLE, BROWN AND COMPANY /*Emily Dickinson*/ "After great pain a formal feeling comes," from *The Complete Poems of Emily Dickinson*. Copyright 1929, © 1957 by Mary L. Hampson, by permission of Little, Brown and Co.

LIVERIGHT PUBLISHING CORPORATION /*Hart Crane*/ "Garden Abstract," "Moment Fugue," from *The Collected Poems of Hart Crane*. By permission of Liveright, Publishers, N.Y. Copyright © 1961, by Liveright Publishing Corp.

THE MACMILLAN COMPANY, NEW YORK /*E. A. Robinson*/ "Eros Turannos," from *Collected Poems* by E. A. Robinson. Copyright 1916 by E. A. Robinson, Renewed 1944 by Ruth Nivison. /*W. B. Yeats*/ "When You Are Old," Copyright 1906 by The

ACKNOWLEDGMENTS

Macmillan Company, Renewed 1934 by W. B. Yeats. "No Second Troy," "The Coming of Wisdom with Time," "On Hearing that the Students . . . ," Copyright 1912 by The Macmillan Company, Renewed 1940 by Bertha Georgie Yeats. "The Wild Swans at Coole," Copyright 1919 by The Macmillan Company, Renewed 1946 by Bertha Georgie Yeats. "The Second Coming," Copyright 1924 by The Macmillan Company, Renewed 1952 by Bertha Georgie Yeats. "Sailing To Byzantium," "Leda and the Swan," "Among School Children," Copyright 1928 by The Macmillan Company, Renewed 1956 by Bertha Georgie Yeats. "Crazy Jane Talks with the Bishop," "After Long Silence," Copyright 1933 by The Macmillan Company, Renewed 1961 by Bertha Georgie Yeats. "Lapis Lazuli," "The Spur," "The Circus Animals' Desertion," Copyright 1940 by Georgie Yeats. "To a Squirrel at Kyle-na-no," Copyright 1919 by The Macmillan Company, Renewed 1946 by Bertha Georgie Yeats, all from *Collected Poems* by W. B. Yeats, reprinted with permission of The Macmillan Company, New York, The Macmillan Company of Canada, Limited, A. P. Watt & Son, London, and Mr. M. B. Yeats. /*Thomas Hardy*/ "Epitaph on a Pessimist," from *Collected Poems* by Thomas Hardy, Copyright 1925 by The Macmillan Company, Renewed 1953 by Lloyds Bank Ltd.

THE MACMILLAN COMPANY OF CANADA LIMITED /*Thomas Hardy*/"On an Invitation to the United States," "The Darkling Thrush," "The Ruined Maid," "In Tenebris," "The Convergence of the Twain," "When I Set Out for Lyonnesse," "The Going," "Regret Not Me," "His Heart," "The Wound," "Transformations," "At the Piano," "Epitaph on a Pessimist," "In Time of 'The Breaking of Nations,' " from *The Collected Poems of Thomas Hardy* by permission of The Estate of Thomas Hardy, Macmillan & Co., Ltd., London, and The Macmillan Company of Canada Limited.

MANCHESTER UNIVERSITY PRESS /*John Clare*/ "Song Last Day," "March Violet," by permission of the publishers.

NEW DIRECTIONS /*Ezra Pound*/ "The Tomb at Akr Çaar," "A Virginal," from *Personae* by Ezra Pound. Copyright 1926, 1954 by Ezra Pound. /*Wilfred Owen*/ "Has Your Soul Sipped?," "Shadwell Stair," "Insensibility," "Greater Love," "Anthem for Doomed Youth," "A Terre," from *Collected Poems of Wilfred Owen*. Copyright © Chatto & Windus, Ltd., 1963. /*Dylan Thomas*/ "The Force that Through the Green Fuse Drives the Flower," "A Refusal to Mourn the Death by Fire of a Child in London," "In My Craft or Sullen Art," from *The Collected Poems of Dylan Thomas*. Copyright 1953 Dylan Thomas. Reprinted by permission of the publisher, New Directions, New York.

OXFORD UNIVERSITY PRESS, INC. /*Gerard Manley Hopkins*/ "The Habit of Perfection," "God's Grandeur," "The Lantern Out of Doors," "The Windhover," "Spring and Fall," from *Poems of Gerard Manley Hopkins*, Third Edition, edited by W. H. Gardner. Copyright 1948 by Oxford University Press, Inc. Reprinted by permission. /*Conrad Aiken*/ "Dead Leaf in May," from *Selected Poems* by Conrad Aiken. Copyright © 1961 by Conrad Aiken. Reprinted by permission of Oxford University Press, Inc.

RANDOM HOUSE, INC., ALFRED A. KNOPF, INC. /*Wallace Stevens*/ "Thirteen Ways of Looking at a Blackbird," (*Harmonium*), "Domination of Black," copyright 1923, 1951 by Wallace Stevens; "The House Was Quiet and the World Was Calm" (*Transport to Summer*), copyright 1942, 1947 by Wallace Stevens. Reprinted from *Collected Poems of Wallace Stevens* by permission of Alfred A. Knopf, Inc.

CHARLES SCRIBNER'S SONS /*Edwin Arlington Robinson*/ The following poems by Edwin Arlington Robinson are reprinted with the permission of Charles Scribner's Sons: "Richard Cory," "The House on the Hill," and "Luke Havergal," from *The Children of the Night* (1897) and "For a Dead Lady," from *The Town Down the River*. Copyright 1910 Charles Scribner's Sons; renewal copyright 1938 Ruth Nivison.

THE SOCIETY OF AUTHORS /*A. E. Housman*/ "In the morning, in the morning,"

ACKNOWLEDGMENTS

"They say my verse is sad: no wonder," "I did not lose my heart in summer's even," "Epitaph on an Army of Mercenaries," "The chestnut casts his flambeaux," "Be Still, My Soul," " 'Is my team ploughing,' " "1887," reprinted by permission of The Society of Authors as the literary representative of the Estate of the late A. E. Housman, and Messrs. Jonathan Cape Ltd., publishers of A. E. Housman's *Collected Poems.*

A. P. WATT & SON /*Arnold Bennett*/ "There was a young man of Montrose," used by permission of Mrs. Cheston Bennett.

THE VIKING PRESS, INC. /*D. H. Lawrence*/ "The Song of a Man Who Has Come Through," "What Ails Thee?—," "Tortoise Shout," "To Be Superior," "Puss-puss," "The English Are So Nice!," "Glory of Darkness" (two versions), "Bavarian Gentians" (two versions), from *The Complete Poems of D. H. Lawrence,* ed. Vivian de Sola Pinto and F. Warren Roberts. Copyright 1923, 1929 by Frieda Lawrence Ravagli, Copyright 1933 by Frieda Lawrence, Copyright 1950 by Frieda Lawrence Ravagli, Copyright © 1964 by Angelo Ravagli and C. M. Weekley, Executors to the Estate of Frieda Lawrence. All Rights Reserved. Reprinted by permission of The Viking Press, Inc.

YALE UNIVERSITY PRESS /*George Starbuck*/ "Fable for Flipped Lid," from *Bone Thoughts* by George Starbuck. Reprinted by permission of the publisher.

———

Some details of this book draw upon the writings of Richard Harter Fogle, *The Imagery of Keats and Shelley,* John F. Lynen, *The Pastoral Art of Robert Frost,* I. A. Richards, *Principles of Literary Criticism,* and George Wright, *The Poet in the Poem.* I would like to thank James Rosier of the University of Pennsylvania for advice on the Middle English material, and John Wallace of Johns Hopkins University for suggesting several poems for the anthology.

PREFACE

This text aims at once to serve those teachers who wish to have detailed discussions and exercises covering the chief familiar elements of poetry, and to serve those who desire an anthology large enough to use by itself. The discussions proceed from relatively simple matters to more complex; the exercises for each discussion are similarly arranged. The approach is analytical, and presupposes no special knowledge on the part of the student. The anthology covers in chronological order two hundred and fifty poems of all the major and some of the minor English and American poets. It contains ten poems of more than a hundred lines each, and represents six poets—Shakespeare, Donne, Blake, Hardy, Yeats, and Frost—with fourteen to seventeen poems apiece. The principle of selection was to rely upon standard poems for somewhat more than two-thirds of the material and for the rest to offer good and great poems that have rarely if ever appeared in an introductory text before.

The Byron selection needs explanation. The choice seemed to be between a truncated and marred canto of *Don Juan* or *Childe Harold* and several of the pretty, conventional lyrics such as "She Walks in Beauty." In the end, some unfamiliar poems were chosen that, despite defects, may be more satisfactory.

The Middle English poems have an introductory note on pronunciation that some teachers may want to use. Throughout the book all *ed*, *es*, and *e* endings normally silent to the modern reader are marked with an accent when they are to be pronounced as syllables. Annotating of unfamiliar words and allusions has been generally confined to Middle English poems and to others such as "Lycidas" which offer too many problems for the student to be expected to handle on his own. The intention is to make a reasonable demand upon the student's independent awareness of the unfamiliar. Most of such words and allusions can be found in the ordinary desk dictionary or their meanings adequately inferred from the context.

JAMES G. HEPBURN
University of Rhode Island

CONTENTS

(Chronological anthology of 250 poems. Italicized page
numbers refer to poems appearing in Parts One and
Two.)

INTRODUCTION

Among the old-fashioned ways of regarding poetry, the most respectful was to treat it as wisdom, something remote from ordinary life and observed at an exalted height. Among the new-fashioned ways, the most familiar is to treat it as fun, something indulged in by babies who rhyme sounds in their cradles and by used-car salesmen who say cash for your car. These two views suggest different things not only about the nature of poetry but also about the way to write it, teach it, study it, and read it.

Here is an untitled poem that has wisdom in it and fun, but does not tell us much and fails to make us laugh.

> In the morning, in the morning,
>   In the happy field of hay,
> Oh they looked at one another
>   By the light of day.
>
> In the blue and silver morning
>   On the haycock as they lay,
> Oh they looked at one another
>   And they looked away.

The poet, A. E. Housman, has omitted two seemingly important pieces of information: who *they* are, and why they look away from one another. Let us supply an answer. *They* are eight farm dogs that ought to be out herding the sheep, and they look away from one another when they hear the farmer coming after them. Not a satisfactory answer, but why not? And suppose we find a satisfactory answer, and explain why it is satisfactory: we have still to ask why Housman chose not to provide the information—what the difference is between a poem

1

with the information in it and Housman's with the information only implied.

There are other curious things about the poem. One piece of information Housman gives four times: the fact that it is morning. Why should he do that? And why should he say that a field of hay is happy? Why should he say that the morning is blue and silver rather than that the sky is? Why did he make the second stanza rhyme with the first? Why did he repeat the whole line *Oh they looked at one another*? Why indeed did he write a poem instead of saying something like this: On a beautiful morning in a hayfield, two lovers looked at one another and realized that their feelings were no longer romantic.

The following chapters attempt to deal with such problems in a certain systematic fashion: by close examination of the elements of poetry. (There are other ways, equally good, that are usually dealt with in advanced courses.) Eventually the student should be able to return to Housman's poem and offer a reasoned explanation of why it is the way it is. What view of poetry seems to be implicit in such a program? Certainly not that poetry is wisdom, most certainly not that poetry is fun, but rather that in its instances—poem by poem—it is a kind of machine that can be taken apart and put back together again, or perhaps a flower that can be examined under a microscope. And the student is a mechanic or scientist, the teacher a master technician, and the result knowledge (not wisdom). Then there is another question: of what use is it to learn how a poem ticks? This question is similar to a long-familiar question: why read poetry to begin with? The answer that is often provided may be unconvincing: understanding poetry makes us able to enjoy it, and poetry (whether it is wisdom or fun or a machinelike flower) is worth enjoying. One of the great English poets, William Wordsworth, took a dim view of the first part of this answer. He said: "We murder to dissect." The flower wilts under the microscope. Most modern teachers would agree with him only to the extent of acknowledging that understanding poetry does not necessarily make us able to enjoy it. Presumably one student might write a fine analysis of a poem without appreciating it as much as a less analytically inclined student. Such complications are perhaps summed up in the words of another English poet, Oscar Wilde, when he said: "Education is an admirable thing, but it is well to remember from time to time that nothing that is worth knowing can be taught."

Poetry is one of the things worth knowing—knowing now in the sense of both understanding and enjoying. It is, of course, neither a machine nor a flower; and the fundamental way of knowing it remains, as always, to read it. Read it aloud, slowly, articulating meaning, rhythm, rhyme, beauty, energy.

PART ONE

Aspects of a Poem

1

THE GENERAL SENSE OF A POEM: PART 1

Words Unknown and Known

Omar Khayyam, who spoke English and Persian, thought that all he needed for paradise was a book of verse, a tree, a jug of wine, and the person he loved. But if the first poem in the book of verse were "Canis Major," he would also have needed a dictionary. Without knowing the meaning of the Latin phrase *Canis Major,* he might mistakenly have thought the poem was about a man and his dog, or even about two dogs.

CANIS MAJOR

The great Overdog.
That heavenly beast
With a star in one eye,
Gives a leap in the east.

He dances upright   5
All the way to the west
And never once drops
On his forefeet to rest.

I'm a poor underdog,
But tonight I will bark   10
With the great Overdog
That romps through the dark.

—Robert Frost

The phrase *Canis Major,* along with many other frequently used foreign words, appears in even small English dictionaries. It refers to a group of stars named the Greater Dog that includes the very bright star Sirius. The speaker of the poem (not Robert Frost but the *I* in the last stanza who refers to himself as an underdog) is evidently looking up at these stars as they cross the sky and is feeling unusually happy.

In paradise, of course, no one would require Omar Khayyam to know what the phrase *Canis Major* means, or even what the general sense of the poem is, so perhaps he would have declined the dictionary. But in college the student may need a dictionary to prevent his poetry course from being the opposite of paradise. He will use it much more for English words than for foreign:

DELIGHT IN DISORDER

A sweet disorder in the dress
Kindles in clothes a wantonness:
A lawn about the shoulders thrown
Into a fine distraction,
An erring lace, which here and there   5
Enthralls the crimson stomacher,
A cuff neglectful, and thereby
Ribands to flow confusedly,
A winning wave (deserving note)
In the tempestuous petticoat,   10
A careless shoe-string, in whose tie
I see a wild civility,
Do more bewitch me than when art
Is too precise in every part.

—*Robert Herrick*

Here the general sense may seem clear enough immediately. The speaker (again not the poet but the *I* of the third from last line) is saying that he likes a woman to wear clothes in a seemingly casual way. But at least one line probably appears nonsensical: who ever heard of a woman throwing a lawn about her shoulders? Recognition of such nonsense suggests an answer: *lawn* must have a special meaning. What would a woman throw about her shoulders? The dictionary says that *lawn* can mean *a fine, thin linen or cotton fabric*. There are other words, too—*enthralls, stomacher, ribands*—that may need looking up to clarify the details of the poem. And there is one word, *wantonness,* whose meaning poses a special problem. If we think we know what the word means—immodest conduct—we will infer that the speaker is recommending a carelessness of dress that suggests a carelessness of morality in the wearer. Is he? If we turn to the dictionary we find that the word also means *being untied*. Is the speaker simply recommending a sweet untidiness? The problem is different from that with *lawn*, for there the one familiar meaning, *a grass plot*, cannot possibly apply, whereas here someone might argue that *immodesty* applies as much as does *untidiness*. His argument might be as follows: *wantonness, erring, enthralls, tempestuous, careless*, and *bewitch* are all words that suggest that the speaker is thinking about the sexual attractiveness of a woman as part of his concern for the way she dresses; and while he is not recommending immoral behavior, he seems clearly to be opposed to prissy and prudish women as well as to prissy and prudish wearing of clothes. What we have is a word with two meanings that are both in some degree appropriate in the particular poem. This complexity of meaning is called *ambiguity;* and when it is properly handled, it is considered a desirable poetic quality. We can also see that the complex meaning of a single word has bearing upon the general sense of a poem. Earlier in this paragraph the general sense of "Delight in Disorder" was summarized thus: *the speaker . . . is saying that he likes a woman to wear clothes in a seemingly casual way.* It needs amending to include the speaker's saying that he is attracted to the woman who likes to wear clothes in a seemingly casual way.

The dictionary, then, is useful in understanding the general sense of a poem, and the student will be expected as an automatic part of his work to look up unknown words, known words that seem to make no sense, and known words that he might guess have relevant unknown meanings. Sometimes he will not so much need a dictionary as a moment's thought. What, for example, are two familiar meanings of *heavenly* that are used simultaneously by Robert Frost in the second line of "Canis Major"? At other times neither thought nor the ordinary dictionary will be enough. When the student comes across a name from history or mythology, the dictionary reference, if there is one, may be too brief to be meaningful. He should turn to an encyclopedia, a dictionary of mythology, or another likely source.

EXERCISES

1. The following poem concerns a person's reflection upon his impending death, which he imagines as a return to the sea from which he came.

CROSSING THE BAR

Sunset and evening star,
    And one clear call for me!
And may there be no moaning of the bar,
    When I put out to sea,

But such a tide as moving seems asleep,   5
    Too full for sound and foam,
When that which drew from out the boundless deep
    Turns again home.

Twilight and evening bell,
    And after that the dark!   10
And may there be no sadness of farewell,
    When I embark;

For tho' from out our bourne of Time and Place
    The flood may bear me far,
I hope to see my Pilot face to face   15
    When I have crossed the bar.

—Alfred Lord Tennyson

a. Look up the following words and find meanings for them appropriate to the general sense of the poem: *bar, moaning, drew, deep, bourne.*

b. Explain why the specific nautical meaning of *deep*—the interval between two successive marked fathoms on a sounding line—is inappropriate to the poem.

c. Explain why Tennyson chooses the word *Pilot* to refer to God.

d. Keeping in mind the general sense of the poem as given at the beginning of the exercise, show that *moaning* is used in an ambiguous sense.

  2.

WHEN I SET OUT FOR LYONNESSE

When I set out for Lyonnesse,
    A hundred miles away,
    The rime was on the spray,
And starlight lit my lonesomeness
When I set out for Lyonnesse   5
    A hundred miles away.

What would bechance at Lyonnesse
    While I should sojourn there
    No prophet durst declare,

Nor did the wisest wizard guess   10
What would bechance at Lyonnesse
While I should sojourn there.

When I came back from Lyonnesse
With magic in my eyes,
All marked with mute surmise   15
My radiance rare and fathomless,
When I came back from Lyonnesse
With magic in my eyes!

—*Thomas Hardy*

a. Look up the following words if you do not know their appropriate meanings: *rime, spray, bechance, sojourn, durst, wizard, marked, surmise, rare, fathomless.*

b. Do *rime, spray, marked,* and *rare* have ambiguities of meaning—multiple meanings—that are relevant to the poem? Explain your answer in each case.

c. Look up the word *Lyonnesse.* If you cannot find it in a college dictionary, try a large dictionary. (Note that some dictionaries list names of places separately in an appendix.) If you cannot find it there, or cannot find enough information there, try an encyclopedia, a dictionary of mythology, or a book on Hardy's poetry.

d. Suppose that what happened at Lyonnesse was that the speaker of the poem fell in love. Given what Lyonnesse refers to, explain the double meaning (not necessarily dictionary meaning) of *magic* in the third stanza. Again knowing what Lyonnesse refers to, explain how it can be *a hundred miles away.* As a corollary, explain why Hardy chooses to use Lyonnesse rather than an actual place.

e. What meaning of Lyonnesse emerges from the poem itself, different from, or more general than, the meaning given in the dictionary? Your answer may help explain why the supposition that the speaker fell in love does not say very much—since according to Hardy, not the wisest wizard could guess what would happen at Lyonnesse.

3. In the following poem the speaker reflects upon past and present attempts to describe such beauty as his beloved possesses.

SONNET 106

When in the chronicle of wasted time
I see descriptions of the fairest wights,
And beauty making beautiful old rhyme
In praise of ladies dead and lovely knights,
Then, in the blazon of sweet beauty's best,   5

Of hand, of foot, of lip, of eye, of brow,
I see their antique pen would have expressed
Even such a beauty as you master now.
So all their praises are but prophecies
Of this our time, all you prefiguring;   10
And, for they looked but with divining eyes,
They had not skill enough your worth to sing:
For we which now behold these present days,
Have eyes to wonder, but lack tongues to praise.

—*William Shakespeare*

    a. What single or multiple meanings of the following words are appropriate to the poem? *Chronicle, wasted, wights, rhyme, blazon, antique, master, prefiguring, for, but, divining.*

    b. Two of the preceding words have meanings that suggest what might be the sex of the person addressed in the poem. Explain.

    c. What other words in the poem have dictionary meanings that might suggest an answer contradictory to the previous answer? Given the way Shakespeare uses both sets of words, what is the probable sex of the person addressed?

ADDITIONAL EXERCISES

The following poems may be particularly useful: Sir Walter Ralegh, "The Wood, the Weed, the Wag," p. 192; William Shakespeare, "Sonnet 33," p. 198; Sir Thomas Wyatt, "Who so List to Hunt," p. 190; John Keats, "On the Sonnet," p. 258; Wilfred Owen, "A Terre," p. 331; Gerard Manley Hopkins, "The Habit of Perfection," p. 293.

Sentence Construction and Sentence Sense

    A few pages ago "Delight in Disorder" was spoken of as an easy poem to understand in a general way. But anyone reading the poem for the first time might find it a muddle, and the reason would probably be its complicated sentence construction.

DELIGHT IN DISORDER

A sweet disorder in the dress
Kindles in clothes a wantonness:
A lawn about the shoulders thrown
Into a fine distraction,
An erring lace, which here and there   5
Enthralls the crimson stomacher,

> A cuff neglectful, and thereby
> Ribands to flow confusedly,
> A winning wave (deserving note)
> In the tempestuous petticoat,   10
> A careless shoe-string, in whose tie
> I see a wild civility,
> Do more bewitch me than when art
> Is too precise in every part.

The first two lines are easy enough: disorder kindles wantonness: sub-ject-verb-object. Anyone can look up *wantonness* in the dictionary without feeling that his grasp on the two lines will fall apart while he is gone. The next two lines, though, provide only a subject, *lawn,* with a modifying phrase. Where is the verb, or verb and object, to make the new thought complete? The next two lines do not have it, but have instead another subject, *lace,* modified by a subordinate clause, *which . . . enthralls;* and the new subject itself lacks a main verb. The same thing happens in the next two lines, the next two after that, and again the next two. All the while, *lawn* and *lace* dangle without their verb. The verb finally appears in the next-to-last line: *do bewitch.* Lawn and lace and cuff and so forth *do bewitch* the speaker.

```
       disorder                    kindles
        lawn
        lace
   cuff and ribands              do bewitch
   wave in the petticoat
      shoe-string
```

Once we see what the sentence structure is, we can more easily grasp the sense of the whole poem. We can also realize that Herrick arranged his complicated material neatly. Beginning with lines 3 and 4, every two lines gives a new item in his series.

Compare "Delight in Disorder" with "Canis Major," and observe how much simpler Frost's poem is.

CANIS MAJOR

> The great Overdog.
> That heavenly beast
> With a star in one eye,
> Gives a leap in the east.
>
> He dances upright   5
> All the way to the west

> And never once drops
> On his forefeet to rest.
>
> I'm a poor underdog,
> But tonight I will bark   10
> With the great Overdog
> That romps through the dark.

The first line lacks a verb for its subject, but the period at the end makes clear that the line is an announcement, just like the title, or like Herrick's title. The reader is not left waiting for something. The basic construction of the rest proceeds thus:

Stanza 1   beast------------gives

Stanza 2   He-------------dances . . . (and never) drops

Stanza 3   I-------------am (but)
            I------------will bark

The main stumbling block to understanding Frost's poem lies not with the sentence construction but with the Latin phrase. Poems differ, and have to be met individually. When the general drift of a poem is unclear, analyzing sentences will usually be of some help. As the following exercises show, the problems are not always solved by finding subjects and their verbs. There are problems of omitted words, unusual placing of modifiers, reference of pronouns—all the problems of the way a sentence is put together.

EXERCISES

1.

AT THE PIANO

> A woman was playing,
>   A man looking on;
>   And the mold of her face,
>   And her neck, and her hair,
>   Which the rays fell upon   5
>   Of the two candles there,
> Sent him mentally straying
>   In some fancy-place
>   Where pain had no trace.
> A cowled Apparition   10
>   Came pushing between;
>   And her notes seemed to sigh;
>   And the light to burn pale,

As a spell numbed the scene.
But the maid saw no bale,   15
And the man no monition;
And Time laughed awry,
And the Phantom hid nigh.

—Thomas Hardy

a. Look up the following words if you do not know their appropriate meanings: *cowled, apparition, bale, monition, awry, phantom.*

b. Analyze the sentence construction. Try to solve the problems of the first sentence before proceeding to the second, of the second before proceeding to the third. Your analysis should include answers to the following questions. Sentence 1: what understood word is omitted between *man* and *looking?* What verb is the predicate of the subject *mold?* What word does the prepositional phrase *of the candles* modify? Sentence 2: To which of the three figures in the poem does *her* refer? What understood phrase is omitted between *light* and *to burn?* Sentence 3: To which of the three figures does *maid* refer? What understood word is omitted between *man* and *no?*

c. State the general sense of the poem as you understand it from your analysis.

2.

WHEN I HAVE FEARS

When I have fears that I may cease to be
    Before my pen has gleaned my teeming brain,
Before high-piléd books, in charact'ry,
    Hold like rich garners the full-ripened grain;
When I behold, upon the night's starred face,   5
    Huge cloudy symbols of a high romance,
And think that I may never live to trace
    Their shadows, with the magic hand of chance;
And when I feel, fair creature of an hour,
    That I shall never look upon thee more,   10
Never have relish in the faery power
    Of unreflecting love!—then on the shore
Of the wide world I stand alone, and think
Till Love and Fame to nothingness do sink.

—John Keats

a. Look up the following words: *gleaned, teeming, charactery, garners.*

b. The poem consists of a single sentence. Identify the subjects and verbs of the three chief subordinate clauses that precede the main subject and verb of the sentence. (You may seem to find four such subordinate clauses; if so, explain how the extra one is properly part of one of the others.) Identify the main subject and verb. What is the subject for *hold* (line 4)? What is the verb of which *symbols* (line 6) is the object? To what does *their* (line 8) refer? To what does *thee* (line 10) refer?

    c. State the general sense of the poem that emerges from your analysis.

  3. Poets are not required to write complete grammatical sentences, and in earlier centuries people had different notions from those we have now about sentence construction. In the following modern poem, and in the succeeding earlier one, there occur some unusual constructions.

THE PHILOSOPHER

Three blank walls, a barred window with no view,
A ceiling within reach of the raised hands,
A floor blank as the walls.

And, ruling out distractions of the body—
Growth of the hair and nails, a prison diet,   5
Thoughts of escape—

Ruling out memory and fantasy,
The distant tramping of a jailer's boots,
Visiting mice and such,

What solace here for a laborious mind!   10
What a redoubtable and single task
One might attempt here:

Threading a logic between wall and wall,
Ceiling and floor, more accurate by far
Than the cob-spider's.   15

Truth captured without increment of flies—
Spinning and knotting till the cell became
A spacious other head

In which the emancipated reason might
Learn in due time to walk at greater length   20
And more unanswerably.

—Robert Graves

    a. Look up the following words: *solace, redoubtable, increment, emancipated.*

    b. In grammatical terms, what is the single repeated thing that the first stanza consists of? Identify the parts.

c. Show that stanza 3 is grammatically parallel to stanza 2. What is the general grammatical relationship of the two stanzas to the first line in the fourth stanza? What understood word is omitted from the first line of the fourth stanza?

d. Show that stanza 6 is broadly parallel to stanza 5, and describe their relationship to the end of stanza 4.

e. Stanza 7 is an adjective. Explain.

f. State the general sense of the poem that emerges from your analysis.

4.

SONNET 1

from ASTROPHEL AND STELLA

Loving in truth, and fain in verse my love to show,
That She, dear She, might take some pleasure of my pain,
Pleasure might cause her read, reading might make her know,
Knowledge might pity win, and pity grace obtain,
I sought fit words to paint the blackest face of woe;   5
Studying inventions fine, her wits to entertain,
Oft turning others' leaves, to see if thence would flow
Some fresh and fruitful showers upon my sun-burned brain.
But words came halting out, wanting Invention's stay;
Invention, Nature's child, fled stepdame Study's blows;   10
And others' feet still seemed but strangers in my way.
Thus, great with child to speak, and helpless in my throes,
Biting my truant pen, beating myself for spite,
"Fool," said my Muse to me, "look in thy heart and write."

—Sir Philip Sidney

a. Look up the following words: *fain, fit, inventions, leaves, wanting, stay, great.*

b. What are the subject and verb of the sentence that occupies the first eight lines? What relationship to the subject is borne by the phrases beginning *Loving in truth, Studying inventions,* and *Oft turning?*

c. What word would modern practice normally place between *her* and *read* in line 3? What would be conventional modern word-order in prose for line 6?

d. Describe the subject-verb structure of the second sentence, lines 9–11.

e. Given lines 12 and 13 as they are, what would conventional modern grammar require as the opening word in the last line?

f. State the general sense of the poem that emerges from the preceding questions.

5. The key to the general sense of the following poem is in its title. Use it as well to unlock the sentence structure.

A REFUSAL TO MOURN THE DEATH, BY FIRE, OF A CHILD IN LONDON

Never until the mankind making
Bird beast and flower
Fathering and all humbling darkness
Tells with silence the last light breaking
And the still hour   5
Is come of the sea tumbling in harness

And I must enter again the round
Zion of the water bead
And the synagogue of the ear of corn
Shall I let pray the shadow of a sound   10
Or sow my salt seed
In the least valley of sackcloth to mourn

The majesty and burning of the child's death.
I shall not murder
The mankind of her going with a grave truth   15
Nor blaspheme down the stations of the breath
With any further
Elegy of innocence and death.

Deep with the first dead lies London's daughter,
Robed in the long friends,   20
The grains beyond age, the dark veins of her mother,
Secret by the unmourning water
Of the riding Thames.
After the first death, there is no other.

—*Dylan Thomas*

a. Look up the following words: *Zion, synagogue, sackcloth, stations, elegy, Thames.*

b. What are the subjects and verbs for the subordinate clause beginning *Never until*? Identify the main clause (subject and verbs) that *Never until . . .* is subordinate to.

c. Thomas has a reason for making his first sentence so long and his last sentence so short, and also for piling up the phrasing in the first sentence. Can you infer what that reason is?

ADDITIONAL EXERCISES

The following poems may be particularly useful: George Herbert, "Virtue," p. 213; William Blake, "Ah! Sun-Flower," p. 235; E. A. Robinson, "For a Dead Lady," p. 309; William Butler Yeats, "After Long Silence," p. 304;

Dylan Thomas, "In My Craft or Sullen Art," p. 340; Wallace Stevens, "Domination of Black," p. 314.

Paraphrasing and Condensing

A paraphrase is not the same thing as a poem. A paraphrase is not the same thing as the meaning of a poem. A paraphrase is a sometimes useful instrument in trying to grasp the general sense of a poem.

Suppose we know the words and understand the sentence structure of "Delight in Disorder," and have twice tried to express the general sense of the poem: the speaker is saying that he likes a woman to wear clothes in a seemingly casual way; the speaker is saying that he is attracted to the woman who likes to wear clothes in a seemingly casual way. Let us try a paraphrase—a rephrasing in our own words—that parallels the poem more exactly.

DELIGHT IN DISORDER

A sweet disorder in the dress
Kindles in clothes a wantonness:
A lawn about the shoulders thrown
Into a fine distraction,
An erring lace, which here and there   5
Enthralls the crimson stomacher,
A cuff neglectful, and thereby
Ribands to flow confusedly,
A winning wave (deserving note)
In the tempestuous petticoat,   10
A careless shoe-string, in whose tie
I see a wild civility,
Do more bewitch me than when art
Is too precise in every part.

Our paraphrase: Untidiness in dress can suggest a pleasantly wanton quality: a careless shawl, ribbon, shoe-string are instances of the greater attractiveness of art when it is not too precise. Does the paraphrase make sense? If it does, it suggests that the poem may be as much about the art of painting or of poetry as it is about the art of clothing or of female attractiveness. Perhaps the first twelve lines are no more than an example for the point about art in the last lines. Perhaps the casual tidiness of the poem itself, in which Herrick's art is not too precise, is another illustration for the last lines. And yet there are those twelve lines all about clothes, and those words like *wantonness, erring,* and *bewitch* all about women. What our paraphrase does for us is only to bring into the foreground a part of the meaning that we might otherwise have ignored.

For the most part, paraphrase performs the function of sentence analysis on a larger scale: to clarify the general sense of a poem. It may be particularly helpful in understanding complex poems or poems of several stanzas.

IN THE BLEAK MID-WINTER

In the bleak mid-winter
   Frosty wind made moan,
Earth stood hard as iron,
   Water like a stone;
Snow had fallen, snow on snow,   5
   Snow on snow,
In the bleak mid-winter
   Long ago.

Our God, Heaven cannot hold Him,
   Nor earth sustain;   10
Heaven and earth shall flee away
   When He comes to reign:
In the bleak mid-winter
   A stable-place sufficed
The Lord God Almighty   15
   Jesus Christ.

Enough for Him, whom cherubim
   Worship night and day,
A breastful of milk
   And a mangerful of hay;   20
Enough for Him, whom angels
   Fall down before,
The ox and ass and camel
   Which adore.

Angels and archangels   25
   May have gathered there,
Cherubim and seraphim
   Thronged the air;
But only His mother
   In her maiden bliss   30
Worshipped the Beloved
   With a kiss.

What can I give Him,
  Poor as I am?
If I were a shepherd   35
  I would bring a lamb,
If I were a Wise Man
  I would do my part,—
Yet what I can give Him,
  Give my heart.   40

—*Christina Rossetti*

Here is a condensed paraphrase for each stanza:

1. Long ago occurred a bleak and cold mid-winter.
2. All-powerful God was incarnated then, in a stable.
3. Such a humble place was enough for Him.
4. A humble mother was enough for Him.
5. I have only my heart to give Him.

Though the poem is not difficult to understand line by line or stanza by stanza, the paraphrase helps to show the movement of thought, which makes a broad leap from the first to the last stanza. The speaker contemplates the bleak and poor situation of Christ's birth, and is comforted to think that his own poor heart might thus be a worthy gift. The progress of the thought of the poem is like a delicate argument: if Almighty God found a bleak and poor scene appropriate for His incarnation, He might find my poor heart an appropriate gift. Underlying the argument is the realization that one's heart is the gift that matters.

With many poems, paraphrase will go only halfway in unlocking the general sense.

HELL

Husks, rags and bones, waste-paper, excrement,
  Denied a soul whether for good or evil
And casually consigned to unfulfilment,
  Are pronged into his bag by the great-devil.

Or words repeated, over and over and over,   5
  Until their sense sickens and all but dies,
These the same fellow like a ghoulish lover
  Will lay his hands upon and hypnotize.

From husks and rags and waste and excrement
    He forms the pavement-feet and the lift-faces;   10
He steers the sick words into parliament
    To rule a dust-bin world with deep-sleep phrases.

When healthy words or people chance to dine
    Together in this rarely actual scene,
There is a love-taste in the bread and wine,   15
    Nor is it asked: "Do you mean what you mean?"

But to their table-converse boldly comes
    The same great-devil with his brush and tray,
To conjure plump loaves from the scattered crumbs,
    And feed his false five thousands day by day.   20

—Robert Graves

Here is a condensed paraphrase for each stanza:

1. The devil puts all sorts of waste into his bag.
2. The devil puts dead words into his bag.
3. The devil takes this waste, including dead words, and makes people out of it.
4. Sometimes healthy people and healthy words dine together.
5. The devil comes to this healthy table and manages to get scraps enough to feed his own people.

The paraphrase leaves the poem a puzzle, but may help to bring to mind the vital question that needs to be asked and answered: who are the people who are made out of dead words by the devil—Shakespeare and John Keats, or lying politicians and plagiarizers of Shakespeare and Keats? The general sense of the poem emerges: many people speak nothing but clichés and lies; such people are often the rulers of the world; and oddly enough they draw their clichés and lies from originally vivid and true speech.

EXERCISES

1.

I DID NOT LOSE MY HEART IN SUMMER'S EVEN

I did not lose my heart in summer's even,
    When roses to the moonrise burst apart:
When plumes were under heel and lead was flying,
    In blood and smoke and flame I lost my heart.

I lost it to a soldier and a foeman,   5
  A chap that did not kill me, but he tried;
That took the sabre straight and took it striking,
  And laughed and kissed his hand to me and died.

                              —*A. E. Housman*

    a. What are the relevant meanings of *even, plumes,* and *sabre* in the poem?
    b. Show that *When roses . . .* and *When plumes . . .* are not two clauses in series. (Show how they are matched against each other as part of a general matching of lines 1 and 2 with lines 3 and 4.)
    c. Provide a condensed paraphrase of the poem. Decide to what extent it covers the meanings expressed in each of the following statements: the speaker is saying that he loved the man he killed more deeply than he ever loved a woman; he is saying that the emotions of war are more profound than those of love; he is saying that because he went to war he had no opportunity to give the depths of his feeling to anyone but his enemy. Which of the statements do you think comes closest to the poem?

    2.

DESERT PLACES

Snow falling and night falling fast, oh, fast
In a field I looked into going past,
And the ground almost covered smooth in snow,
But a few weeds and stubble showing last.

The woods around it have it—it is theirs.   5
All animals are smothered in their lairs.
I am too absent-spirited to count;
The loneliness includes me unawares.

And lonely as it is that loneliness
Will be more lonely ere it will be less—   10
A blanker whiteness of benighted snow
With no expression, nothing to express.

They cannot scare me with their empty spaces
Between stars—on stars where no human race is.
I have it in me so much nearer home   15
To scare myself with my own desert places.

                              —*Robert Frost*

    a. What are the relevant meanings of *lairs, ere,* and *benighted* in the poem?

b. What understood verb forms are omitted from the sentence in the first stanza? Can you suggest a reason why Frost chose not to use them? What is the grammatical position of *whiteness* in the sentence in the third stanza?

c. Provide a condensed paraphrase of the poem, stanza by stanza. Then state the idea of the poem in a manner to express the leap in thought from the first stanza to the last.

3.

INSENSIBILITY

I

Happy are men who yet before they are killed
Can let their veins run cold.
Whom no compassion fleers
Or makes their feet
Sore on the alleys cobbled with their brothers.   5
The front line withers,
But they are troops who fade, not flowers
For poets' tearful fooling:
Men, gaps for filling:
Losses, who might have fought   10
Longer; but no one bothers.

II

And some cease feeling
Even themselves or for themselves.
Dullness best solves
The tease and doubt of shelling,   15
And Chance's strange arithmetic
Comes simpler than the reckoning of their shilling.
They keep no check on armies' decimation.

III

Happy are these who lose imagination:
They have enough to carry with ammunition.   20
Their spirit drags no pack,
Their old wounds, save with cold, can not more ache.
Having seen all things red,
Their eyes are rid
Of the hurt of the color of blood for ever.   25
And terror's first constriction over,
Their hearts remain small-drawn.
Their senses in some scorching cautery of battle
Now long since ironed,
Can laugh among the dying unconcerned.   30

IV

Happy the soldier home, with not a notion
How somewhere, every dawn, some men attack,
And many sighs are drained.
Happy the lad whose mind was never trained:
His days are worth forgetting more than not.   35
He sings along the march
Which we march taciturn, because of dusk,
The long, forlorn, relentless trend
From larger day to huger night.

V

We wise, who with a thought besmirch   40
Blood over all our soul,
How should we see our task
But through his blunt and lashless eyes?
Alive, he is not vital overmuch;
Dying, not mortal overmuch;   45
Nor sad, nor proud,
Nor curious at all.
He cannot tell
Old men's placidity from his.

VI

But cursed are dullards whom no cannon stuns,   50
That they should be as stones;
Wretched are they, and mean
With paucity that never was simplicity.
By choice they made themselves immune
To pity and whatever mourns in man   55
Before the last sea and the hapless stars;
Whatever mourns when many leave these shores;
Whatever shares
The eternal reciprocity of tears.

—Wilfred Owen

a. What are the relevant meanings of *insensibility, fleers, cobbled, decimation, cautery, besmirch, dullards, paucity, hapless,* and *reciprocity* in the poem?

b. Analyze the first stanza for parallel phrasing. To whom does *some* refer in the first line of the second stanza? To whom does *his* refer in the fourth line of the fifth stanza? To whom does *they* refer in several lines of the last stanza?

c. Keeping in mind the title of the poem as a key to its general sense, provide condensed paraphrases of each stanza. Describe the relationship in idea of the first five stanzas to the sixth.

ADDITIONAL EXERCISES

The following poems may be particularly useful: Emily Dickinson, "Because I Could Not Stop for Death," p. 284; William Butler Yeats, "On Hearing That the Students of Our New University Have Joined the Agitation Against Immoral Literature," p. 123; A. E. Housman, "The Chestnut Casts His Flambeaux, and the Flowers," p. 297; Percy Bysshe Shelley, "Ode to the West Wind," p. 255; John Donne, "The Canonization," p. 203; William Butler Yeats, "Among School Children," p. 302.

2

THE GENERAL SENSE OF A POEM: PART 2

Diction

When a poet is feeling desperate, he may write a poem about despair. When another poet is feeling cheerful, he may write a poem about despair too. The differences between the poems may in part be in their *diction,* which is the kind of language they each use. In the first of the following poems, the speaker tells about the lack of concern of God and himself for the tragic condition of mankind. In the second, the speaker thinks about the tragic condition of mankind, and believes that a person is better off unborn or dead.

NOT ALL THERE

I turned to speak to God
About the world's despair;
But to make bad matters worse
I found God wasn't there.

God turned to speak to me   5
(Don't anybody laugh)
God found I wasn't there—
At least not over half.

—*Robert Frost*

BE STILL, MY SOUL, BE STILL;
THE ARMS YOU BEAR ARE BRITTLE

Be still, my soul, be still; the arms you bear are brittle,
   Earth and high heaven are fixed of old and founded strong.
Think rather,—call to thought, if now you grieve a little,
   The days when we had rest, O soul, for they were long.

Men loved unkindness then, but lightless in the quarry   5
  I slept and saw not; tears fell down, I did not mourn;
Sweat ran and blood sprang out and I was never sorry:
  Then it was well with me, in days ere I was born.

Now, and I muse for why and never find the reason,
  I pace the earth, and drink the air, and feel the sun.   10
Be still, be still, my soul; it is but for a season:
  Let us endure an hour and see injustice done.

Ay, look: high heaven and earth ail from the prime foundation;
  All thoughts to rive the heart are here, and all are vain:
Horror and scorn and hate and fear and indignation—   15
  Oh why did I awake? when shall I sleep again?

                                              —*A. E. Housman*

Robert Frost's poem is filled with the ordinary words and phrases of both speech and writing known as *informal diction: I turned to speak, God, despair, make bad matters worse.* Two of his phrases, *not all there* and *half* [*there*], are much more common to speech than writing, and are known as *colloquial diction.* The contractions, *wasn't* and *don't,* are likewise used much more in speech than in writing, except in personal letters. The overall effect of the diction is of casual conversation. If the colloquialisms, the contractions, and other words and phrases that tend in their direction are eliminated, the general diction may remain informal, but the effect may be more of ordinary writing.

> I turned to speak to God
> About the despair of the world;
> But to make a bad situation worse
> I found that God was not there.
>
> God turned to speak to me
> (No one should imagine that it was amusing);
> God found that I was not there;
> At least I was being inattentive.

A. E. Housman's poem illustrates the further range of language into *formal diction,* which is the characteristic language of the dignified occasion: *of old, call to thought, grieve, lightless, mourn, muse, pace, endure, high heaven, prime foundation.* Two or three of his words, *rive, ere,* and perhaps *but* (in the sense of *only*) have the special formality of being *archaic* or tending in that direction: they are words once standard but now used rarely and with a sense of artifice. Much of Housman's language is informal but tending in the direction of formality rather than colloquialism: *still, soul, arms, bear, brittle.* Only one or two informal words and phrases tend in the direction of the colloquial: *sorry, a little.* And only one is distinctly colloquial: *ay.* Another word, *sweat,* is thought by a few people to be indecently colloquial.

The reason for observing the diction of a poem may become obvious if we make Frost's language even more formal than Housman's.

> I turned to address the Almighty
> Concerning the despair that afflicts the world;
> However, to worsen an already desperate condition,
> I perceived that the Almighty had absented himself . . .

Although in a superficial sense, the formal paraphrase says the same thing as Frost's original informal and colloquial diction, a fundamental change of meaning has occurred. Frost's diction is flippant and familiar; it treats God disrespectfully and shrugs its shoulders at despair. It is inappropriate to an occasion that would conventionally be thought of as awesome; and it thereby makes light of the occasion and implies a light-hearted view of life.

Housman, on the other hand, has done the expected thing. He is treating what is usually thought of as a solemn subject, and his formal-informal diction makes his reader accept the subject in as solemn a fashion as the speaker. To transform his diction into the colloquial-informal diction of Frost's poem would be to transform the meaning of the poem. The present diction implies meaning almost the opposite of Frost's diction: it treats human tears respectfully, and droops its shoulders as at a formal funeral.

The two poems illustrate the fact that distinctions of colloquial, informal, and formal diction are distinctions of the way people customarily use words, and a poet is free to obey or disobey customary usage to obtain his special meanings. Colloquial diction is by definition language that is not formal, and we know what formal diction is by observing the sort of language that is usually chosen for formal occasions. Frost contradicts the rules by describing a formal occasion, an attempted conversation with the deity, in language that would not ordinarily be chosen. If enough people start saying *not all there* in formal contexts, the phrase may slip from being a colloquialism into being an unobtrusive phrase appropriate for both formal and informal occasions. Until then, it will be out of place, and a poet will use it out of place to imply a special viewpoint.

The range in level of diction from formal to informal to colloquial includes special forms such as *archaisms* (illustrated above) and *slang,* which is newly coined and usually short-lived colloquial language such as *square* and *cool.* There are a variety of other ways of categorizing diction than these. All of them are interrelated, and all the terms overlap. Some of them are left for the student to infer in the exercises below. One of the most common ways is to divide the meanings of individual words into *denotative* and *connotative* meanings. Denotation refers to the basic meaning or meanings of a word, connotation to implications of meaning. Denotatively *speak* and *address* are words that can mean the same thing: to say something. Connotatively they can be said to differ: *speak* suggests an ordinary occasion, *address* a dignified one. It is through these connotative meanings that *speak* and *address* are respectively informal and formal diction. *God* and the *Almighty* denotatively identify the deity, and the *Almighty* has in it the additional denotative meanings of the words *all* and *mighty.* Connotatively *God* and *Almighty* are perhaps the same, both suggesting dignity and respect. The fact that *Almighty* is more formal diction than *God* derives in part from its additional denotative meanings and its more elaborate sound.

As Question 7 in the exercise below suggests, distinctions between denotative and connotative meanings are often unreal, but the difficulties of analysis should not obscure the fact that in their overtones and undertones words that superficially seem to mean the same thing can have important differences. Whether a poet chooses to say *speak* and *God* or *address* and *Almighty* affects fundamentally the sense of what he is saying. This fact is evident in examining the words either from the standpoint of formal versus informal diction or from that of denotative and connotative meaning.

EXERCISES

1.

ROSE AYLMER

Ah what avails the sceptered race,
Ah what the form divine!
What every virtue, every grace!
Rose Aylmer, all were thine.

Rose Aylmer, whom these wakeful eyes   5
May weep, but never see,
A night of memories and of sighs
I consecrate to thee.

—*Walter Savage Landor*

a. Identify the most obviously formal diction in the poem.

b. Identify the diction that is informal and tends in the direction of formality.

c. Identify the distinctly colloquial diction.

d. What general effect does the choice of diction have upon the poem?

e. Assume that Landor considered the following alternatives of words to express the same basic meaning. Distinguish among the connotations.

profits————avails
ruling————sceptered
shape————form
yours————thine
devote————consecrate

2. How do you know that Housman himself did not regard the word *sweat* as indecently colloquial in "Be still, my soul, be still; the arms you bear are brittle"? See the comments on the poem on p. 29.

3. The following poem contains words, phrases, and pronunciations that are known as *localisms,* since they are used only in certain areas. *Scraight* is a localism that means *wail; tha canna* suggests a local pronunciation of *thou canst not.* The locality is the English Midlands. The reference to Burns is to his poem "O, Wert Thou in the Cauld Blast," p. 238.

WHAT AILS THEE?—

What ails thee then, woman, what ails thee?
doesn't ter know?
If tha canna say't, come then an' scraight it out on my bosom
Eh?—Men doesna ha'e bosoms? 'appen not, on'y tha knows what I mean.
Come then, tha can scraight it out on my shirt-front   5
an' tha'lt feel better.

    —In the first place, I don't scraight.
    And if I did, I certainly couldn't *scraight it out.*
    And if I could, the last place I should choose
    would be your shirt-front   10
    or your manly bosom either.
    So leave off trying to put the Robbie Burns touch over me

and kindly hand me the cigarettes
if you haven't smoked them all,
which you're much more likely to do   15
than to shelter anybody from the cau-auld blast.—

—*D. H. Lawrence*

a. Characterize the diction of each stanza according to its degree of formality. Take particular note of *thee* and *thou,* which in English and American usage today would ordinarily be considered archaic.

b. The most obvious purpose served by the diction is to distinguish between the two speakers. Explain. Which of the speakers do you suppose Lawrence likes better? Why do you suppose so? And what does the diction have to do with it?

4. The following poem describes a person who walks at night along a passage by the Thames River in London.

SHADWELL STAIR

I am the ghost of Shadwell Stair.
    Along the wharves by the water-house,
    And through the dripping slaughter-house,
I am the shadow that walks there.

Yet I have flesh both firm and cool,   5
    And eyes tumultuous as the gems
    Of moons and lamps in the lapping Thames
When dusk sails wavering down the pool.

Shuddering the purple street-arc burns
    Where I watch always; from the banks   10
    Dolorously the shipping clanks,
And after me a strange tide turns.

I walk till the stars of London wane
    And dawn creeps up the Shadwell Stair.
    But when the crowing sirens blare   15
I with another ghost am lain.

—*Wilfred Owen*

a. Characterize the general level of diction in the poem, illustrating it from each stanza.

b. What two or three words are most formal? What two or three are least?

c. Assume that Owen considered the following alternatives of words to express the same basic meaning. Distinguish between the connotations in each pair; then distinguish the general sort of connotation that Owen rejected in each set; then define precisely the sort of connotation that his own six words give.

    (1)   specter_____ghost
        sanguinary_____dripping
        stalks_____walks

    (2)   substance_____flesh
        solid_____firm
        contained_____cool

    d. Question "c" may suggest the possibility of categorizing diction according to degree of abstraction. It may suggest one or two other ways. Discuss the matter, and characterize Owen's poem accordingly, using other examples than his words given in Question "c."

    5. The following poem concerns a real or imagined painting or sculpture of a reclining woman. Among other things, the observer reflects that she was created without having to grow up and that she represents the mind of her creator.

SO-AND-SO RECLINING ON HER COUCH

On her side, reclining on her elbow,
This mechanism, this apparition,
Suppose we call it Projection A.

She floats in air at the level of
The eye, completely anonymous,   5
Born, as she was, at twenty-one,

Without lineage or language, only
The curving of her hip, as motionless gesture,
Eyes dripping blue, so much to learn.

If just above her head there hung,   10
Suspended in air, the slightest crown
Of Gothic prong and practick bright,

The suspension, as in solid space,
The suspending hand withdrawn, would be
An invisible gesture. Let this be called   15

Projection B. To get at the thing
Without gestures is to get at it as
Idea. She floats in the contention, the flux

Between the thing as idea and
The idea as thing. She is half who made her.   20
This is the final Projection, C.

> The arrangement contains the desire of
> The artist. But one confides in what has no
> Concealed creator. One walks easily
>
> The unpainted shore, accepts the world   25
> As anything but sculpture. Good-bye,
> Mrs. Pappadopoulos, and thanks.

—Wallace Stevens

a. Characterize the major diction of the poem, taking into account such language as *reclining, anonymous,* and *lineage* on the one hand and *mechanism, projection,* and *let this be called* on the other. What is the general effect of the diction?

b. At what two points in the poem, aside from the title, does the diction radically shift? Define the level of diction at each of these points and explain the purpose of the shift.

c. Stevens is concerned with art, mind, and reality in the poem. If your answer to Question "b" has not already done so, show that the varying diction is itself an expression of his ideas. (The last three and a half lines may be easiest to start with.)

d. *Pappadopoulos* is the name of the woman who becomes the work of art. Her name is her name, and cannot be classified as formal, colloquial, or the like. But Stevens chose the word for an obvious reason, and his choice suggests another basis for classifying diction. What is it? Show with the example of *Pappadopoulos* that meaning is involved in choices according to such classification.

6. The substituted formal diction for Robert Frost's poem, p. 29, does not make the four lines altogether serious. Why not? In what way might it be said then that Frost's diction is in keeping with the situation he describes?

7. If one of the fundamental meanings of *address* is *a set discourse,* the distinction of denotation and connotation between it and *speak* must be stated differently from the way given on p. 30. Discuss the matter, and discuss generally whether Frost is choosing among denotations or connotations when he chooses *speak* rather than *address, bad* rather than *tragic, despair* rather than *troubles.*

ADDITIONAL EXERCISES

1. Analyze the diction in the following poems: Ezra Pound, "A Virginal," p. 320; Robert Frost, "Fire and Ice," p. 310; Thomas Hardy, "Transformations," p. 292; A. E. Housman, "The chestnut casts his flambeaux, and the flowers," p. 297; Wilfred Owen, "A Terre," p. 331; John Donne, "The Canonization," p. 203.

2. Review the questions in the regular exercises above, and list and illustrate the several classifications of diction used and suggested there.

Meaning, Truth, Morality, and Criticism

Thomas Hardy was a fine poet but a wicked man. Witness the following poem.

THE RUINED MAID

"O 'Melia, my dear, this does everything crown!
Who could have supposed I should meet you in Town?
And whence such fair garments, such prosperi-ty?"—
"O didn't you know I'd been ruined?" said she.

—"You left us in tatters, without shoes or socks,   5
Tired of digging potatoes, and spudding up docks;
And now you've gay bracelets and bright feathers three!"—
"Yes: that's how we dress when we're ruined," said she.

—"At home in the barton you said 'thee' and 'thou,'
And 'thik oon,' and 'theäs oon,' and 't'other'; but now   10
Your talking quite fits 'ee for high compa-ny!"—
"Some polish is gained with one's ruin," said she.

—"Your hands were like paws then, your face blue and bleak
But now I'm bewitched by your delicate cheek,
And your little gloves fit as on any la-dy!"—   15
"We never do work when we're ruined," said she.

—"You used to call home-life a hag-ridden dream,
And you'd sigh, and you'd sock; but at present you seem
To know not of megrims or melancho-ly!"—
"True. One's pretty lively when ruined," said she.   20

—"I wish I had feathers, a fine sweeping gown,
And a delicate face, and could strut about Town!"—
"My dear—a raw country girl, such as you be,
Cannot quite expect that. You ain't ruined," said she.

    —*Thomas Hardy*

A ruined maid is a girl who sells her virtue, and a girl who sells her virtue may end up buying dope, penicillin, and Hell-fire. Such a fate is sad and should be a warning for all. Unfortunately, Hardy emphasizes the other things she buys: clothes, leisure, and a good time; and he shows another girl who would like to be ruined too, or at least have some of the things that can go with being ruined. He fails to shake his finger at either girl; and he treats female sin so lightly that one might suspect that he is in favor of it. The question to ask—and we have already answered it—is whether a man who favors sin or shows it in a favorable light can be a good poet. There is a related question: can a man who believes in the Ten Commandments write bad poetry? And there is another question that may already have come to mind: is female sin a sin? or is Hardy a wicked man? In our present age, which prides itself on being tolerant, these questions are often handled in the following way. Morality, the age says, has nothing to do with poetry: the wicked man may know the art of poetry, and the good man may know only clichés about loving his mother and father. Morality, the age says, is relative: what seems sin to me may not seem so to Hardy, and I allow him the right to his beliefs. It follows, the age says, that one reads poetry not for right ideas, right morals, but for excellence; one judges a poet to be good not because his ideas, his morality, agree with one's own, but because his ideas, his morality—offensive or comforting—are presented excellently.

There are difficulties about such a viewpoint. Many great poets have been inspired by what they themselves took to be right views, and many of their readers have responded deeply to these views in their poetry. It is even arguable that wisdom, compassion, love, and delight underlie all the greatest poetry in the English language—or to put it differently, that wicked men and criminal views do not conspire to produce great poems. Thus what the age says must be taken not as final truth but as a proper warning against simple-minded responses to poetry. Avoid the reaction that says, *I like this poet's views, therefore his poem is good,* or *I dislike his views, therefore his poem is bad.*

Suppose now we are a moral person reading "The Ruined Maid." A woman who is not chaste is an offense to us; but we do not want to be simple-mindedly offended by the poem. One thing we ought to do is to ask how we know what Hardy's viewpoint is. For he says nothing in his own person in the poem: it consists of an address by an unruined maid along with responses by a ruined maid. Should we take his silence and his humorous treatment of the subject as approval or at least unconcern? Here is an alternative: his silence is a refusal to scorn and a refusal to encourage scorning; he would no more condemn the ruined maid than Christ would condemn the woman taken in adultery; his silence and humor imply a sympathy for the two maids and an understanding of how hardship and longing can lead to sin; his silence is an implicit condemnation of the social conditions that encourage feminine weakness. We might end by thinking that Hardy is fundamentally as moral as we are, and then fall into the trap again: I approve of Hardy's compassion, and therefore his poem is good.

Nevertheless our approach has shown the sophistication of asking an important question: where is the poet in a poem, and what does he think? A full answer to this question occupies all the succeeding chapters in this book, particularly Chapters 9, 10, and 11; but some observations need to be made now. Sometimes a poet hides his views in a poem, and they have to be inferred: either he creates distinct characters who do all the speaking or he says *I* supposedly in his own person but is pretending. Sometimes a poet may seem to speak directly in his own person in a poem, but he may be a hypocrite or he may fail to see himself clearly, and the reader still has to infer what his views are. The consequence of these difficulties is that in ordinary analysis of poetry, it is important always to distinguish between the speaker or speakers of a poem and the poet himself. In such a poem as "The Ruined Maid" this is easy enough to do, and the difficulty lies in inferring Hardy's views. In a poem such as "Delight in Disorder" (page 8) the initial task is difficult: it is tempting to say *Herrick* rather than *the speaker of the poem;* but the latter phrase must be used. It is the speaker of the poem who expresses delight in disorder, not Herrick. After we understand the speaker's views, we may then ask whether it seems likely that they coincide with Herrick's. We may guess from the artful artlessness of the poem itself that Herrick does share his speaker's views; and if we have time we can analyze other poems of Herrick's and read about his life to find either supporting or contradictory evidence. In any event, the initial distinction between speaker and poet must be made.

Suppose now once again we are a moral person reading "The Ruined Maid," and we are avoiding a simple-minded response. We have decided, perhaps, that Hardy is compassionate, but we do not add: therefore his poem is good. Or we have decided that he is flippant and indifferent, but we do not add: therefore his poem is bad. Our restraint rests upon our awareness that a poem is more than an expression of a viewpoint—just as it is more than a prose paraphrase or more than the sum of the dictionary definitions of its words. Nothing has been said about the color of language in Hardy's poem, as in the phrase *spudding up docks,* nothing about the peculiar emphasis of *la-dy* and *melancho-ly,* nothing about the rhythmic structure of question and answer in each stanza up to the last. These and other aspects of the poem require the reader's awareness before he can understand the whole poem and have a respectable opinion about its merit. The meaning of a poem—the whole poem—resides as much in sound, rhythm, structure, and other parts as in ideas, views, and word definitions. The following chapters are further explorations of meaning.

EXERCISES

1.

HE THAT IS DOWN, NEEDS FEAR NO FALL

He that is down, needs fear no fall,
He that is low, no pride:
He that is humble, ever shall
Have God to be his guide.

I am content with what I have,　　　　　5
Little be it, or much:
And, Lord, contentment still I crave,
Because thou savest such.

Fullness to such a burden is
That go on pilgrimage:　　　　　10
Here little, and hereafter bliss,
Is best from age to age.

—John Bunyan

a. What does *crave* mean? What does *such* refer to in the eighth line? What does *such* refer to in the ninth?

b. Characterize the diction, and state its effect upon the poem.

c. Do you feel that the speaker of the poem is expressing views with which Bunyan would agree? Can you in very general terms explain why you think so?

d. Do you yourself agree with the views expressed in the poem? Would you say that most people in our society preach and practise such views, preach them and practise something else, or both preach and practise something else?

e. If you think the poem is a fine poem, try to suggest an explanation ·

other than that it expresses profound Christian views. If you think the poem is bad, offer reasons other than dislike of its views.

2.

THE ENGLISH ARE SO NICE!

The English are so nice
so awfully nice
they are the nicest people in the world.

And what's more, they're very nice about being nice
about your being nice as well!   5
If you're not nice they soon make you feel it.

Americans and French and Germans and so on
they're all very well
but they're not *really* nice, you know.
They're not nice in *our* sense of the word, are they now?   10

That's why one doesn't have to take them seriously.
We must be nice to them, of course,
of course, naturally—
But it doesn't really matter what you say to them,
they don't really understand   15
you can just say anything to them:
be nice, you know, just nice
but you must never take them seriously, they wouldn't understand.
just be nice, you know! oh, fairly nice,
not too nice of course, they take advantage   20
but nice enough, just nice enough
to let them feel they're not quite as nice as they might be.

—D. H. Lawrence

    a. Define the character of the diction more precisely than by saying that it is colloquial-informal.

    b. Do you feel that the views expressed by the speaker, or speakers, of the poem are ones with which Lawrence would agree? Can you in a very general way explain why you feel so?

    c. Would you say that the views expressed are ones which most people openly feel about their own kind (Americans about Americans, Frenchmen about Frenchmen, Protestants about Protestants), secretly feel but pretend not to, or frankly disbelieve?

    d. Are the views of the speaker more truly in accord with your own views than those of the speaker of Bunyan's poem, and do you like this poem better?

3.

A DRUMLIN WOODCHUCK

One thing has a shelving bank,
Another a rotting plank,
To give it cozier skies
And make up for its lack of size.

My own strategic retreat   5
Is where two rocks almost meet,
And still more secure and snug,
A two-door burrow I dug.

With those in mind at my back
I can sit forth exposed to attack   10
As one who shrewdly pretends
That he and the world are friends.

All we who prefer to live
Have a little whistle we give,
And flash, at the least alarm   15
We dive down under the farm.

We allow some time for guile
And don't come out for a while
Either to eat or drink.
We take occasion to think.   20

And if after the hunt goes past
And the double-barreled blast
(Like war and pestilence
And the loss of common sense),

If I can with confidence say   25
That still for another day,
Or even another year,
I will be there for you, my dear,

It will be because, though small
As measured against the All,   30
I have been so instinctively thorough
About my crevice and burrow.

—*Robert Frost*

a. What are the relevant meanings of *drumlin, guile, pestilence?*
b. Describe the broad structure of the sentence that occupies the last three stanzas of the poem.

   c. Identify the general level of diction and show whether it is appropriate to the situation that the poem describes.

   d. Identify the speaker of the poem, and summarize his views.

   e. In what obvious way cannot Frost be the speaker of the poem? What in the last three stanzas of the poem changes the character of the speaker somewhat? Are the speaker's views mainly like or unlike those of the speaker in "Not all There," p. 27, and what can you make of the fact?

ADDITIONAL EXERCISES

Read an encyclopedia article on the life of Bunyan, Lawrence, or Frost, and write a brief opinion on whether it offers evidence that the poet shares the views of the speaker of his poem above.

3

RHYME AND SOUND, ALLITERATION AND ASSONANCE

Repetition is one of the facts of life. A young man taps his foot in time with music, a young woman visits her mother once every week, an old man watches a child take the same steps he himself took, and in the process their hearts beat. The heartbeats vary under emotion, the steps are never exactly the same, each visit is unique, and the tapping ceases if the music is dull. In poetry, repetition is to be found everywhere, and explaining it is like explaining why the heart beats and why the music is dull or not. The present chapter and the next chapter are concerned with two kinds of poetic repetition: rhyme and rhythm. They involve sound.

There are several sorts of rhyme. The familiar kind is the repetition of vowel and consonant sounds at the ends of lines. Such rhyme is often called *end rhyme*.

> All Nature is but art, unknown to thee;
> All chance, direction, which thou canst not see.
>
> *—Alexander Pope*

(Here the end rhyme involves a single vowel sound: *ee—ee*. This is single rhyme.)

> Know then thyself, presume not God to scan;
> The proper study of mankind is Man.
>
> *—Alexander Pope*

(Here the end rhyme involves a single vowel sound and a succeeding consonant sound: *an—an*. This is also single rhyme.)

> But—Oh! ye lords of ladies intellectual,
> Inform us truly, have they not henpecked you all?
>
> *—Lord Byron*

(Here the end rhyme involves three vowel sounds and succeeding consonant sounds: *ect-u-al—ecked-you-all*. This is triple rhyme.)

Another kind of rhyme occurs within the line rather than from line to line at the end. In the following passage, *ew—ew* and *irst—urst* in the first and third lines are examples. Such rhyming matches sections of the individual line in the same way that end rhyme matches whole lines with one another. It is called *internal rhyme*.

> The fair breeze blew, the white foam flew,
> The furrow followed free;
> We were the first that ever burst
> Into that silent sea.
>
> *—Samuel Taylor Coleridge*

This passage is notable also for two special kinds of internal rhyming. The terms *alliteration* and *assonance* are customarily used to identify them rather than the term internal rhyme. Alliteration refers to the repetition of isolated consonantal sounds within the line and from line to line, as most noticeably with the three *f*'s in the first line, another three *f*'s in the second line, and the single *f* in the third. There are also several repeated *r*'s in the words *fair, breeze, furrow, free, were, first, ever, burst*. What other alliteration occurs in the passage? Assonance refers to the repetition of isolated vowel sounds, as with the modified *u* sounds in *furrow* in the second line and *were, first, ever*, and *burst* in the third.*

Why should a poet bother to rhyme sounds? Here is an anonymous poet going to a lot of trouble with his end rhymes.

> There was a young curate of Kidderminster
> Who very unwillingly chid a spinster
> For some words on the ice
> Which were far from being nice
> When he, quite accidentally, slid aginst her.   5

---

* Alliteration and assonance are often defined differently from the way they are defined here. See the Glossary on these points and also on *consonance*.

Quadruple rhyme (rhyming four vowel sounds and succeeding consonant sounds) is so difficult in the English language that the mere
fact of doing it is amusing. Even the slight cheating (*aginst*) is
amusing. Such rhyming is self-justifying. But what is the purpose of
the ordinary sort of single rhyming of *ice* and *nice?* Imagine a carica-
ture of a spinster: she is a woman who is icily nice, nicely iced. What
happens to her iced niceness when a nice young curate un-nicely
bumps into her on the ice? The rhyming of *ice* and *nice* brings the
words and their related connotations to the foreground and thus neatly
emphasizes the humorous predicament that the limerick describes.

Sometimes a poet uses rhyme for other reasons. Read the following
poem aloud, listening not only to the end rhyme but also to the alliteration and assonance.

THE WOUND

> I climbed to the crest,
>   And, fog-festooned,
> The sun lay west
>   Like a crimson wound:
>
> Like that wound of mine   5
>   Of which none knew,
> For I'd given no sign
>   That it pierced me through.
>
>   —*Thomas Hardy*

All the end rhymes are echoed in the alliteration and assonance of the
poem. *Crest* goes not only with *west* but also with *fest.* Fes*tooned* goes
not only with *wound* at the end of the fourth line but also with *wound*
in the fifth line. The *i* sounds in *mine* and *sign* appear elsewhere in *I,
climbed, like* (twice), and *I'd.* The *oo* sounds in *knew* and *through*
repeat those in *wound* and *festooned.* The incidental alliteration includes *c*limbed, *c*rest, and *c*rimson; *c*rest and *c*rimson; *f*og and *f*est;
*w*est and *w*ound. What Hardy achieves by all this rhyming of sounds
is a mournfulness (particularly in the *oo*'s), a heaviness (in the *i*'s),
and a slight harshness (particularly in the hard *c*'s). These qualities
suit his scene and subject, and give them greater force.

Another poet, Algernon Charles Swinburne, uses sometimes the same sounds but achieves a different effect in a stanza describing the coming of spring.

> For winter's rains and ruins are over,
>   And all the season of snows and sins;
> The days dividing lover and lover,
>   The light that loses, the night that wins;
> And time remembered is grief forgotten,   5
> And frosts are slain and flowers begotten,
>   And in green underwood and cover
> Blossom by blossom the spring begins.

It is not heavy *i* sounds that predominate, nor harsh *f*'s, *b*'s, and *d*'s, but softer *i* sounds as in *winter, ruins,* and *sins,* and softer *r*'s, *l*'s, and *s*'s. Compare *frosts are slain and flowers begotten* with *fog-festooned.* Swinburne surrounds his *f*'s with soft *r*'s, *s*'s, *l*'s, and soft vowel sounds (except for *ai* in *slain*). Hardy keeps his two *f*'s close together and puts between them a hard *g.* In Swinburne the *f*'s become part of a generally delicate variation of sound; in Hardy they become harsh. The same difference in effect can perhaps be seen in *blossom by blossom* and *climbed to the crest.* Swinburne's *b*'s are surrounded by soft *l*'s, *s*'s, *m*'s, and *o*'s. Hardy's hard *c*'s are followed by an *l* and *r* that emphasize the harsh sound. Note in the first line of Swinburne's stanza the profusion of soft *r*'s (six of them), in the first two lines of soft *s*'s (nine).

In achieving his delicacy of sound, Swinburne relies on his end rhymes as much as on his alliteration and assonance. Instead of the sharp *t*'s and *d*'s with which Hardy closes his rhyming words in his first stanza, Swinburne has *r*'s, *s*'s, and *n*'s; instead of Hardy's long *i* and *oo* sounds in the rhyming words in his second stanza, Swinburne has short *i*'s and *e*'s as in *sins* and *forgotten.* He also makes use of double rhyme in the first, third, fifth, sixth, and seventh lines, and again softens his sound. The double rhyme that he uses, in which the first vowel is accented and the second not (*ōver, lōver, cōver*), is called *feminine rhyme,* the name given because its characteristic effect is softening. Contrast Hardy's single accented final vowels with their consonants: *crēst, tōoned, wēst, wōund.* Ordinary single rhyme receiving an accent is called *masculine rhyme.* Swinburne uses it with *sins, wins,* and *begins,* but with generally softening sounds.

Rhyme, alliteration, and assonance are not always deliberately used

by poets, and some of the alliteration and assonance that can be found
in any poem is there simply because the English language has a limited
number of sounds, inevitably repeated. But no one will think the artful alliteration in the following two lines of Swinburne is accidental:

> The lilies and languors of virtue,
> The roses and raptures of vice.

And no one should assume that the decision to use or avoid rhyme is
casually taken. What is gained has to be weighed against what is lost.
To use rhyme means generally, but not always, to sacrifice freedom,
naturalness, and forward movement in favor of order, artful recurrence, and emphasis. It is apparent, too, that certain rhyme patterns can
have a powerful effect on what the rest of the poem is like. Consider
a poem in which two lines are rhymed together, then the next two
lines, and so on without break (conventionally noted as rhyming
aabbccddee etc.). This pattern was used by Robert Herrick in some
lines on the pleasures of wine:

O thou the drink of gods and angels! Wine	*a*	
That scatter'st spirit and lust; whose purest shine,	*a*	
More radiant than the summer's sunbeams shows,	*b*	
Each way illustrious, brave; and like to those	*b*	
Comets we see by night; whose shagg'd portents	*c*	5
Foretell the coming of some dire events:	*c*	
Or some full flame, which with a pride aspires,	*d*	
Throwing about his wild and active fires.	*d*	
'Tis thou, above nectar, O divinest soul!	*e*	
(Eternal in thyself) that canst control	*e*	10
That which subverts whole nature, grief and care;	*f*	
Vexation of the mind, and damned despair.	*f*	

He derived from his rhyme the normal benefits of order and artful
recurrence, but he did not exploit the fact that each pair of rhyming
lines forms a unit. A century later Alexander Pope wrote poems in
which the thought and phrasing are generally fitted into the two-line
unit that the rhyme suggests, and the rhyming words are often made
to be the key words of the thought and phrase, as with the rhyming
words of the first four lines here:

Know then thyself, presume not God to scan;	*a*
The proper study of mankind is Man.	*a*
Placed on this isthmus of a middle state,	*b*

```
A being darkly wise, and rudely great:              b
With too much knowledge for the skeptic side,       c    5
With too much weakness for the Stoic's pride,       c
He hangs between; in doubt to act, or rest,         d
In doubt to deem himself a god, or beast.           d
```

Such emphasis of the rhyme, of the rhyme unit, such enforced economy of thought and phrase, can make for an extraordinary combination of elegance and energy. (In which two lines does the phrasing least fit the rhyme unit?) Only Pope and a very few other poets mastered the form. A little more than a century after Pope, another poet took the same rhyme pattern and played the game of making it as unobtrusive and casual as could be:

```
That's my last duchess painted on the wall,           a
Looking as if she were alive. I call                  a
That piece a wonder, now: Frà Pandolf's hands         b
Worked busily a day, and there she stands.            b
Will't please you sit and look at her? I said         c    5
"Frà Pandolf" by design, for never read              c
Strangers like you that pictured countenance,         d
The depth and passion of its earnest glance . . .     d
```

—Robert Browning

How Browning achieved his particular de-emphasis of rhyme is as much a matter of phrasing as Alexander Pope's emphasis is. Analysis of it leads into rhythm and the next chapter.

Rhyme, alliteration, and assonance, then, can be handled in many ways, and each way has its particular effect in determining the shape of a poem, the color of its sound, and the focus of its words. When a poet uses rhyme, he thus deeply affects the overall quality, mood, and idea of his poem.

EXERCISES

1. In each of the following examples decide whether the rhyming words relate to each other in grammatical structure or meaning in such a way as to strengthen their emphasis. (Re-examine *ice-nice* in the limerick and *scan-man* in the fragment from Pope.)

a. A. E. Housman describing the human predicament:

> We for a certainty are not the first
> Have sat in taverns while the tempest hurled

> Their hopeful plans to emptiness, and cursed
> Whatever brute and blackguard made the world.

b. Alexander Pope describing destruction:

> Atoms or systems into ruin hurled,
> And now a bubble burst, and now a world.

c. Pope describing man:

> Sole judge of truth, in endless error hurled:
> The glory, jest, and riddle of the world!

d. Aphra Behn describing Cupid taking his qualities from a pair of lovers:

> From thy bright eyes he took his fire,
> Which round about, in sport he hurled;
> But 'twas from mine he took desire,
> Enough to undo the amorous world.

e. Henry Vaughan describing eternity:

> I saw eternity the other night
> Like a great ring of pure and endless light,
> All calm as it was bright;
> And round beneath it, Time, in hours, days, years,
> Driven by the spheres,
> Like a vast shadow moved, in which the world
> And all her train were hurled. . .

5

f. Andrew Marvell describing a cataclysm:

> While round the rattling thunder hurled,
> As at the fun'ral of the world.

2. Analyze the alliteration and assonance in the first Pope couplet and the Marvell couplet, and distinguish between their overall effects on each couplet.

3.

GOD'S GRANDEUR

> The world is charged with the grandeur of God.
>   It will flame out, like shining from shook foil;
>   It gathers to a greatness, like the ooze of oil
> Crushed. Why do men then now not reck his rod?
> Generations have trod, have trod, have trod;
>   And all is seared with trade; bleared, smeared with toil;
>   And wears man's smudge and shares man's smell: the soil
> Is bare now, nor can foot feel, being shod.

5

And for all this, nature is never spent;
  There lives the dearest freshness deep down things;   10
And though the last lights off the black West went
  Oh, morning, at the brown brink eastward, springs—
Because the Holy Ghost over the bent
  World broods with warm breast and with ah! bright wings.

             —Gerard Manley Hopkins

    a. Compare the end rhymes in the first stanza with those in the second for general heaviness of sound. Take into account the use of masculine or feminine rhyme.

    b. Point out the major elements of alliteration and assonance in the poem, and make a general comparison of their quality of sound in the two stanzas.

    c. Contrast the dominant ideas in the two stanzas, and show whether or not Hopkins uses the sound of his rhyme, alliteration, and assonance to support the contrast.

    4. The following three stanzas are the opening of a poem by Wilfred Owen, "A Terre" (the whole poem is given on page 331). It is the speech of a wounded soldier to a friend.

Sit on the bed. I'm blind, and three parts shell.
Be careful; can't shake hands now; never shall.
Both arms have mutinied against me,—brutes.
My fingers fidget like ten idle brats.

I tried to peg out soldierly,—no use!   5
One dies of war like any old disease.
This bandage feels like pennies on my eyes.
I have my medals?—Discs to make eyes close.
My glorious ribbons?—Ripped from my own back
In scarlet shreds. (That's for your poetry book.)   10

A short life and a merry one, my buck!
We used to say we'd hate to live dead-old,—
Yet now. . . . I'd willingly be puffy, bald,
And patriotic. Buffers catch from boys
At least the jokes hurled at them. I suppose   15
Little I'd ever teach a son, but hitting,
Shooting, war, hunting, all the arts of hurting.
Well, that's what I learnt,—that, and making money.

    a. The rhymes that Owen uses are called approximate or imperfect rhymes. Identify the rhyming words, and decide what effect Owen gains by using this sort of rhyme. Which rhymes illustrate the effect best? Why should he choose not to use all such rhymes?

    b. Analyze the alliteration and assonance, and discuss its contribution to the character of the three stanzas.

    5. Outline the rhyme schemes of the following two poems and compare the extent to which each poet has allowed the scheme to control his sentence phrasing and thought. In which poem is the rhyme more evident as one reads, and what is the general difference in effect upon the poems?

SONNET 65

Since brass, nor stone, nor earth, nor boundless sea
But sad mortality o'er-sways their power,
How with this rage shall beauty hold a plea,
Whose action is no stronger than a flower?
O, how shall summer's honey breath hold out   5
Against the wreckful siege of battering days,
When rocks impregnable are not so stout,
Nor gates of steel so strong, but Time decays?
O fearful meditation! where, alack,
Shall Time's best jewel from Time's chest lie hid?   10
Or what strong hand can hold his swift foot back?
Or who his spoil of beauty can forbid?
O, none, unless this miracle have might,
That in black ink my love may still shine bright.

                    —William Shakespeare

BRIGHT STAR

Bright star, would I were steadfast as thou art—
    Not in lone splendor hung aloft the night
And watching, with eternal lids apart,
    Like nature's patient, sleepless Eremite,
The moving waters at their priestlike task   5
    Of pure ablution round earth's human shores,
Or gazing on the new soft fallen mask
    Of snow upon the mountains and the moors—
No—yet still steadfast, still unchangeable,
    Pillowed upon my fair love's ripening breast,   10
To feel forever its soft fall and swell,
    Awake forever in a sweet unrest,
Still, still to hear her tender-taken breath,
And so live ever—or else swoon to death.

                    —John Keats

ADDITIONAL EXERCISES

1. Discuss Byron's use of rhyme in his epigrams on Castlereagh, p. 253.

2. Analyze and compare the character of the alliteration, assonance, and end rhyme in the following poems: Ezra Pound, "A Virginal," p. 320; John Donne, "Holy Sonnet 14," p. 78; Robert Frost, "Dust of Snow," p. 83.

3. Compare the relationship of rhyme pattern to sentence phrasing and thought in the sonnets by Sir Philip Sidney, pp. 196–97.

4. Discuss what Keats' poem "On the Sonnet," p. 258, argues and illustrates about rhyme.

5. Examine the several conjectural readings for the opening of the second line of Shakespeare's "Sonnet 146," p. 200, and decide which one best suits the line and the poem in alliteration, assonance, and sense.

4

RHYTHM AND SOUND

Meter

Rhythm in its familiar sense in poetry, in which there is a discernible regular beat within each line and from line to line, is called *meter*. Recognizing meter in a poem may be as difficult as recognizing rhythm in a new piece of music, and there are people who are rhythm-deaf just as there are people who are tone-deaf. But the following anonymous poem (in which the word *party* means *person*) relies upon meters that are recognizable to almost everyone.

> There was an old party of Lyme
> Who married three wives at one time.
>   When asked: "Why the third?"
>   He replied: "One's absurd,
> And bigamy, sir, is a crime."   5

Here is another almost the same. The word *brass* in it means *money*.

> There was a young man of Montrose
> Who had pockets in none of his clothes.
>   When asked by his lass
>   Where he carried his brass,
> He said: "Darling, I pay through the nose."   5

> *—Arnold Bennett*

Both poems follow closely, but not exactly, an abstract pattern of rhythm common to thousands of other poems that bear the name of limerick. The marking of rhythm in a poem is often done with the following symbols: ‾ to indicate an accented syllable and ˘ to indicate an unaccented syllable. The abstract limerick pattern calls for the following arrangement.

$$\smile - \smile\smile - \smile\smile -$$
$$\smile - \smile\smile - \smile\smile -$$
$$\smile - \smile\smile -$$
$$\smile - \smile\smile -$$
$$\smile - \smile\smile - \smile\smile -$$

The anonymous limerick follows the pattern exactly except for the addition of a single unaccented syllable at the beginning of the fourth line.

There was an old party of Lyme

Who married three wives at one time.

When asked: "Why the third?"

He replied: "One's absurd,

And bigamy, sir, is a crime."   5

Mark off the Bennett limerick, and note in what ways it varies from the abstract limerick pattern. That both poems do vary from the abstract pattern illustrates the fact that abstract patterns are not meant to be followed exactly; for part of the interest of the rhythm of a poem is the way it plays both with and against an abstract pattern. Even the most regular poem will have many irregularities that marking symbols cannot adequately catch: variations in heaviness of accent and in length of syllable. Question 4 on page 57 touches on this point.

The fundamental problem in analyzing the meter of any poem is to decide where the accents go; and in most poems there is room for difference of opinion. But no one is likely to argue that the accents in the first line of the anonymous limerick should be distributed thus: *Thĕre wăs ăn ŏld părtў ŏf Lўme.* Why not? One reason is the normal accenting of words. The two-syllable word *party* is ordinarily pronounced with the accent on the first syllable, and the poet has done nothing to force the reader to pronounce it otherwise. (Normal accenting is also followed with *married, replied, absurd,* and the trisyllabic *bigamy* in the rest of the poem.) Secondly, some words are more important than others, and they are likely to receive more weight. *Par*ty and *Lyme* are more important than *there* and *of* in the line, and the accents fall naturally on them. Thirdly, the notion of a beat implies a fairly regular gap between each beat; and although poets sometimes

force two accents together without the gap of an unaccented syllable
in between, there is no reason to believe the poet has done so with the
two normally weak sounds *ty* and *of.* Fourthly, the metrical pattern
that the poet uses and that the reader falls into helps to determine
accenting; and thus anyone who is familiar with limerick rhythm will
give a beat to *was* despite the fact that it is not an important word in
the line. Try rearranging the line, and observe the extent to which the
normal accenting of *party,* the relative importance of the words, and
the implied metrical pattern juggle one another and make for success
or failure in the rhythm.

Ŏf Lȳme thĕre wăs ăn ōld pārtў

Ŏf Lȳme ăn ōld pārtў thĕre wās

Ŏf Lȳme ăn ōld pārtў wăs thēre

Thĕre wās ŏf Lȳme ăn ōld pārtў

Thĕre wās ŏf ōld ă Lȳme pārtў

Ă pārtў ŏf ōld Lȳme thĕre wās

Ă Lȳme pārtў ŏf ōld wăs thēre

Purely from the standpoint of rhythm, which lines would not do as
the opening of the limerick? Observe the fact that although the second
variation, *Ŏf Lȳme ăn ŏld pārtў thĕre wās,* has exactly the same order
of accented and unaccented syllables as the original line, and accents
the same words as well, it has a different rhythmic quality. *Lyme* as
the second syllable receives more of an accent than *was* receives as the
second syllable: *Lyme* is a more important word in the whole clause,
and *Of Lyme* is an artificial and abrupt opening phrase, and makes for
a heavier accent. *Was* in the final position receives more accent than
it does in the second, largely because the last accented syllable in any
line of poetry usually does receive a heavier accent as part of its being
at the end. The conventional marks of accenting can not show all such
differences. For that matter, the conventional words *accented* and *unaccented* obscure the fact that every syllable receives some degree of
accent merely by being spoken or read. When we say *unaccented,* we
mean *significantly lesser degree of accent than a nearby syllable receives.*

Perhaps the most apparent problem in accenting the anonymous limerick is in not marking with an accent *Why* and *One's* in lines 3 and 4. They do receive more emphasis than the immediately succeeding syllables *the* and *a,* and it would be permissible to mark them *Why* and *One's.* The choice not to mark them perhaps at best makes clear how imprecise and relative the markings – and �‿ are. Ordinarily the beat of a meter means an accented syllable followed by a gap and then by another accented syllable, and thus despite the relative importance of *Why* and *One's,* the fact that they follow the heavy accents of *asked* and *plied* (in *replied*) tends to reduce them. They also occupy the same position (third syllable) as the unaccented *an* and *ied* in the first two lines, and the reader is inclined to continue the pattern.

Now read the limerick aloud and accent strongly *three* and *One's.* Read it aloud and minimize the same words. The fact is that there are at least three metrical patterns involved in most poems: (1) the pre-established abstract pattern—as, for example, the abstract pattern of the limerick or sonnet that the poet knows before he writes his poem, (2) the variation imposed by the poet—as illustrated by the enforced extra syllable in the fourth line of the anonymous limerick and the similar additions in the one by Arnold Bennett, and (3) the reasonable variation that the reader can bend the poet's imposed variation to—as evidenced by the various legitimate accenting that can be given to *three* or *One's.* To these three metrical patterns must be added non-metrical rhythms, which will be considered in detail later. They include sentence phrasing—as illustrated by the rhythmic difference between *There was an old party of Lyme* and *Of Lyme an old party there was.* The ordinary sort of metrical analysis of a poem is meant to uncover the second pattern in relationship to the first, but it always draws upon the third and needs to take nonmetrical rhythms into account.

EXERCISES

1.

> There was a young lady of Lynn
> Who was so excessively thin
> That when she essayed
> To drink lemonade
> She slipped through the straw and fell in.   5

—*Anonymous*

a. Mark off accented and unaccented syllables. Does the limerick follow the abstract pattern for limericks (p. 53) exactly? Point out any differences.

b. Does the poet distort the normal pronunciation of any of the multisyllabic words?

c. What ordinarily insignificant word is rather heavily accented? Why does it happen to be?

d. Point out any legitimate variations in accenting that a person reading the poem aloud might want to impose.

2.

DUST OF SNOW

The way a crow
Shook down on me
The dust of snow
From a hemlock tree

Has given my heart   5
A change of mood
And saved some part
Of a day I had rued.

—Robert Frost

a. Mark off accented and unaccented syllables. State what the overall abstract metrical pattern of the poem is; note any variations that Frost imposes; and point out any legitimate variations that a person reading the poem aloud might want to impose.

b. Suggest a reason why the one line that differs most from the others in metrical analysis is made so by Frost. Does your answer suggest that the difference is real or apparent? (If you cannot answer this question directly, study Question 4.)

3.

SUCCESS IS COUNTED SWEETEST

Success is counted sweetest
By those who ne'er succeed.

To comprehend a nectar
Requires sorest need.

Not one of all the Purple Host   5
Who took the Flag today
Can tell the Definition
So clear of Victory

As he defeated—dying—
On whose forbidden ear   10
The distant strains of triumph
Burst agonized and clear!

—*Emily Dickinson*

a. Mark off accented and unaccented syllables. State the abstract pattern of total number of syllables per line for the three sets of four lines. Do the same for the accented syllables.

b. What variations of meter does the poet impose? Which line offers the most distinct variation in total number of syllables, and what influence does this line have on its matching line in its stanza?

4. In the anonymous limerick on p. 52 the first two syllables in line 3, *When asked*, take longer to pronounce than the first two syllables in line 4, *He re-*. Thus although the fourth line was shown to have one more syllable than the abstract pattern of the limerick calls for (p. 53), the extra syllable helps to make the line equal to the third in actual rhythmic length. The observed irregularity makes for regularity. Examine the extra syllables in the Bennett limerick (p. 52) and any extra syllables in the Frost and Dickinson poems above to see if the same can be said of them.

5. Compare the rhymes in the limerick in Question 1, the two limericks on p. 52, and the limerick on p. 43, considering the extent to which the rhyming words are related to one another grammatically or in meaning. Can you offer a generalization about the characteristic chief use of rhyme in limericks? (Suggestion: the generalization could concern rhythm.)

ADDITIONAL EXERCISES

The following poems may be particularly useful: Walter Savage Landor, "Rose Aylmer," p. 30; William Blake, "The Tiger," p. 141; A. E. Housman, "In the morning, in the morning," p. 1; Thomas Hardy, "In Time of 'The Breaking of Nations,'" p. 293; John Donne, "Song" (Go and catch a falling star), p. 201; Gerard Manley Hopkins, "God's Grandeur," p. 48.

Meter and Feet

The beating of the meter of a poem divides the poem into parts. Each division, each unit—marked by the beat, the accent—is called a *foot,* and includes the accented syllable and surrounding unaccented syllables. The whole process of marking accents and distinguishing feet is called *scansion,* and it is based upon an awareness of (1) the abstract pattern of rhythm that a poem relies on, (2) the units of spaced accented and unaccented syllables that the abstract pattern of rhythm suggests, and (3) the changes in rhythm and units that the poet enforces. Here is the abstract rhythmic pattern of the limerick again, along with the units, the feet, that it suggests. Sound the pattern aloud with nonsense syllables, emphasizing the divisions.

˘‿|˘˘‿|˘˘‿|	3 feet
˘‿|˘˘‿|˘˘‿|	3 feet
˘‿|˘˘‿|	2 feet
˘‿|˘˘‿|	2 feet
˘‿|˘˘‿|˘˘‿|	3 feet

Observe the fact that the first two feet of every line are ˘‿ \| ˘˘‿, and that the whole limerick contains only two kinds of feet: ˘‿ and ˘˘‿ . The abstract schemes that most poems are based upon are similarly regular. With this abstract scheme in mind, scan Arnold Bennett's limerick:

There was a young man of Montrose	3 feet
Who had pock ets in none of his clothes.	3 feet
When asked by his lass	2 feet
Where he ca rried his brass,	2 feet
He said: "Dar ling, I pay through the nose."	3 feet

The limerick falls into the scheme exactly, except that it adds a syllable to the first foot in the second, fourth, and fifth lines. Note that in the first and third lines the divisions of the feet coincide with normal phrase pauses, whereas in the other lines the divisions sometimes cut a word in half. In the latter case, the rhythmic units of the limerick pattern override the natural rhythmic unity that an individual word possesses. As will be seen below, a poet sometimes makes use of the natural rhythmic unity of a word or phrase to override the regular pattern.

There are conventional terms to describe kinds of feet and numbers of feet per line.

⌣–| as in *agaín*————————*iamb* (*iambic*), the most common foot in English poetry.

–⌣| as in *hítting*————————*trochee* (*trochaic*).

⌣⌣–| as in *interfére*————————*anapest* (*anapestic*).

–⌣⌣| as in *hórrible*————————*dactyl* (*dactylic*).

⌣–⌣| as in *behávior*————————*amphibrach* (*amphibrachic*).

The feet above form the bases of the metrical rhythms of most English poetry. Two unusual feet occasionally appear among them:

– –|as in *héad-stárt*————————*spondee* (*spondaic*).

⌣ ⌣|————————————*pyrrhic* (*pyrrhic*). For an example, see line 11 in "Sonnet 18," p. 60, and the discussion following.

The number of feet per line are identified as follows. One foot of any sort per line is *monometer;* two feet of any sort is *dimeter;* three feet *trimeter;* four feet *tetrameter;* five feet *pentameter;* six feet *hexameter;* seven feet *heptameter;* eight feet *octameter.* To apply this terminology to Bennett's limerick, we would say that it consists entirely of iambic and anapestic feet, with the first, second, and fifth lines trimeter and the third and fourth dimeter. The second and fifth lines are anapestic trimeter. The abstract limerick pattern calls for the second and fifth lines and also the first to be mixed iambic and anapestic.

Bennett's limerick and the anonymous limerick analyzed in the preceding section are rhythmically simple, and their rhythmic character is easy to describe. The rhythm in both is emphatic rather than weak, and light rather than serious. It trips along at a good pace, and the shortening in lines 3 and 4 tends to make the last line come at even a faster clip—noticeable especially in the anonymous limerick, Bennett making his rhythm stumble slightly with the extra syllable at the beginning of his last line. It is hardly a rhythm suitable for a funeral, and very suitable for frivolity.

Unless a person is familiar with the rhythms of English poetry, he will need to read a poem two or three times before trying to scan it, picking up the abstract rhythm or rhythms that the poem plays with and against. Scan the following poem on your own before looking at the analysis that follows. Note that *ow'st* and *grow'st* are to be regarded as one-syllable words and *wander'st* as a two-syllable word.

SONNET 18

Shall I compare thee to a summer's day?
Thou art more lovely and more temperate:
Rough winds do shake the darling buds of May,
And summer's lease hath all too short a date:
Sometime too hot the eye of heaven shines,   5
And often is his gold complexion dimmed;
And every fair from fair sometime declines,
By chance or nature's changing course untrimmed;
But thy eternal summer shall not fade,
Nor lose possession of that fair thou ow'st,   10
Nor shall death brag thou wander'st in his shade,
When in eternal lines to time thou grow'st:
So long as men can breathe, or eyes can see,
So long lives this, and this gives life to thee.

—*William Shakespeare*

Shall I compare thee to a sum mer's day?

Thou art more love ly and more tem perate:

Rough winds do shake the dar ling buds of May,

And sum mer's lease hath all too short a date:

Sometime too hot the eye of hea ven shines,   5

And of ten is his gold complex ion dimmed;

And ev́ ery fair from fair sometime declines,

By chance or na ture's chang ing course untrimmed;

But thy eter nal sum mer shall not fade,

Nor lose posses sion of that fair thou ow'st,   10

Nor shall death brag thou wan der'st in his shade,

When in eter nal lines to time thou grow'st:

So long as men can breathe, or eyes can see,

So long lives this, and this gives life to thee.

The basic pattern that Shakespeare has relied upon throughout is iambic pentameter, and he has followed it so closely that every line divides readily into five feet of two syllables apiece, with most of the feet iambic. So predictable is the rhythm that it gives accent to insignificant words like *of* in line 10 and *in* in line 12. The main problem of the scansion is the irregular eleventh line, which could well be given as

Nor shall death brag thou wan der'st in his shade

and in other ways. Note that when three accents come together, as with *shăll deáth brăg,* they still have a gap between them, not a visible syllable gap but the time involved in pronouncing—an aspect of all movement from syllable to syllable. There are several other points in the poem where alternative scansion would be legitimate. Consider whether each of the following possibilities is legitimate, providing an explanation of your opinion in each case: *Shăll Ī* and *theē tŏ,* line 1; *thoū ărt* and *lŏve / lў,* line 2; *roŭgh wīnds,* line 3; *toō shŏrt,* line 4; *ănd ōf / tĕn ĭs,* line 6; *frŏm făir,* line 7; *līves thīs,* line 14.

The quality of Shakespeare's rhythm is easily perceived. The rhythm does not trot along like the limerick rhythm, but moves sedately. The greater number of feet per line tends to restrain the pace, and iambic feet seem generally to proceed more slowly than anapestic. The risk that Shakespeare runs with his very regular iambic pentameter is a plodding, jerky rhythm, and it is easy enough to read the poem in such a way, emphasizing the abstract pattern at the expense of the actual pattern. Shakespeare avoids the fault in part by slight variations such as some of the proposed alternative scansions in the previous paragraph suggest. The total effect is a gracefulness that suits the occasion of the poem.

In the following sonnet Shakespeare once again uses iambic pentameter as his abstract pattern, but he wrenches it. The poem may need reading several times before the actual rhythm emerges. Scan the poem on your own before looking at the analysis. Note that *Th' expense* is pronounced as two syllables and that the accented *ed* in *despiséd* means that it is pronounced as a separate syllable.

SONNET 129

Th' expense of spirit in a waste of shame

Is lust in action; and till action, lust

Is perjured, murderous, bloody, full of blame,

Savage, extreme, rude, cruel, not to trust;

Enjoyed no sooner but despiséd straight;   5

Past reason hunted; and no sooner had,

Past reason hated, as a swallowed bait,

On purpose laid to make the taker mad:

Mad in pursuit, and in possession so;

Had, having, and in quest to have, extreme;   10

A bliss in proof, and proved, a very woe;

Before, a joy proposed; behind, a dream.

All this the world well knows; yet none knows well

To shun the heaven that leads men to this hell.

—William Shakespeare

˘ — | ˘ — ˘ | ˘ ˘ — | ˘ — |
Th' expense of spirit in a waste of shame

˘ — | ˘ — ˘ | ˘ ˘ — | ˘ — |
Is lust in action; and till ac tion, lust

˘ — ˘ | — ˘ ˘ | — ˘ | ˘ ˘ — |
Is perjured, murderous, bloody, full of blame,

— ˘ | ˘ — | — | — ˘ | ˘ ˘ — |
Savage, extreme, rude, cruel, not to trust;

˘ — | ˘ — ˘ | ˘ ˘ — | ˘ — |
Enjoyed no sooner but despi sed straight;   5

Past reason hunted; and no soon er had,

Past reason hated, as a swall owed bait,

On pur pose laid to make the ta ker mad:

Mad in pursuit, and in posses sion so;

Had, having, and in quest to have, extreme;   10

A bliss in proof, and proved, a ver y woe;

Before, a joy proposed; behind, a dream.

All this the world well knows; yet none knows well

To shun the heaven that leads men to this hell.

As the poem is scanned, Shakespeare is seen to have so wrenched the iambic pentameter frame that in the first seven lines it exerts little control over the rhythmic divisions. A word like *pockets* in Bennett's limerick allows itself to be split to accommodate a clear rhythm (p. 58), but a word like *murderous* and a phrase like *Past reason hunted* maintain their unity. Both *murderous* and *Past reason hunted* could be scanned with the same accenting to fit the iambic pentameter mold (treating the second two syllables of *murderous* as one):

Is per jured mur derous blood y full of blame,

Past rea son hun ted; and no soon er had,

But the mold is a dimly perceived outline, and such scanning does not show the wrenching, and is inadequate. The original scanning of these and the other lines of the poem shows six of the fourteen lines to have four feet rather than five and more than one-third of the seventy feet to be irregularly non-iambic. The overall effect of the meter is one of harshness and energy, particularly apparent in lines 3 and 4, tapering off in the last lines. The appropriateness of it to the lust that Shakespeare is describing hardly needs saying. Other things than the meter account for the extraordinary rhythm of the poem, and these are discussed in the next section.

EXERCISES

1. Identify the kinds of feet in "Sonnet 129" as scanned.

2. Mark off the feet in the three poems given on pages 55–57. Identify the metrical pattern—the characteristic foot or feet, and characteristic number of feet per line. Identify all variations from the norm, and justify regarding them as variations.

3. Here are alternative scansions of two lines from Bennett's limerick. One or more of them are unacceptable under any condition. One or more are acceptable if they are regarded in isolation, not as part of Bennett's limerick or of any conventional limerick. None are acceptable if seen as part of Bennett's limerick. Explain each case.

There was a young man of Montrose

There was a young man of Montrose

There was a young man of Montrose

There was a young man of Mon trose

Who had pockets in none of his clothes

Who had pockets in none of his clothes

ADDITIONAL EXERCISES

Complete the scansion of the poems given in the additional exercises on p. 57.

Nonmetrical Rhythm

> Th' expense of spirit in a waste of shame
> Is lust in action; and till action, lust
> Is perjured, murderous, bloody, full of blame,
> Savage, extreme, rude, cruel, not to trust; . . .

> *—William Shakespeare*

The harshness and energy of the meter in this sonnet (analyzed in full on pages 62–63 may be said to strengthen the harshness and energy of the idea of the poem. The reverse is also true: the violence of the idea helps to determine the character of the rhythm. It does so both metrically (helping the *regular beat*) and nonmetrically (helping the *irregular flow and movement*). The powerful words *perjured, murderous, bloody* in line 3 provide metrical units, metrical beats; and the overall force of the language throughout the poem makes for a turgid flow, slowly diminishing, that is independent of meter. Alliteration and assonance likewise can serve both metrical and nonmetrical rhythms. Observe first in the following lines how the alliteration and assonance in *rains-ruins, season-snows-sins,* and *light-loses-night* help to emphasize the regularity of accent in the metrical pattern:

> For winter's rains and ruins are over,
>
> And all the season of snows and sins;
>
> The days dividing lover and lover,
>
> The light that loses, the night that wins;
>
> —*Algernon Charles Swinburne*

Such emphasis, though, does not give the lines an emphatic beat, and the reason is in part that Swinburne uses alliteration and assonance in unaccented syllables as well, and smoothes out the meter with their nonmetrical flow. This is most apparent with the six *r*'s and nine *s*'s in the first two lines. (If need be, see the fuller discussion of the alliteration and assonance in these same lines on page 45.) In general it can be said that every aspect of a poem can bear upon rhythm both metrically and nonmetrically: the choice of short or long words, the ending of sentences in the middle or at the ends of lines, the use or avoidance of repeated phrasing, and so forth. The ensuing discussion mainly concerns the devices known as *caesura, end-stopped line,* and *run-on line* in their nonmetrical use. There is some comment on free verse—nonmetrical verse. Larger structural elements of nonmetrical rhythm are discussed in Chapter 8.

Caesura refers to internal breaks in the rhythm of a line of poetry caused by phrasal pauses and punctuation.* Such pauses will be found in most lines of poetry, and when the individual line is four feet or more, the pause tends to become noticeable. It is indicated by a double vertical: ||. Marking caesuras is sometimes as difficult as marking accents, and there is room for disagreement. In a line in which there is no heavy pause, the single most noticeable pause (if there is one) is

* The term is often defined differently. See the Glossary.

regarded as the caesura. In a line in which there is at least one heavy pause, that pause is a caesura along with any other heavy pauses. Compare Shakespeare's use of caesura in "Sonnet 18" and "Sonnet 129."

Shall I compare thee || to a summer's day?
Thou art more lovely || and more temperate:
Rough winds do shake || the darling buds of May,
And summer's lease || hath all too short a date:
Sometime too hot || the eye of heaven shines,   5
And often || is his gold complexion dimmed;
And every fair || from fair sometime declines,
By chance || or nature's changing course untrimmed;
But thy eternal summer || shall not fade,
Nor lose possession || of that fair thou ow'st,   10
Nor shall death brag || thou wander'st in his shade,
When in eternal lines || to time thou grow'st:
So long as men can breathe, || or eyes can see,
So long lives this, || and this gives life to thee.

Th' expense of spirit || in a waste of shame
Is lust in action; || and till action, || lust
Is perjured, || murderous, || bloody, || full of blame,
Savage, || extreme, || rude, || cruel, || not to trust;
Enjoyed no sooner || but despiséd straight;   5
Past reason hunted; || and no sooner had,
Past reason hated, || as a swallowed bait,
On purpose laid || to make the taker mad:
Mad in pursuit, || and in possession so;
Had, || having, || and in quest to have, || extreme;   10
A bliss in proof, || and proved, || a very woe;
Before, || a joy proposed; || behind, || a dream.
All this the world well knows; || yet none knows well
To shun the heaven || that leads men to this hell.

In "Sonnet 18" there is only one caesura per line. For the most part it falls near the center of the line, and it is a very light pause. It establishes throughout the poem a nonmetrical rhythm of two light and even phrase units per line. A comparison of caesuras and metrical divisions in the poem will show that although the caesuras occasionally break into the metrical feet, they do so very lightly, without disrupting the metrical beat. The caesuras give an even, light nonmetrical rhythm, and they sometimes assist the metrical rhythm. Here are the first four lines with both caesura and foot divisions. (See page 60 for a metrical analysis of the whole poem.) In the first two lines, the caesuras break into the third foot; in the next two lines they coincide with the end of the second foot.

Shall I | compare | thee || to | a sum | mer's day? |
Thou art | more love | ly || and | more tem | perate: |
Rough winds | do shake | || the dar | ling buds | of May, |
And sum | mer's lease | || hath all | too short | a date: |

In contrast, the caesuras in "Sonnet 129" are very unevenly spaced, and in six of the lines there are from two to four caesuras. In the first line the caesura is very light, and in the second line the first caesura is very heavy, almost a full stop. The rest of the poem is similarly irregular. The caesura rhythm is thus as ragged, abrupt, and harsh as the caesura rhythm in "Sonnet 18" is light and even. Since the metrical rhythm of the poem, as analyzed on pages 62–63, is itself ragged and verges on being nonmetrical, the caesuras often coincide with the foot divisions— or to put it differently, the irregular caesuras are sometimes so strong that they control the foot divisions. They again make evident the shifting speed, the large irregularity of rhythm of the sonnet. Here are the first four lines with both caesura and foot divisions:

Th' expense | of spirit | || in a waste | of shame |
Is lust | in action; | || and till ac | tion, || lust |
Is perjured, | || murderous, | || bloody, | || full of blame, |
Savage, | || extreme, | || rude, | || cruel, | || not to trust; |

Another way of describing the difference between "Sonnet 18" and "Sonnet 129" is to say that in "Sonnet 18" Shakespeare puts all his heavy pauses at the ends of the lines, whereas in "Sonnet 129" he has many more heavy pauses to begin with and puts them irregularly within the lines as well as at the ends. All the lines in "Sonnet 18" are *end-stopped:* the end of the poetic line coincides with the end of a grammatical phrase. In contrast, some of the lines of "Sonnet 129" are *run-on:* that is, the ends of such lines do not coincide with grammatical pauses, and the rhythm presses forward to the next line. The marking used here for end-stopped lines is the same as for caesuras: ||. The run-on lines are unmarked.

Shall I compare thee to a summer's day? ||
Thou art more lovely and more temperate: ||
Rough winds do shake the darling buds of May, ||
And summer's lease hath all too short a date: ||
Sometime too hot the eye of heaven shines, || 5
And often is his gold complexion dimmed; ||
And every fair from fair sometime declines, ||
By chance or nature's changing course untrimmed; ||
But thy eternal summer shall not fade, ||
Nor lose possession of that fair thou ow'st, || 10
Nor shall death brag thou wander'st in his shade, ||
When in eternal lines to time thou grow'st: ||
So long as men can breathe, or eyes can see, ||
So long lives this, and this gives life to thee. ||

Th' expense of spirit in a waste of shame
Is lust in action; and till action, lust
Is perjured, murderous, bloody, full of blame,
Savage, extreme, rude, cruel, not to trust; ||
Enjoyed no sooner but despiséd straight; || 5
Past reason hunted; and no sooner had, ||
Past reason hated, as a swallowed bait, ||
On purpose laid to make the taker mad: ||
Mad in pursuit, and in possession so; ||
Had, having, and in quest to have, extreme; || 10
A bliss in proof, and proved, a very woe; ||
Before, a joy proposed; behind, a dream. ||

> All this the world well knows; yet none knows well ||
> To shun the heaven that leads men to this hell. ||

The fourteen end-stopped lines in "Sonnet 18" add up to a large non-metrical rhythm of fourteen phrasal strokes. And each line, with a caesura falling generally in the middle and the end end-stopped, divides more neatly into two parts than the caesuras alone indicated. The whole nonmetrical rhythm of the poem has a balanced, even quality that is in character with the highly regular meter. The two rhythms together give the poem its smooth, sedate flow. The run-on lines in "Sonnet 129" have, of course, a different effect. They contribute to the shifting rhythm of the poem. Observe the variety with which the lines run on. In the first line the subject *expense* comes at the beginning and has to wait for *is lust in action* several feet away in the next line to complete the large phrasal unit. In the second line the subject *lust* comes as the last syllable and is backed against its verb *is perjured* in the next line to continue its large phrasal unit. The whole of line 3 is a string of adjectives, and the string carries over to line 4, with the consequence that despite the heavy pauses between each of these adjectives, they belong together in a single phrasal unit, and thus the third line is run-on. The string comes to a kind of pause only at the end of line 4, which may be described as end-stopped. But Shakespeare is only shifting the form of his adjectives in line 5, and given the pressure of the rhythm, line 4 comes close to being run-on. The same may be said of one or two of the later lines, such as line 8, which is marked as end-stopped.

Compare now the heavy pauses in the first three lines of the two poems, ignoring any light caesuras:

> Shall I compare thee to a summer's day? ||
> Thou art more lovely and more temperate: ||
> Rough winds do shake the darling buds of May, ||
>
> Th' expense of spirit in a waste of shame
> Is lust in action; || and till action, || lust
> Is perjured, || murderous, || bloody, || full of blame

Nothing better shows how evenly patterned the nonmetrical rhythm of "Sonnet 18" is, how fluctuating and jammed up that of "Sonnet 129" can be.

It is evident from the first lines of "Sonnet 129" that one cannot always sense whether a line is run-on or end-stopped in a first reading. Had the first two lines read thus:

> Th' expense of spirit in a waste of shame,
> The death of spirit in a pool of lust,

they would have been two parallel noun phrases, with an end-stopped first line. On the other hand, no alteration in line 3 could prevent the original line 2 from being run-on, and the reader sees that line 2 is run-on as he first reads the poem:

> Is lust in action; and till action, lust

When nonmetrical rhythm is made the whole rhythm of a poem, the result is what is called *free verse*. Robert Frost once likened free verse to playing tennis with the net down, but the fact is that writing good free verse requires special talent. Characteristically, free verse avoids rhyme as well as meter. The poem below—which is one of a group that describe a man's pleasure in his marriage—illustrates the fluid rhythm of free verse at its best. Some of the sense of the poem may not be clear, and need not be. Mark the accents and significant pauses (whether caesuras or end-stops) before looking at the analysis that follows.

THE SONG OF A MAN WHO HAS COME THROUGH

Not I, not I, but the wind that blows through me!
A fine wind is blowing the new direction of Time.
If only I let it bear me, carry me, if only it carry me!
If only I am sensitive, subtle, oh, delicate, a winged gift!
If only, most lovely of all, I yield myself and am borrowed   5
By the fine, fine wind that takes its course through the chaos of the
    world
Like a fine, an exquisite chisel, a wedge-blade inserted;
If only I am keen and hard like the sheer tip of a wedge
Driven by invisible blows,
The rock will split, we shall come at the wonder, we shall find the
    Hesperides.   10

Oh, for the wonder that bubbles into my soul,
I would be a good fountain, a good well-head,
Would blur no whisper, spoil no expression.

What is the knocking?
What is the knocking at the door in the night?   15
It is somebody wants to do us harm.

No, no, it is the three strange angels.
Admit them, admit them.

--D. H. Lawrence

Not I, not I, but the wind that blows through me!

A fine wind is blowing the new direction of Time.

If only I let it bear me, carry me, if only it carry me!

If only I am sensitive, subtle, oh, delicate, a winged gift!

If only, most lovely of all, I yield myself and am borrowed   5

By the fine, fine wind that takes its course through the chaos of the
        world

Like a fine, an exquisite chisel, a wedge-blade inserted;

If only I am keen and hard like the sheer tip of a wedge

Driven by invisible blows,

The rock will split, we shall come at the wonder, we shall find
        the Hesperides.   10

Oh, for the wonder that bubbles into my soul,

I would be a good fountain, a good well-head,

Would blur no whisper, spoil no expression.

What is the knocking?

What is the knocking at the door in the night?   15

It is somebody wants to do us harm.

No, no,   it is the three strange angels.

Admit them,   admit them.

Perhaps in line 16 the rhythm tends to fall into a metrical pattern, but by and large the rhythm is free—and inevitably the markings of accent and pause are open to question. The accenting relies upon the usual devices except an abstract metrical pattern: (1) conventional accenting of multisyllabic words, as with *diréction* in line 2; (2) ordinary importance of words, as with the accenting of *wind* but not *the* in line 1; (3) alliterative emphasis, as with *course* and *chaos* in line 6; (4) repeated phrasal patterns, as in line 3, in which the phrase tends to establish the accenting throughout: *beār mĕ* suggests *cārrŷ mĕ, cārrŷ mĕ* rather than *cārrŷ mē, cārrŷ mē*. Accents per line vary from two in line 14 to perhaps seven in line 6; the total number of syllables per line ranges from five to nineteen. The chief rhythmic units are grammatical phrases, highly irregular in length. Most but not all of the lines are end-stopped. Pauses within the lines vary widely in number and position.

Such irregularity more easily yields slack disorderliness than rhythm. Lawrence holds things together in large part by his repetitions of phrasing and by his unbalanced grammatical constructions that maintain a forward movement. The poem begins with the relatively intense *Not I, not I* that the rest of the first line leaves grammatically incomplete. The second line begins as repeated phrasing of part of the incomplete first line, and then shifts to become uneasily complete on its own. With the opening of the third line, Lawrence begins his subordinate *if only* clauses, increasing their length until in lines 5 to 7 the grammatical structure is nearly lost; he re-establishes the structure with *if only* in line 8, and then draws the stanza up with the brief main clauses of line 10. The rhythm moves from an intensity to a fullness, and then diminishes. The succeeding stanzas offer a similar movement on a smaller scale. The second stanza begins with the intensity of the first, and turns to another series of phrases. The questions in the third stanza bring to a pause the rhythmic overflowing of expressive statement. The first line of the last stanza recalls the opening of the poem, and the second line closes the poem in the diminishing rhythm of the close of the first stanza.

Other elements contribute to the fluid character of the rhythm. The phrasal pauses, though frequent, are rarely heavy; and the phrasing itself avoids awkwardness or roughness. The accenting is fairly light, even in lines where it is profuse. The word sounds and word meanings are seldom harsh; the words tend to be monosyllabic but are not blunt. *Wedge-blade inserted* is the single brief exception to these qualities, and it is still a far cry from *Is perjured, murderous, bloody, full of blame, / Savage, extreme, rude, cruel, not to trust.* The overall rhythmic movement of the poem is relatively swift and intense without losing a sense of ease. It is neither harsh nor emphatic. The image of the wind in the first stanza suggests the quality of the rhythm, and both suggest the delicate intensity of spirit that Lawrence is describing.

The tools for analyzing the rhythm of a poem are inexact, even when the poem is a simple limerick. A good reader will be able to hear the rhythm of a poem better than he is able to analyze it. The usefulness of analysis is to sharpen one's sense of rhythm. For rhythm is central to poetry, whether for the sake of its beat or flow, the sounds it conveys, or the meanings it implies.

EXERCISES

1. Explain the phrasal means by which Alexander Pope emphasizes his rhymes and Robert Browning de-emphasizes his in the fragments on pages 46–47. What different rhythmic effects are achieved by the two poets?

2.

SONNET

> She took the dappled partridge flecked with blood,
>   And in her hand the drooping pheasant bare,
>   And by his feet she held the woolly hare,
> And like a master painting where she stood,
> Looked some new goddess of an English wood.   5
>   Nor could I find an imperfection there,
>   Nor blame the wanton act that showed so fair—
> To me whatever freak she plays is good.

Hers is the fairest Life that breathes with breath,
And *their* still plumes and azure eyelids closed   10
Made quiet Death so beautiful to see
That Death lent grace to Life and Life to Death
And in one image Life and Death reposed,
To make my love an Immortality.

—Alfred Lord Tennyson

HOLY SONNET 7

At the round earth's imagined corners, blow
Your trumpets, Angels, and arise, arise
From death, you numberless infinities
Of souls, and to your scattered bodies go,
All whom the flood did, and fire shall o'erthrow,   5
All whom war, dearth, age, agues, tyrannies,
Despair, law, chance, hath slain, and you whose eyes,
Shall behold God, and never taste death's woe.
But let them sleep, Lord, and me mourn a space,
For, if above all these, my sins abound,   10
'Tis late to ask abundance of Thy grace,
When we are there; here on this lowly ground,
Teach me how to repent; for that's as good
As if Thou hadst sealed my pardon, with Thy blood.

—John Donne

a. Scan both of the poems, and explain any variations from iambic pentameter that you observe in the first five lines of each poem.

b. Mark the caesuras in each poem, noting any unusual uses. Mark off all the heavy internal pauses in the lines, and make a general contrast between the two poems in their use of internal pause.

c. Mark off the end-stopped and run-on lines in each poem.

d. Compare the degree of consistency in length of grammatical units in the two poems.

e. On the basis of your preceding analyses, contrast the rhythmic characters of the two poems, and show the appropriateness of each rhythm to its poem.

3.

BREAK, BREAK, BREAK

Break, break, break,

  On thy cold gray stones, O Sea!

And I would that my tongue could utter

  The thoughts that arise in me.

O well for the fisherman's boy,   5

  That he shouts with his sister at play!

O well for the sailor lad,

  That he sings in his boat on the bay!

And the stately ships go on

  To their haven under the hill;   10

But O for the touch of a vanished hand,

  And the sound of a voice that is still!

Break, break, break

  At the foot of thy crags, O Sea!

But the tender grace of a day that is dead   15

  Will never come back to me.

—Alfred Lord Tennyson

a. Scan the poem and identify all the kinds of feet in it.

b. Characterize the general strength with which the lines are either run-on or end-stopped.

c. To what extent do the grammatical units coincide with individual lines? When the units are larger than individual lines, what is their characteristic size?

d. Show how Tennyson uses internal pause and sound to maintain metrical regularity in the first and last stanzas. (On sound, see Question 4, p. 57.)

e. On the basis of your answers to the preceding questions, describe the general character of Tennyson's rhythm, and discuss its relationship to the idea of the poem.

4. The following two excerpts from poems illustrate an unusual kind of metrical verse. In reading them, assume that each one has a regular number of beats per line.

from CHRISTABEL

'Tis the middle of the night by the castle clock,
And the owls have awakened the crowing cock;
Tu—whit!——Tu—whoo!
And hark again! the crowing cock,
How drowsily it crew.   5

Sir Leoline, the Baron rich,
Hath a toothless mastiff bitch;
From her kennel beneath the rock
She maketh answer to the clock,
Four for the quarters, and twelve for the hour;   10
Ever and aye, by shine and shower,
Sixteen short howls, not over loud;
Some say she sees my lady's shroud. . .

—Samuel Taylor Coleridge

from PIERS PLOWMAN

In a summer season when soft was the sun
I shaped me into a shroud as I a shep were;
In habit as a Hermit, unholy of works,
Went wide in this world wonders to hear.
But on a May morning on Malvern Hills   5
Me befel a ferly, of fairy me thought:
I was weary for wandering and went me to rest
Under a broad bank by a bourne side,
And as I lay and leaned and looked on the waters
I slumbered into a sleeping, it swithed so merry. . . .   10

—William Langland

2. *shep:* shepherd; 6. *ferly:* marvel; 8. *bourne:* brook; 10. *swithed:* sounded.

a. Mark the accented and unaccented syllables in each line, and total
the number of syllables per line. Using Tennyson's Sonnet in Question 1
as a typical example of ordinary metrical verse, state the apparent differ-.

ence between it and the two excerpts. (One way of approaching the difference is to notice what happens to the unaccented syllables in the fragments
when the regularity of beat of the accented syllables is maintained.)

   b. Relying upon your answer to Part "d" of Question 3, discuss whether
the first and last stanzas of "Break, Break, Break" should be regarded as
ordinary metrical verse or as the unusual sort of the two fragments.

   c. Compare and contrast the chief devices by which the authors of the
two fragments indicate and control the accenting. Which poet more strictly
controls the accenting, and by means of what device?

   d. Which of the two fragments seems closer to ordinary poetry in its
meter? Discuss.

   5. Relying solely upon analyses of word-length, grammatical-phrase-
length, and quality of word sound (pleasant, harsh, full, plain, etc.), make
a comparison of the rhythms of the following three poems.

LORD, IT BELONGS NOT TO MY CARE

> *Lord,* it belongs not to my care,
>   Whether I die or live;
> To love and serve Thee is my share,
>   And this Thy grace must give.
>
> If life be long I will be glad,   5
>   That I may long obey;
> If short—yet why should I be sad
>   To soar to endless day?
>
> *Christ* leads me through no darker rooms
>   Than He went through before;   10
> He that unto *God's* kingdom comes,
>   Must enter by this door.
>
> Come, *Lord,* when grace has made me meet
>   Thy blesséd face to see;
> For if Thy work on earth be sweet,   15
>   What will Thy glory be!
>
> Then shall I end my sad complaints,
>   And weary, sinful days;
> And join with the triumphant saints,
>   To sing *Jehovah's* praise.   20
>
> My knowledge of that life is small,
>   The eye of faith is dim;
> But 'tis enough that *Christ* knows all,
>   And I shall be with Him.
>
>   —*Richard Baxter*

HOLY SONNET 14

Batter my heart, three personed God; for You
As yet but knock, breathe, shine, and seek to mend;
That I may rise, and stand, o'erthrow me, and bend
Your force, to break, blow, burn and make me new.
I, like an usurped town, to another due,   5
Labor to admit You, but O, to no end,
Reason Your viceroy in me, me should defend,
But is captived, and proves weak or untrue.
Yet dearly I love You, and would be loved fain,
But am betrothed unto Your enemy: 10
Divorce me, untie, or break that knot again,
Take me to You, imprison me, for I
Except You enthrall me, never shall be free,
Nor ever chaste, except You ravish me.

—*John Donne*

ON THE LATE MASSACRE IN PIEDMONT *

Avenge, O Lord, thy slaughtered saints, whose bones
Lie scattered on the Alpine mountains cold,
Even them who kept thy truth so pure of old
When all our fathers worshipped stocks and stones,
Forget not: in thy book record their groans   5
Who were thy sheep and in their ancient fold
Slain by the bloody Piemontese that rolled
Mother with infant down the rocks. Their moans
The vales redoubled to the hills, and they
To Heaven. Their martyred blood and ashes sow   10
O'er all th' Italian fields where still doth sway
The triple tyrant: that from these may grow
A hundredfold, who having learnt thy way
Early may fly the Babylonian woe.

—*John Milton*

ADDITIONAL EXERCISES

1. Analyze the rhythm of "Lullaby," p. 188.

2. Analyze the rhythmic effect of the repeated phrasing and incremental repetition (see *Glossary,* p. 170) in "A Lyke-Wake Dirge," p. 186, and "Edward," p. 183.

* The Catholic Piedmontese massacred a local sect with Protestant leanings.

3. Analyze the rhythm of "Bavarian Gentians," p. 159, along the lines suggested by the discussion of "The Song of a Man Who Has Come Through."

4. Analyze the rhythm in Gerard Manley Hopkins' "The Windhover," p. 295. Compare it with the two fragments given in Question 4 above, and decide whether it is metrical like them, metrical in the manner of ordinary verse, or nonmetrical.

5. Write a summary of the opinions on the conventional and linguistic approaches to rhythm contained in the following articles: W. K. Wimsatt, Jr., and Monroe C. Beardsley, "The Concept of Meter: An Exercise in Abstraction," *PMLA,* LXXIV (December 1959), 585–598, and George B. Pace, "The Two Domains: Meter and Rhythm," *PMLA,* LXXVI (September 1961), 413–419. Report also on the two responses to Wimsatt and Beardsley in *PMLA* June 1961 and December 1962.

5

METAPHOR

The language of poetry is metaphorical, and some people believe that this means saying pretty things such as *my love's like a red, red rose* or *the moon, a golden galleon* or *Queen Anne's Lace*. It does. To speak metaphorically is to describe or identify one thing in terms of another, and to say that a woman is like a rose or the moon like a galleon or a flower like lace is to use metaphor. Customarily the word *simile* is applied when the one thing is said explicitly to be similar to the other—usually using *like* or *as*. Thus *my love's like a red, red rose* is a simile but can be called a metaphor. *The moon, a golden galleon* and *Queen Anne's Lace* are metaphors. Observe the progressive condensation in the metaphors: *the moon, a golden galleon* omits *like,* and *Queen Anne's Lace* omits both *like* and the thing compared, the flower.

To speak metaphorically may also mean saying trite things, prosaic things, ugly things.

> He's square
>
> —*Author Unknown*

> The iron curtain
>
> —*Winston Churchill*

> The round squat turret, blind as the fool's heart
>
> —*Robert Browning*

In the first of these, the personality of a man is compared to a geometrical shape. In *iron curtain* the foreign policy of Communist

Europe is compared to an imagined iron curtain. When Churchill first used the phrase, he made clear what it referred to, and it has since been used so often that the reference is understood without being given. In Browning's line, a turret is said to be blind, and thus is compared to a living creature, presumably a human being. And then Browning disrupts his metaphor by adding that this blind turret is blind in the way that a fool's heart is blind, and thus he has at least two more metaphors, in which the turret is compared to the heart of a fool and the heart of a fool is said to be blind. If this assortment of metaphors seems to make no sense, it illustrates the fact that all metaphors display an element of nonsense: men are not square, and foreign policies are not like iron curtains.

Despite the nonsense, metaphors are used for two good reasons: they are inescapable and invaluable. Suppose you are a hard-headed businessman and despise metaphors, being interested only in whether the stock-market is rising. Your hard head is as metaphorical as a soft head: a quality of mind in such a phrase is being compared to a physical condition of the head. Does the stock-market rise? Does it give its seat to a lady? A financial condition is thus likened to a physical movement. The metaphor of a rising stock-market is so common, so unnoticeable, that it is called a *dead metaphor*. *Hard-headed* is almost dead. All the other words in the same sentence are metaphorical too, but the metaphorical meanings have been used to death for so long that they are called *buried metaphors,* and one has to go to a dictionary of the history of words to find them out. For instance:

Suppose once meant to place under.
Business once meant busy-ness.
Interested once meant to lie between.
Metaphor once meant to transfer.

In the history of language, every word has metaphorical roots, even such words as *you, are, a,* and *and,* and a single word may have a dozen metaphors buried in it, one underneath the other. Ordinarily, neither the writer nor the reader knows about such metaphors, and in effect they are not metaphors. The rest of the discussion will not consider them.

All metaphors consist of two elements: the thing described or identified (commonly called the *tenor*) and the means by which it is described or identified (commonly called the *vehicle*).

Tenor	Vehicle
my love	rose
moon	galleon
(a flower)	Queen Anne's Lace
he	square
(Communist foreign policy)	iron curtain
turret	blind
turret	fool's heart
(practical)	hard-headed
(economically improving)	rising

The list tells several things: (1) the tenor is often omitted—being understood or implied, as with *a flower, Communist foreign policy, practical,* and *economically improving;* (2) a dead metaphor, such as *rising* or perhaps *hard-headed,* is one in which the distinction between vehicle and tenor goes unobserved; and (3) the describing or identifying that the vehicle does can be various and can be incidental to other aims: *Queen Anne's Lace* describes a physical object through physical comparison; *square* describes a nonphysical quality through physical comparison; *galleon* is more decorative than descriptive; *blind as the fool's heart* perhaps aims mainly to arouse emotion. Note particularly that metaphors are often pointed to by naming the vehicle alone. Thus *hard-headed* is called a metaphor; it is the vehicle of the whole metaphor that includes the practical quality of mind it refers to. The same is the case with *rising, iron curtain,* and *Queen Anne's Lace.*

When metaphors are used well, they are accurate or economical or suggestive or beautiful or ugly or unobtrusive or ridiculous or anything else that the wit of the poet wants to make them. If *my love's like a red, red rose,* Robert Burns has said economically that she is young but more woman than virgin, and that she is lovely but with a rosy, full face rather than a pale, delicate one. If *she walks in beauty, like the night / Of cloudless climes and starry skies,* Lord Byron has said less economically that she is young and lovely, but with a dark, serene beauty, and his simile suggests such beauty better than *young, lovely, dark, serene* do. If *the witch that came (the withered hag) / To wash the steps with pail and rag, / Was once the beauty Abishag,* Robert Frost has used *witch* and *hag* to call to mind another sort of woman. The poet uses original metaphors, familiar ones, and dead ones. He can be obvious about them or subtle. He can pile a multitude of them together or draw out a single one. He can choose vehicles all of one sort, or of a dozen sorts. Whatever he does, he affects the quality of what he is saying.

The following poem is about as plain metaphorically as a poem can be.

DUST OF SNOW

The way a crow
Shook down on me
The dust of snow
From a hemlock tree

Has given my heart · 5
A change of mood
And saved some part
Of a day I had rued.

—Robert Frost

There are several metaphors in the poem, but most of them are unobtrusive, being dead: *way, given, heart, change, saved.* (Each of these terms is the vehicle of each whole metaphor.) *Way* is a path used to describe a manner of doing something; *given* is a physical act applied to the effect of that manner of doing something; *heart* is an organ that stands for a person's feelings; and so forth. There is only one noticeable metaphor in the poem: *dust of snow;* and it is as plain as a noticeable metaphor can well be. Frost might have said *diamonds of snow* or a *stream of snow,* but apparently he wanted to keep his poem unadorned and unself-conscious. He relied upon plain and dead metaphors, and his poem has an ordinariness of a simple though meaningful experience.

Here is William Butler Yeats being self-conscious:

THE COMING OF WISDOM WITH TIME

Though leaves are many, the root is one;
Through all the lying days of my youth
I swayed my leaves and flowers in the sun;
Now I may wither into the truth.

Most of the metaphors are obvious and artful. The most important one, in which the speaker compares himself to a plant (the vehicle, unnamed), is extended through the third and fourth lines of the poem and retrospectively includes the first line. It is called an *extended metaphor,* and embraces the following individual metaphors (vehicles): *leaves, root, swayed, flowers, wither,* and in association *sun.* Until the reader consciously considers these metaphors he will not understand the poem. And when he considers them, he will see that they are curious: their references (their tenors) are not easy to pin down. What does *flowers* refer to—that is, what is the tenor for the vehicle? Are the flowers the poems of a speaker who is a poet? Are they the physical beauty of a speaker who once was handsome? Are they the sensual life that the speaker once enjoyed? Yeats' metaphor is suggestive rather than exact. The metaphor *root* is difficult in another way: it has a precise reference, but what it refers to is intangible and hidden: the root, the core, the integrity of a person's individual existence. Part of the importance of metaphor is that it thus identifies intangible and hidden aspects of human existence.

The poem has other somewhat less noticeable metaphors. *Lying days* describes *days* as a liar. The metaphor is a shorthand way of saying *days when I lied. Lying* in itself does not mean literal telling of lies; it is a metaphor (vehicle) of the same suggestive sort as *flowers:* it refers to caring more for beauty or pleasure or art than for truth. In the title of the poem there are dead metaphors, which can be described either of two ways: *wisdom* and *time* are described as persons who are coming somewhere, or *coming* is used to describe a mental development. Such ambiguity in pointing out metaphor is inevitable and common—testimony to the fact that language is metaphor piled on metaphor.

Yeats' metaphors help to make his poem different from Frost's, and then in a way similar to it. His chief metaphor is elaborate rather than simple, beautiful rather than plain, suggestive rather than precise. To state these qualities is in large part to say what his poem is like. But observe that in the third line, *I swayed my leaves and flowers in the sun,* the metaphor takes on a life of its own, and becomes a simple description like *The way a crow / Shook down on me / The dust of snow / From a hemlock tree.* Yeats uses a metaphor of nature to say something about the natural course of life of his speaker. Frost talks of the influence of nature upon his speaker.

Metaphor assumes various shapes that have special names, and is intimately related to other non-literal language. Two of the most common of these are *synecdoche* and *personification.* In synecdoche part of something is made to stand for the whole thing. The phrase *the black-board jungle* combines synecdoche with ordinary metaphor. *Blackboard* stands for *school,* and *jungle* is the vehicle that describes what the school is like. In personification an inanimate or abstract thing is given human quality, as in the trite phrase *mother nature* and in William Wordsworth's more poetical expression of the same thought: *Nature never did betray the heart that loved her.* Some degree of personification can be found in a large proportion of metaphorical language. Browning's blind turret and Yeats' lying days are examples. In general, describing and identifying one thing in terms of another may be regarded as a fundamental activity by which language grows and people see. That metaphor is so obvious an element of poetry illustrates the fact that poets are professional users of words, and are preoccupied with describing and identifying things, whether those things are snow-laden hemlock trees or leaves and flowers in the soul.

EXERCISES

1. The lines *my love's like a red, red rose* and *the round squat turret, blind as the fool's heart* have each a dead metaphor unidentified in the discussion on pp. 80–81. What are they? (The discussion of "Dust of Snow" on p. 83 will help on the second one.)

2.

THEY SAY MY VERSE IS SAD: NO WONDER

> They say my verse is sad: no wonder;
>   Its narrow measure spans
> Tears of eternity, and sorrow,
>   Not mine, but man's.
>
> This is for all ill-treated fellows   5
>   Unborn and unbegot,
> For them to read when they're in trouble
>   And I am not.

—A. E. Housman

a. The following phrases are metaphorical; each may involve more than one metaphor: *verse is sad, narrow measure spans, tears of eternity.* Distinguish between tenor and vehicle in each case, state whether the poet has supplied the tenor or not, and identify any personification.

b. *Ill-treated fellows* and *in trouble* are dead metaphors. Explain.

c. Where is the poem most obviously metaphorical? Where least?

How original are the metaphors? Relying upon the discussions of "Dust of Snow" and "The Coming of Wisdom with Time" as examples, describe the general effect of Housman's metaphors upon his poem.

3. In the following poem, the speaker describes his feelings before a girl's death (*she* in line 3), and then describes her dead.

A SLUMBER DID MY SPIRIT SEAL

A slumber did my spirit seal;
   I had no human fears:
She seemed a thing that could not feel
   The touch of earthly years.

No motion has she now, no force;   5
   She neither hears nor sees;
Rolled round in earth's diurnal course,
   With rocks, and stones, and trees.

               —William Wordsworth

a. The following words and phrases are metaphors: *slumber, seal, touch of earthly years, motion, force, rolled, earth's diurnal course.* With each one distinguish between tenor and vehicle, state whether the poet has supplied the tenor or not, and identify any personification.

b. In general, are the metaphors in this poem more or less ordinary than those in Housman's poem in Question 2? Describe their general effect upon the poem.

4. An extended metaphor of a self-consciously exaggerated sort, in which tenor and vehicle seem to have little in common, is often called a *conceit*. In the following sonnet, Shakespeare uses legal and business language to describe love. Such words as *possessing, charter,* and *misprison* (in modern spelling *misprision*) are part of his conceit.

SONNET 87

Farewell! thou art too dear for my possessing,
And like enough thou know'st thy estimate:
The charter of thy worth gives thee releasing;
My bonds in thee are all determinate.
For how do I hold thee but by thy granting?   5
And for that riches where is my deserving?
The cause of this fair gift in me is wanting,
And so my patent back again is swerving.
Thyself thou gavest, thy own worth then not knowing,
Or me, to whom thou gavest it, else mistaking;   10
So thy great gift, upon misprison growing,

Comes home again, on better judgment making.
Thus have I had thee, as a dream doth flatter,
In sleep a king, but waking no such matter.

a. List in order of their appearance ten words other than *possessing,
charter,* and *misprison* that are part of Shakespeare's conceit. Distinguish between tenor and vehicle of the first five.

b. Given your preceding account of the tenors, would you say that Shakespeare's metaphors are economical in the sense that Burns' metaphor of the woman as a rose is (see page 82)? Explain.

c. What is the general effect of Shakespeare's metaphors upon his poem? (Make a contrast with both the Wordsworth and the Housman poems, and also consider the shift in metaphors that occurs with the final couplet.)

5. It was remarked on page 81 that all metaphors are somewhat nonsensical. Women are not like roses: they do not have petals, thorns, a stem. But metaphors still make sense. Women and roses can have things in common: beauty, brightness of color, brief fulfillment. Review the list of tenors and vehicles on page 82, and note the various degrees and kinds of similarity (or dissimilarity) each vehicle brings to its tenor—taking into account what the writer presumably wants to call to mind and what he wants to be ignored.

6. Keeping in mind your analysis in Question 5, discuss whether Yeats' extended metaphor in "The Coming of Wisdom with Time" (page 83) qualifies as a conceit according to the definition at the beginning of Question 4.

7.

HOLY SONNET 14

Batter my heart, three-personned God; for You
As yet but knock, breathe, shine, and seek to mend;
That I may rise and stand, o'erthrow me, and bend
Your force to break, blow, burn, and make me new.
I, like an usurped town, to another due,   5
Labor to admit You, but O, to no end;
Reason, Your viceroy in me, me should defend,
But is captived, and proves weak or untrue.
Yet dearly I love You, and would be loved fain,
But am betrothed unto Your enemy.   10
Divorce me, untie or break that knot again;
Take me to You, imprison me, for I,
Except You enthrall me, never shall be free,
Nor ever chaste, except You ravish me.

a. Identify the two or three extended metaphors that Donne relies on, and list under each of them the individual metaphors associated with it (as with Yeats' "The Coming of Wisdom with Time" on pages 83–84).

b. Identify the single most striking metaphor in the poem. Comment upon the relationship of tenor and vehicle in it in the light of Question 5. Comment generally upon the relationship between tenor and vehicle in the extended metaphors of the poem. (It may be useful to consider how close Donne's metaphors are to some of the conventional religious metaphors applied to God.)

c. What is the general effect of Donne's metaphors upon his poem? In your answer make a contrast with each of the poems given in the preceding questions.

ADDITIONAL EXERCISES

1. Analyze the metaphorical language in Thomas Hardy, "In Time of 'The Breaking of Nations,'" p. 293; A. E. Housman, "Epitaph on an Army of Mercenaries," p. 127; Robert Frost, "The Subverted Flower," p. 312; and William Shakespeare, "Sonnet 73," p. 110.

2. Look up the definition of *mixed metaphor* in the *Glossary,* p. 172, and discuss "Holy Sonnet 14" (above) in relation to it.

3. Look up the definition of *metaphysical conceit* in the *Glossary,* p. 172, and discuss "Holy Sonnet 14" (above) and "A Valediction: Forbidding Mourning," p. 207, with regard to it. Compare and contrast the general character of the conceits in "Holy Sonnet 14," "A Valediction: Forbidding Mourning," and Shakespeare's "Sonnet 87" (above).

6

SENSE IMAGERY

> Though leaves are many, the root is one;
> Through all the lying days of my youth
> I swayed my leaves and flowers in the sun;
> Now I may wither into the truth.
>
> *—William Butler Yeats*

> The way a crow
> Shook down on me
> The dust of snow
> From a hemlock tree . . .
>
> *Robert Frost*

As was pointed out at the end of the previous chapter, Yeats' flowering bush is a metaphor and at the same time (in line 3) a simple description comparable to Frost's literal snow-laden tree. Both bush and tree are visual images.

The word *image* has several meanings in poetry, some of them mentioned in the *Glossary*, page 170. In the present chapter a distinct kind of image is discussed. Sometimes called free sense imagery (and here simply called sense imagery), it refers to word, phrase, and passage meanings that identify, describe, or evoke physical sensation, acts, and objects and scenes. *Dizziness, running,* and *leaves and flowers in the sun* are sense images. Such imagery may be metaphorical or literal or both, and may concern a single sense or several senses together. Since distinctions of physical experience are often subtle, and since readers vary widely in their reactions to sense imagery, analysis of this aspect of poetry is difficult. The following list offers one way in which sense imagery can be categorized.

Visual imagery refers to objects and scenes identified and described, and also to the act of seeing. Note that the following image is both literal and metaphorical.

> The sun was gone now; the curled moon
> Was like a little feather . . .
>
> *—Dante Gabriel Rossetti*

Auditory imagery refers to sounds identified, described, and evoked, and also to the act of hearing. (Excluded from the present discussion is auditory imagery in the meaning of alliteration, onomatopoeia, etc.) Note that the following image is also visual.

> Ring out, wild bells, to the wild sky
>
> *—Alfred Lord Tennyson*

Tactual imagery refers to sensations of touch identified, described, or evoked. The following image is also visual and perhaps slightly auditory.

> Whenas in silks my Julia goes,
> Then, then, methinks, how sweetly flows
> That liquefaction of her clothes.
>
> *—Robert Herrick*

Olfactory imagery refers to sensations of smell identified, described, or evoked. The following image is also visual.

> . . . jessamine faint, and the sweet tube rose,
> The sweetest flower for scent that blows . . .
>
> *—Percy Bysshe Shelley*

Gustatory imagery refers to sensations of taste and eating identified, described, or evoked. The following image is also visual.

> . . . whose strenuous tongue
> Can burst Joy's grape against his palate fine . . .
>
> *—John Keats*

Kinesthetic imagery refers to bodily position and muscle sense identified, described, or evoked.

> . . . whose strenuous tongue

Organic imagery refers to sensations of the organs of the body (such as breathing) and to other local and nonlocal internal sensations (such as dizziness or wakefulness) identified, described, or evoked. It includes imagery of the act of seeing and hearing, and likewise embraces tactual, olfactory, gustatory, and kinesthetic images when the reader is made to respond to them intimately.

> They lay calm-breathing on the bedded grass;
> Their arms embracéd, and their pinions too;
> Their lips touched not, but had not bade adieu . . .
>
> —*John Keats*

Calm-breathing is the organic image. The bodily position described is a kinesthetic image, and the embracing arms and almost-touching lips are tactual images. The intimacy with which the reader experiences the kinesthetic and tactual images makes them organic as well. (In contrast, Herrick's tactual image above seems nonorganic. A reading of the whole of Keats' poem, page 259, may make the difference clearer.) All three lines are visual too.

Note. Visual and kinesthetic images—and other images to a lesser extent—can be usefully divided into two types: static and kinetic, that is, nonmoving and moving. Keats' image of the lovers is almost static; Herrick's of Julia is kinetic.

The difficulties of labelling images is evident in most of the preceding examples. One more illustration may be useful. Tennyson's *Ring out, wild bells, to the wild sky* was said to be both auditory and visual. *Ring* and *wild* give the image a kinetic quality, and the kinetic quality perhaps makes the image kinesthetic as well.

Despite the hazards of analysis, an awareness of sense imagery is fundamental to understanding poetry. Here is a poem notable for its visual imagery.

SONNET

> She took the dappled partridge flecked with blood,
> And in her hand the drooping pheasant bare,
> And by his feet she held the woolly hare,

And like a master painting where she stood,
Looked some new goddess of an English wood.   5
    Nor could I find an imperfection there,
    Nor blame the wanton act that showed so fair—
To me whatever freak she plays is good.
Hers is the fairest Life that breathes with breath,
    And *their* still plumes and azure eyelids closed   10
        Made quiet Death so beautiful to see
That Death lent grace to Life and Life to Death
    And in one image Life and Death reposed,
        To make my love an Immortality.

                              —Alfred Lord Tennyson

The whole poem presents a single visual image—a description—of a girl holding a partridge, a pheasant, and a hare. Lovely and clear as the image is, its effectiveness has little to do with photographic realism. Is the girl young or mature? What sort of dress is she wearing? In which hand does she bear the pheasant? Is the pheasant Ringneck or Golden? Any visual image in words makes its appeal to an inward eye rather than to a physical eye. Some incidental details of the image are relatively precise and literal: *partridge flecked with blood, azure eyelids closed*. Other details are general and metaphorical: like *a master painting,* looked *some new goddess*. All these details, literal and metaphorical, are themselves properly called visual images, just as collectively they constitute a visual image. They are complemented by a few other images that connect to other senses. *Took, drooping, bare, held, stood, eyelids closed,* and *reposed* concern bodily position and muscle sense, and are thus kinesthetic images. *Breathes* is organic. *Eyelids closed* and *partridge flecked with blood* may evoke organic sensation. Along with *quiet, breathes* suggests a silence of scene, and thus is additionally an auditory image. Observe the fact that although such a line as *Nor could I find an imperfection there* can barely be said to contain any sense imagery, in context it contributes to the visual image that the preceding lines have been establishing. Note also that such kinetic images as *act* and *plays* lose all force by the abstractness of the lines in which they appear and by the static imagery of the preceding lines. Taken together, and overlapping one another as they do, all the images of the poem make Tennyson's scene quiet, static, composed. The character of the rest of the poem, perhaps most evidently in the rhythm, is in keeping with these qualities; and the total effect is a master painting.

In the following poem the imagery has a different character.

BRIGHT STAR

Bright star, would I were steadfast as thou art—
  Not in lone splendor hung aloft the night
And watching, with eternal lids apart,
  Like nature's patient, sleepless Eremite,
The moving waters at their priestlike task   5
  Of pure ablution round earth's human shores,
Or gazing on the new soft fallen mask
  Of snow upon the mountains and the moors—
No—yet still steadfast, still unchangeable,
  Pillowed upon my fair love's ripening breast,   10
To feel forever its soft fall and swell,
  Awake forever in a sweet unrest,
Still, still to hear her tender-taken breath,
And so live ever—or else swoon to death.

             —*John Keats*

The visual imagery concerns the star in the night sky, the oceans lapping the continents, the snow on the land, and the man and woman. These images, though brief, are powerful. They are accompanied by equally powerful organic images: *steadfast, watching, with eternal lids apart, patient, sleepless, gazing, steadfast* again, *pillowed, ripening breast, fall and swell, awake, sweet unrest, still, still, tender-taken breath, swoon*. Some of these organic images have kinesthetic and visual elements: *steadfast, watching, gazing, pillowed, still*. Other powerful images in the poem are tactual: the oceans washing the shores, the snow lying upon the land, and the man feeling the fall and swell of his beloved's breast. The auditory images suggest quietness of sound: the waters at a great distance coming ashore, the snow fallen upon the land, the woman breathing. Such words as *still, still* serve a triple imagistic purpose: auditory, kinesthetic, and organic.

The difference of Keats' sonnet from Tennyson's is clear enough. Whereas Tennyson's visual images seem to stand composed at ten feet from the observer, two or three of Keats' visual images are at once seen at a great distance and no distance at all—especially the star in the sky that becomes a watching, lidless eye. Moreover, although Keats' visual images are not actively kinetic, they have a sweet unrest rather than an almost entirely static quality: the bright star hangs suspended in the sky, the waters are moving, the woman's breast swells. The most obvious difference lies with the profusion and power of Keats' organic imagery, which makes for an intimate sensuousness that Tennyson declines.

EXERCISES

1.

MUSIC, WHEN SOFT VOICES DIE

Music, when soft voices die,
Vibrates in the memory—
Odors, when sweet violets sicken,
Live within the sense they quicken.
Rose leaves, when the rose is dead,   5
Are heaped for the beloved's bed;
And so thy thoughts, when thou art gone,
Love itself shall slumber on.

—*Percy Bysshe Shelley*

a. Identify the visual, auditory, and olfactory images of the poem.

b. What kind, or kinds, of images are the following: *vibrates in the memory, sicken, the sense they quicken, slumber?*

c. On the basis of your previous answers, identify the dominant kind of image in the poem.

d. Describe the character of the poem in terms of the quality of its imagery.

2.

SONNET 73

That time of year thou mayst in me behold
When yellow leaves, or none, or few, do hang
Upon those boughs which shake against the cold,
Bare ruined choirs, where late the sweet birds sang.
In me thou see'st the twilight of such day   5
As after sunset fadeth in the west;
Which by and by black night doth take away,
Death's second self, that seals up all in rest.
In me thou see'st the glowing of such fire,
That on the ashes of his youth doth lie,   10
As the deathbed whereon it must expire,
Consumed with that which it was nourished by.
This thou perceiv'st, which makes thy love more strong,
To love that well which thou must leave ere long.

—*William Shakespeare*

a. Identify the three main visual images of the poem. State whether they are offered metaphorically or literally and what general meaning Shakespeare uses them to suggest.

b. Look up the word *choirs* and find a meaning appropriate for the phrase *bare ruined choirs*. With this meaning in mind, and also the answer to Question "a," use the first four lines of the poem to illustrate the point, made on page 92, that visual imagery must appeal to an inward rather than physical eye.

c. Identify the chief tactual, auditory, and kinesthetic images in the first four lines. Which one is most powerful?

d. Other than the visual images, what are the two or three most powerful single images in the poem? Is your answer here consistent with your answer to the second part of Question "c"?

e. Is the imagery in the poem mainly static or kinetic? Illustrate both sorts.

f. On the basis of your answers to the preceding questions, compare the effect of the imagery upon the poem with the effects of the imagery in the Tennyson and Keats poems above.

3.

LONDON

I wander through each chartered street,
Near where the chartered Thames does flow,
And mark in every face I meet
Marks of weakness, marks of woe.

In every cry of every Man,   5
In every Infant's cry of fear,
In every voice, in every ban,
The mind-forged manacles I hear.

How the Chimney-sweeper's cry
Every blackening Church appalls;   10
And the hapless Soldier's sigh
Runs in blood down Palace walls.

But most through midnight streets I hear
How the youthful Harlot's curse
Blasts the new born Infant's tear,   15
And blights with plagues the Marriage hearse.

—William Blake

a. Identify the several auditory images in the poem, and decide whether or not they have strongly organic qualities. Explain your answer in each case.

b. Stanza 3 has two powerful visual images and two powerful auditory images. Would you say that the stanza as a whole is equally auditory and visual, more one than the other, or more something else than either? Explain your answer.

c. What kind, or kinds, of images are the following phrases? One or another of them may be unusually difficult to identify. *Chartered street, mind-forged manacles, blasts, blights with plagues, Marriage hearse.*

d. On the basis of your answers to the preceding questions, compare the effect of the imagery upon the poem with the effects of the imagery in the Shakespeare and Keats poems above.

4.

HOLY SONNET 14

Batter my heart, three-personed God; for You
As yet but knock, breathe, shine, and seek to mend;
That I may rise and stand, o'erthrow me, and bend
Your force to break, blow, burn, and make me new.
I, like an usurped town, to another due,   5
Labor to admit You, but O, to no end;
Reason, Your viceroy in me, me should defend,
But is captived, and proves weak or untrue.
Yet dearly I love You, and would be loved fain,
But am betrothed unto Your enemy.   10
Divorce me, untie or break that knot again;
Take me to You, imprison me, for I,
Except You enthrall me, never shall be free,
Nor ever chaste, except You ravish me.

—John Donne

a. Identify three general visual images in the poem. Are they weak or strong? Explain what makes them so.

b. In what lines of the poem do kinesthetic images dominate? Are the most powerful of these images of muscle sense or of bodily position?

c. Considered from the perspective of the speaker, what kind, or kinds, of sensations are suggested by the following phrases: *labor to admit You, reason . . . in me . . . is captived, and proves weak, take me to You, enthrall me, ravish me?* Considered from the perspective of the deity, what kind, or kinds, of imagery are *take, enthrall,* and *ravish?* If you see a difference in imagery according to perspective, which perspective and hence which sort of imagery do you suppose is most shared by the reader? If you do not see a difference, sum up the general character of the imagery here.

d. Reconsider Question "b" in the light of Question "c," deciding (1) whether perspective alters the character of the imagery, and (2) whether in the end you feel the effective imagery to be like or unlike the effective imagery in "c."

e. Identify the dominant kind, or kinds, of imagery in the poem, showing any broad shift in the course of the poem, and characterizing the overall effect of the imagery upon the idea of the poem.

ADDITIONAL EXERCISES

1. Analyze Conrad Aiken's "Dead Leaf in May," p. 328, as a montage of visual images.

2. Compare the imagery in three of Shakespeare's sonnets, pp. 197–200.

3. Compare and contrast the dominant imagery in Gerard Manley Hopkins' "The Windhover," p. 295, and William Butler Yeats' "The Wild Swans at Coole," p. 300.

4. Compare the relative importance of visual and organic imagery in establishing the reality of the objects of art in John Keats' "Ode on a Grecian Urn," p. 260, and William Butler Yeats' "Lapis Lazuli," p. 304.

7

SYMBOLISM

Symbolism is a concept at once familiar and mysterious. The flag is a symbol of the country, the beard is a symbol of manhood, and white is a symbol of death. Moreover, white is a symbol of innocence, and also a symbol of weakness. These are conventional and natural symbols. They display readily what a symbol is: something that stands for more than itself. And the thing itself and what it stands for are equally clear in such examples. But then one goes to a Scandinavian or Italian film, and sees a hooded figure playing chess on the seashore, or sees a strange fish cast up on a beach near a party of revellers. The scene is symbolical; it obviously stands for something more than itself; but what does it stand for? And the whole film is symbolical, and what do the symbols add up to? Such a film seems different from an American film about cowboys or about young love on Main Street, and symbolism seems to be something difficult and deep—and sometimes pretentious and fake. And then one is told that cowboy films are really symbolical too.

Symbolism in poetry can have similar transparency and difficulty. It assumes a variety of forms and serves a variety of purposes. It provides an important part of the meaning of a poem, and is intimately linked to imagery and metaphor. Observe it in the flesh. The following poem possesses symbolism in the simple fact that its author, Robert Frost, chose to put it at the head of collections of his poems.

THE PASTURE

I'm going out to clean the pasture spring;
I'll only stop to rake the leaves away

(And wait to watch the water clear, I may):
I sha'n't be gone long.—You come too.

I'm going out to fetch the little calf   5
That's standing by the mother. It's so young
It totters when she licks it with her tongue.
I sha'n't be gone long.—You come too.

Frost was a poet who although he wrote poems about the Pacific
Ocean and Communism was most famous for his poems about rural
New England life, and "The Pasture" seems to stand for all such
poems as "Stopping by Woods on a Snowy Evening," "The Death of
the Hired Man," and "Mending Wall." "The Pasture" is a badge, a
signature, by which Frost announced and acknowledged what he
primarily was. It is thus symbolic.*

Of course Frost could have put "Stopping by Woods on a Snowy
Evening" instead of "The Pasture" at the head of his poems. If he had,
then "The Pasture" would no longer be the express symbol of his
characteristic poetry. Thus a symbol is something that is *chosen* to
stand for more than itself. The context in which a poem is placed, or
in which parts of a poem are placed, will encourage or discourage
particular symbolic significance. Now the fact is that Frost did choose
"The Pasture." Why did he do so? He could not at all have chosen
such a poem as "Once by the Pacific" (page 310) because that poem
has nothing to do with rural New England. Something is chosen to be
a particular symbol only if it has a particular appropriateness. "Stopping by Woods on a Snowy Evening" (page 105) does have the appropriateness of being about rural life. But it does not have the full appropriateness of "The Pasture." "The Pasture" is an address by the speaker
of the poem to an unidentified *you*. The speaker is someone familiar
with farm life, and he extends his invitation to share a farm experience
to *you* who may be unfamiliar with it. For Frost to place this poem at
the head of all his poems is to make the address symbolic: the invitation seems to be from Frost the rural poet to *you* the reader to share
a poetic experience of rural life. Thus particular details of "The Pasture" are appropriate for weighting with particular symbolism.

Suppose now we look at "The Pasture" without any thought of
Frost's having put it first in his collections. Is it symbolic—does it, or

* The comments here and in the following paragraphs on "The Pasture" draw upon
the discussion of John F. Lynen, *The Pastoral Art of Robert Frost*, New Haven, 1960,
pp. 21–23.

does any part of it, stand for something more than itself? The answer is yes, and is yes for any poem: for merely to select and isolate a subject is to imply a special significance that carries beyond the subject. But some poems are more heavily symbolic than others, and some are differently symbolic from others; and anyone who calls "The Pasture" a symbolic poem without being aware that it is also a plain poem that presents a visual image of farm life is being absurd. Some of the symbolism is similar to that which has already been pointed out. The two figures in the poem are presented in the broadest way: the speaker is not Farmer Jones who has a wart on his nose but a generalized farmer, and *you* is not City-slicker Johnson who is wearing vaseline hair tonic but only a person who may not know farm life. In being able to stand for many people, the two figures are symbolic, and the situation between them becomes symbolic. The invitation is to share two farm experiences, cleaning the pasture spring and fetching the new-born calf. Presumably the experiences are worth sharing; and given the generalized persons of the poem, these particular experiences are made to stand for all farm experience: they are symbols of one sort of life, farm life, that is implicitly contrasted with nonfarm life. What is farm life like? Frost had a multitude of details to choose from: shutting the barn door, repairing the tractor, negotiating a lease on an orchard, and so forth. He chose two that have certain shared qualities. They are typically rural activities (in contrast to repairing a machine), innocent (in contrast to negotiating a lease), concerned with fundamental facts of life: obtaining water and giving birth (in contrast to shutting the barn door), and concerned with springtime and the renewal of life. By choosing the pasture spring and the new-born calf, Frost seems to say that farm life is worthwhile because it is simple, fundamental life.

"The Pasture" is typical of Frost's poetry not only in its subject but in its unpretentious, unobtrusive symbolism. Some of his poems are different:

THE LOCKLESS DOOR

It went many years,
But at last came a knock,
And I thought of the door
With no lock to lock.

I blew out the light,
I tiptoed the floor,

5

And raised both hands
In prayer to the door.

But the knock came again.
My window was wide;   10
I climbed on the sill
And descended outside.

Back over the sill
I bade a "Come in"
To whatever the knock   15
At the door may have been.

So at a knock
I emptied my cage
To hide in the world
And alter with age.   20

At what sort of door would a knock not come for many years? At
what sort would a person's response be a gesture of prayer—apparently
to implore the visitor to go away? At what sort would a person's
response ultimately be to climb out the window and then invite the
visitor in? The answers can only be: at a door that is not a door.
Frost's pasture spring is always a pasture spring, even when it is symbolic of farm life, but his lockless door asks to be unlocked.

Unlocking symbolic meanings can be difficult. How do we know
when we have the right meaning? How do we know that there are
not six right meanings? The fact is that critics often disagree about
symbolic interpretations, just as they often disagree about rhythm and
every other aspect of poetry. But they properly disagree within limits.
Consider the following suggestions about "The Lockless Door."

1. The visitor is death, and men try to escape death.
2. The visitor is life, and men are often afraid to accept life.
3. The visitor represents the lower classes who after centuries out in
the cold come to dispossess the aristocracy.
4. The scene represents the indecent prying of psychology into the
minds of people.
5. The visitor is Christian love, which a person accepts only gradually.
6. The visitor is self-knowledge, imperative and inescapable.

The obvious test of these interpretations is to measure them against details of the poem. Do any of the parts fit badly?

1. If the visitor is death, why should death seem to come before the man goes into the world *to alter with age?* If the visitor is death, should not *come in* and entrance into the house imply the death of the occupant?

2. If the visitor is life, what sort of life is being avoided first by living alone and then by living *in the world?*

3. The house does not look like the stately home of an aristocrat, and the occupant does not behave like an aristocrat either in praying or in climbing out the window. The visitor does not appear to be a revolutionary.

4. Is there anything indecent about the visitor? He knocks rather than pries.

5. There is nothing to suggest that the visitor is lovable. The occupant does not gradually accept him but seems to hide from him.

6. How can the visitor be self-knowledge if he is unknown? And if self-knowledge is inescapable, what is the man doing climbing out the window?

If doubts can be raised about all the interpretations, are none of them valid? Here a fundamental fact about symbolism must be recognized. All symbolism that a poet employs will display incongruous details; for symbolism involves one thing standing for another, and there are always differences between any two things. Does farm life totter like a calf? Does it have four legs? Symbolism is built upon suggestiveness, in which differences are submerged under particular likenesses; and the reader trying to puzzle out a poet's symbolism has to distinguish between relevant and irrelevant flaws in the interpretations that come to mind. He does so in part by keeping a watchful eye on the general character of the poem, excluding any interpretation whose own general character does not match it. With "The Lockless Door" the reader must be conscious of at least two qualities: first, that it is a personal poem, about private experience, and is as personal and private when the speaker is hiding in the world as when he is in his house; secondly, that it has an atmosphere of mystery and subdued fear, associated with both the situation of the speaker and the presence of the visitor. The first of these qualities makes the interpretation about social revolution (3) broadly impossible, and lends support to the others. The second renders very doubtful that the poem is concerned with a positive acceptance of life (2) or love (5), and lends varying support to the remaining three. Mystery and fear do surround death (1), and fearful uncovering of mystery is perhaps implied in the interpretations about psychology (4) and self-knowledge (6).

Return now to the objections to the details of the first, fourth, and sixth interpretations, and ask how relevant they are. Curiously enough, although the general character of the poem gives most weight to the first interpretation, the flaws in detail here are more serious than those in the fourth and sixth interpretations. Death arriving and yet the man not dying makes no sense unless the man goes to heaven; whereas a prying psychologist might well knock politely on the door to someone's brain, and self-knowledge is unknown until it is known. But all the objections remain troubling, and the solution to them is to modify the interpretations. The poem describes a man awaiting something he knows not what, fearful of it and defenseless against it. When it comes, he prays and then makes a polite escape. He alters with age in what may be only another sort of hiding and waiting place. Suppose that it is not death arriving but a glimmering awareness of death that comes to a man in middle age; suppose that it is not indecent psychology or pretentious self-knowledge arriving but a glimmering awareness of self, inevitable and fearful, and capable of being ignored by retreating into a public world. The interpretations now meet both the general character of the poem and the main details of it.

One question remains: which is the better interpretation? It may be unnecessary and undesirable to choose between them; for the poem lives in its indefiniteness. But it might be said that the interpretation about death is more in keeping with the general character of the poem in its attention to mystery and fear, and the interpretation about the self more accords with the detail of the contrast between house and world—a contrast that seems to refer to private and public life. It is curious that whereas "The Pasture" does not seem symbolic and its symbolism is plain, "The Lockless Door" is obviously symbolic and its symbolism is obscure.

Both of Frost's poems display the usefulness of symbolism at its best. In very few lines Frost can convey a world of meaning, and the meaning is concrete rather than abstract. He might have argued philosophically about the nobility of farm life; he might have written a long analysis of what the human mind is supposed to be like. Instead he offers two brief images, compelling in themselves, and suggestive. The reader is not bullied; he is not forced to admit a general truth; he sees a stone dropped into water, and watches the enlarging ripples.

EXERCISES

1.

IN DIVÉS' DIVE

It is late at night and still I am losing,
But still I am steady and unaccusing.

As long as the Declaration guards
My right to be equal in number of cards,

It is nothing to me who runs the Dive.   5
Let's have a look at another five.

—Robert Frost

a. The poem describes a man playing cards in a dive. Two words in the poem, *Divé* and *Declaration,* make evident that the dive is not an ordinary one. Look up Divé in a dictionary of mythology, and decide from the second stanza itself what *Declaration* refers to.

b. The poem can be said to be about the game of life. Interpret the following symbolic details: it is late at night; the player is losing; the player is steady and unaccusing; all the player is concerned about is to have the same number of cards as everyone else; the player is ready for another hand. Give appropriate new meanings to *Divé* and *Declaration*.

c. What is unsatisfactory about the following interpretation? The poem is about the game of marriage. The player is an aging woman who endures uncomplainingly a tyrannical husband and who consoles herself with the thought that the law protects her from unusual violence.

d. If your interpretation in Question "b" did not emphasize the speaker's political situation, rephrase it in such a way that it does. This time keep *Declaration* to its ordinary political meaning.

2.

RICHARD CORY

Whenever Richard Cory went down town,
We people on the pavement looked at him:
He was a gentleman from sole to crown,
Clean favored, and imperially slim.

And he was always quietly arrayed,   5
And he was always human when he talked;
But still he fluttered pulses when he said,
"Good-morning," and he glittered when he walked.

And he was rich—yes, richer than a king—
And admirably schooled in every grace: 10
In fine, we thought that he was everything
To make us wish that we were in his place.

So on we worked, and waited for the light,
And went without the meat, and cursed the bread;
And Richard Cory, one calm summer night,   15
Went home and put a bullet through his head.

—Edwin Arlington Robinson

a. Sum up the qualities that Richard Cory is shown to possess in the
first three stanzas. Sum up the qualities *we* are shown to possess in them.

b. Argue that the information about Richard Cory in the last stanza
contradicts what is shown about him before. Then argue that the information is basically consistent.

c. On the basis of your preceding answers, what does Richard Cory
the man symbolize? What does his suicide symbolize? What do the people
on the pavement symbolize?

d. Given your answers to Question "c," do Richard Cory and *we* seem
more alike, or less alike, as symbolic figures than they seem as figures on a
street? Explain.

e. Would there be any difference in the symbolic implication of the
suicide if Robinson had begun the poem with it and then gone on to
describe Cory as he seemed in life? Explain.

3.

STOPPING BY WOODS ON A SNOWY EVENING

Whose woods these are I think I know.
His house is in the village though;
He will not see me stopping here
To watch his woods fill up with snow.

My little horse must think it queer   5
To stop without a farmhouse near
Between the woods and frozen lake
The darkest evening of the year.

He gives his harness bells a shake
To ask if there is some mistake.   10

> The only other sound's the sweep
> Of easy wind and downy flake.
>
> The woods are lovely, dark and deep,
> But I have promises to keep,
> And miles to go before I sleep,
> And miles to go before I sleep.

15

—Robert Frost

a. The symbolism in this poem is not so unobtrusive as that in "The Pasture," not so obvious as that in "The Lockless Door." What two or three details are most immediately symbolic? Why do they seem so?

b. Here are two interpretations of the poem:

(1) Death is attractive, but man must accept his responsibilities in life.

(2) Private esthetic impulses must yield before responsibilities to the community.

Answer the following questions.

(1) Which details of the poem will support each interpretation?

(2) Which details either contradict each interpretation or are irrelevant to it?

(3) To which interpretation does the general character of the poem seem closer?

(4) Does the repetition of the last line seem to strengthen or weaken the sense of decision on the speaker's part? What bearing does your answer here have upon the interpretations? What bearing would the opposite answer have?

(5) Review your preceding answers and decide whether both, neither, or only one of the interpretations of the poem seems satisfactory.

(6) If neither interpretation seems satisfactory, can you suggest a modification or an alternative?

4.

THE SICK ROSE

> O rose, thou art sick!
> The invisible worm
> That flies in the night,
> In the howling storm,
>
> Has found out thy bed
> Of crimson joy,
> And his dark secret love
> Does thy life destroy.

5

—William Blake

a. Treat the rose as a literal rose attacked by a literal worm. Explain what if any metaphorical meanings the following words then have: *sick, invisible, flies, storm, bed, love.*

b. Treat the rose as a literal rose, and the worm as symbolic. Provide an appropriate symbolic meaning for the worm, and explain what if any metaphorical meanings the following words would then have: *sick, storm, bed, love.*

c. Treat the rose as a symbol of womanhood, and give the worm the same general symbolic meaning as in Question "b." Describe the general meaning of the poem, and note whether *sick, storm, bed,* and *love* have necessarily changed in meaning from Question "b."

d. Treat the rose as a symbol of sensuous fulfillment and the bed as a literal matrimonial bed. Is the symbolic meaning of the worm in Question "c" relevant under these conditions? If so, explain the general meaning of the poem that follows. What other symbolic meaning of the worm might be relevant here? Explain the consequent general meaning of the poem.

e. If none of the previous interpretations has implicitly done so, treat the howling storm as a symbol of lust, and describe the general meaning of the poem that follows. Do the same treating the storm as a symbol of puritanical love.

f. Do the ordinary literal meanings of the words that Blake uses suggest that he is primarily concerned with plant life or animal life, human life or nonhuman life? Does the single most important word in the poem support your general answer? Comment on the preceding interpretations of the poem in the light of your answers here.

g. Is it possible to provide a broad interpretation of the poem that will satisfactorily include in it all the previous interpretations? If so, provide it. If not, argue whether it follows that one or another of the previous interpretations must be rejected.

5. In both symbolism and metaphor, one thing is related to another. Are symbolism and metaphor then the same thing—or almost the same thing? Review the discussions in the present chapter and in Chapter 5; review Question 4 on "The Sick Rose"; and write an essay on the subject, using "The Sick Rose" as chief illustration.

6. In the opening of the chapter it was asserted that symbolism, metaphor, and imagery are intimately related; and in the last paragraph of the chapter Robert Frost's pasture and lockless door were described as both images and symbols. Review the implications of Question 5 on the relationship between metaphor and symbol, and write an essay on the connection among all three. Use the poems in this chapter for illustration.

ADDITIONAL EXERCISES

1. Discuss the major symbolism in Emily Dickinson's "Success is counted sweetest," p. 56; William Blake's "The Echoing Green," p. 233; Wallace Stevens' "Thirteen Ways of Looking at a Blackbird," p. 315; and Robert Browning's "Childe Roland to the Dark Tower Came," p. 267.

2. Critics often speak of conventional symbolism (for example, the cross as a conventional symbol of Christ) and natural symbolism (for example, sleep as a natural—obvious, ready—symbol of death). Of which sort is each of the symbols mentioned in the first two sentences in this chapter, p. 98? Compare the use of such symbolism in the major symbols of William Blake's "The Lamb," p. 234; Alfred Lord Tennyson's "Crossing the Bar," p. 10; and Percy Bysshe Shelley's "Ode to the West Wind," p. 255.

3. Review the questions on "Stopping by Woods" above, and discuss whether symbolic meaning or literal image seems more important to the poem.

4. Question 2 immediately above distinguishes two kinds of symbols. What supplementary categories are suggested by the discussion and questions in this chapter? Consider, for example, the difference in character of symbol in "In Divés' Dive," "The Lockless Door," and "The Pasture."

5. It was asserted on p. 100 that every poem is symbolic in that it involves a selection and isolation of material. The following poems may provide a hard test for the assertion. Analyze them and decide whether any of them suggests that symbolic meaning is sometimes non-existent—or if existent, unimportant. Robert Burns, "Epitaph on James Grieve," p. 238; Lord Byron, "Epigrams," p. 253; and Wilfred Owen, "A Terre," p. 331.

8

STRUCTURE

The structure of a poem is like the structure of a house: it is what underlies, supports, and frames the words, the alliteration, the metaphors, the rhymes. It is the integrated pattern and movement of all the parts. Being thus fundamental, the structure of a poem inevitably impinges upon meaning, as the illustrations and exercises below show. The word structure is a metaphor for looking at a poem in a particular light.

Here is a small cottage of a poem:

DUST OF SNOW

The way a crow
Shook down on me
The dust of snow
From a hemlock tree

Has given my heart   5
A change of mood
And saved some part
Of a day I had rued.

—Robert Frost

The most obvious aspect of the structure is the division of the poem into two stanzas. This stanzaic division corresponds with a division between image and idea, or action and reaction: the crow shakes the snow in the first stanza, and the speaker of the poem reflects in the second. Two stanzas, two parts: what could be more clear cut and simple? But look at the poem again, and observe that the poet has crossed this structure with another structure: the two stanzas are both part of a single sentence. The subject of the sentence is *way* (followed by an adjective clause); the verb is *has given . . . , saved*. The reader cannot stop at the end of the first stanza; he has to press on through the second stanza before he has a single complete thought. Frost has emphasized this link between the stanzas by his phrasing of the individual lines, by the absence of all punctuation except the period at the end, and by his placement of subject and verb at the very beginning of each stanza. The lines of the poem flow easily forward, within each stanza and from stanza to stanza. In sum, the two-part stanzaic structure coincides with the two-part division of image and idea, or action and reaction, and with the two-part division of the sentence into subject and verb; and this two-part structure is placed against the single-unit structure of the sentence, which is phrased in such a way as to emphasize simplicity and wholeness. Structurally, the poem is a tidy cottage; and part of the pleasure it affords is this complex neatness that lies behind the plain appearance of diction and scene. Likewise part of the meaning of the poem is this neatness, which counters any suggestion of despair—just as the crow does.

One aspect of the structure of the poem that has been unmentioned—and there are still others—is the rhyme scheme. Decide whether it contributes to the two-part structure, the single-unit structure, or both.

Here is a more complex poem:

SONNET 73

That time of year thou mayst in me behold
When yellow leaves, or none, or few, do hang
Upon those boughs which shake against the cold,
Bare ruined choirs, where late the sweet birds sang.
In me thou see'st the twilight of such day   5
As after sunset fadeth in the west,
Which by and by black night doth take away,
Death's second self, that seals up all in rest.
In me thou see'st the glowing of such fire,
That on the ashes of his youth doth lie,   10
As the death-bed whereon it must expire,
Consumed with that which it was nourished by.
This thou perceiv'st, which makes thy love more strong,
To love that well which thou must leave ere long.

—*William Shakespeare*

First observe that the rhyme (ababcdcdefefgg) has a fourfold structure: abab—cdcd—efef—gg. But equally the repeated pattern of rhyming of the first three sections of it (first and third lines rhyming, and second and fourth), along with the repeated use of four lines, suggests a two-fold structure: *abab-cdcd-efef* || *gg*. The fourfold aspect of the rhyme structure is complemented by and congruent with the four sentences of the poem. The twofold aspect is supported by the structure of idea in the poem: the first twelve lines say that the speaker of the poem is growing old; the last two lines assert a consequence. As in the Frost poem, the two structures coexist harmoniously. And they are set into the overall unitary structure of the nonstanzaic fourteen lines.

Now consider another aspect of structure, the development of image and idea. The first four lines present an image of autumn, the next four of a darkening evening, the next four of a dying fire. These three images can be thought of as constituting a single image of a dying fire on an autumn evening, or they can be seen as separate, essentially repeating images. Individually or together, they say: I am growing old. Again one sees a structure in which the first twelve lines contrast with the last two. The division is further emphasized by the fact that the idea in the first twelve lines is presented in sustained images, whereas the idea in the last two lines is presented more directly. The two parts of the poem look different from each other: in the first twelve lines images are in the foreground, with an idea lying behind them; in the last two lines an idea is in the foreground, served by incidental metaphors.

The arrangement of the three images of the poem offers another element of structure. Perhaps the order could be reversed, so that the poem could begin with the fire and end with the autumn, but the order could not easily be fire-autumn-twilight or twilight-autumn-fire. Why not? The present structure offers a narrowing focus of time and scene in the movement from season to time of day to brief fire. In this increasing particularity and immediacy, Shakespeare implies an end, a conclusion, which comes with the last two lines.

What is the effect of the structure of the poem upon the poem as a whole? There is a neatness, an elegance, in the harmony of rhyming, grammatical, and imagistic structures. There is a sedateness in the progressive, regular repetition of images. At the same time, the twofold and fourfold divisions, the separation of image and idea, never break the poem into parts: the interrelationships among these divisions and the easy forward movement of the images maintain the unity of the poem. If now we transform all of this into some sort of meaning, we might say that the structure restrains the mood of the poem, prevents any sense of anguish from dominating it, lends grace to the speaker's melancholy.

One more aspect of the structure of the poem should be mentioned. Notice that the fourth line could be removed without disturbing the grammatical completeness of the first sentence; it stands as an appositive to *boughs* in the third line. The eighth line, which stands in apposition to *night* in the seventh, could similarly be removed. And the eleventh and twelfth lines could likewise be removed. What is the effect upon the structure of the poem of the presence of such appendages to the grammatical units?

Despite their obvious differences in rhyme scheme and other elements, Shakespeare's Sonnet 73 and Robert Frost's "Dust of Snow" are similar in the general neatness of their structures. Perhaps the most important distinction to be made between them is that Frost's structure was determined when he wrote the poem, whereas Shakespeare's was in part a familiar structure of one kind of sonnet: a poem of fourteen lines, rhymed in a particular fashion, with the last two lines set off from the first twelve. Part of Shakespeare's task as an artist was to use this structure in an original way, complementing it and modifying it with other elements of structure that were not predetermined. Frost had a task at once easier and harder: he did not have to worry about a prescribed structure, and he had to invent his own.

Other poems are not neat, and are not meant to be neat. Here is a poem which in its structure varies radically from the two previous poems.

THERE WAS A BOY

There was a Boy; ye knew him well, ye cliffs
And islands of Winander!—many a time,
At evening, when the earliest stars began
To move along the edges of the hills,
Rising or setting, would he stand alone,   5
Beneath the trees, or by the glimmering lake;
And there, with fingers interwoven, both hands
Pressed closely palm to palm and to his mouth
Uplifted, he as through an instrument,
Blew mimic hootings to the silent owls,   10
That they might answer him.—And they would shout

Across the watery vale, and shout again,
Responsive to his call,—with quivering peals,
And long halloos, and screams, and echoes loud
Redoubled and redoubled; concourse wild   15
Of jocund din! And, when there came a pause
Of silence such as baffled his best skill:
Then sometimes, in that silence, while he hung
Listening, a gentle shock of mild surprise
Has carried far into his heart the voice   20
Of mountain-torrents; or the visible scene
Would enter unawares into his mind
With all its solemn imagery, its rocks,
Its woods, and that uncertain heaven received
Into the bosom of the steady lake.   25

This boy was taken from his mates, and died
In childhood, ere he was full twelve years old.
Pre-eminent in beauty is the vale
Where he was born and bred: the churchyard hangs
Upon a slope above the village-school;   30
And through that churchyard when my way has led
On summer-evenings, I believe that there
A long half-hour together I have stood
Mute—looking at the grave in which he lies!

—*William Wordsworth*

The structure is quite apparently irregular. The poem has no rhyme scheme, in fact no rhyme, to give it neatness of shape. The first stanza (more fittingly called a verse paragraph) is twenty-five lines long, the second is nine. A glance at the details of the second verse paragraph shows no uniformity of treatment: two lines tell of the boy's death, three describe the place where he is buried, four the movement and observation of the speaker of the poem. The main divisions of the first verse paragraph are similarly irregular. One also notices that there are several strong caesuras, as in the opening two lines; that the iambic pentameter rhythm is often broken; and that there are many run-on lines. Such irregularity could, of course, indicate an absence of structure and a defective poem, but Wordsworth has in fact created a structure more subtle than the structures used by Shakespeare and Frost in their two poems. He does not rely upon a conventional form such as the sonnet, and he does not invent his own neat stanzaic structure; rather, he creates a fluid organic pattern.

The structure of the poem might most easily be approached by thinking of an element of it that is in fact traditional. (For however original a poem may be, it necessarily relies on much traditional structure.) Observe again the rhythm: despite irregularities, the clear pattern throughout the poem is iambic pentameter; and in long stretches, as from lines three to fifteen, there is little variation, and the variation is subdued. One might say, then, that an important structural element of the poem is its iambic pentameter line, one laid after the other. Of course the individual line is an important structural element in any poem, and a more complete discussion of the two previous poems would have dealt with it too. The significance of the line in the present poem is enhanced by the absence of a rhyme scheme that would fit it into a pattern, say, of couplets or quatrains. At the same time, the significance is modified by the presence of incongruent grammatical structures: almost every line in the first verse paragraph is run-on, and almost all the heavy grammatical pauses—ends of clauses and sentences —are placed within the lines rather than at the ends. Thus the iambic pentameter stroke of each line is enveloped by a steady forward movement, and the verse paragraph as a whole seems to possess a solid unity of structure—and one that is natural rather than sculptured. The forward movement and unity are themselves assisted by the narrative structure, which advances from the opening phrase in chronological order.

The second verse paragraph is less unified than the first, and lacks something of its forward movement—as evidenced partly by the period at the end of the second line. It seems to be a kind of diminishing afterthought. It could even be removed, and the first verse paragraph could stand alone as a complete poem. By way of contrast, if the second stanza of the Frost poem were removed, the first stanza would be left dangling in mid air. Yet nothing is more certain than that in its own way Wordsworth's second verse paragraph is as important structurally as Frost's. It can be removed as Frost's cannot be, but to remove it is to change radically the structure and thence the substance of the poem. Let us see how this is so.

Like the Frost poem with its neatly disposed subject and object, Wordsworth's has two key words, *listening* and *mute* (one in each verse paragraph, line 19 and line 34), each placed in the rhythm and phrasing in such a way as to be emphasized. They are used virtually as synonyms, and they point up the fact that the two verse paragraphs present parallel images, the first of the boy listening in his heart to nature and the second of the speaker of the poem—presumably an older man—listening to the meaning of nature. Nature speaks to the boy with its sounds, and it speaks when both he and it are silent. It speaks to the man when both he and it are silent. Seen thus, the second verse paragraph deepens the implications of the first; it is no appendage, but a vital structure. Only with the end of the second verse paragraph does the reader himself stand mute, looking at boy and man in nature, listening to the meaning of life.

As a further means of clarifying the structural importance of the second verse paragraph, contrast it now with the quatrains of Shakespeare's poem. Any one of the quatrains (any one of the images contained by them) could be removed without vitally damaging the structure of the poem or the poem itself: something important would be lost, the clear and sedate narrowing of images and implication, but the poem could sustain the loss, and remain much the same as before. In Wordsworth's poem the second image of the listening person reverberates against the first, enhances its meaning, gives the poem a direction into deeper meaning.

The importance of structure to meaning is nowhere else more impressively demonstrated than in this poem. It has been impossible to describe the structure without clarifying the meaning, and it would be equally impossible to state the meaning without discussing the structure. To isolate as clearly as possible the broad structure, one might say that the poem consists of two verse paragraphs, one long and one short, which contain similar images that are so intimately linked that the second seems a brief and profound after-image of the first; and each verse paragraph has a simple unity, with no display of artificial joints or paired and balanced parts.

EXERCISES

1.

THE WOUND

I climbed to the crest,
  And, fog-festooned,
The sun lay west
  Like a crimson wound:

Like that wound of mine   5
  Of which none knew,
For I'd given no sign
  That it pierced me through.

—Thomas Hardy

a. Point out the similarities in structural detail between "The Wound" and Frost's "Dust of Snow" in stanzaic division, image and reflection, sentence use, rhyme.

b. Point out the differences from Frost's poem in sentence structure and punctuation.

c. On the basis of your preceding answers, would you say that Hardy's poem is more tidy than Frost's or less? Does the relative degree of regularity of meter in each poem support your answer?

d. Does the degree of tidiness of structure in Hardy's poem tend to make it more serious than Frost's or less? What single structural element would you select as being most important in achieving the distinction?

e. Review the discussion of sound in "The Wound," page 44. What bearing does it have on the structure of the poem?

2.

SONNET 100

Where art thou, Muse, that thou forget'st so long
To speak of that which gives thee all thy might?
Spend'st thou thy fury on some worthless song,
Darkening thy power to lend base subjects light?
Return, forgetful Muse, and straight redeem   5
In gentle numbers time so idly spent;
Sing to the ear that doth thy lays esteem
And gives thy pen both skill and argument.
Rise, resty Muse, my love's sweet face survey,
If Time have any wrinkles graven there;   10
If any, be a satire to decay,
And make Time's spoils despiséd everywhere.
Give my love fame faster than Time wastes life;
So thou prevent'st his scythe and crooked knife.

—William Shakespeare

a. Point out the similarities in structural detail between "Sonnet 100" and "Sonnet 73" in rhyme and sentence use, noticing any incidental differences.

b. Show that there is a comparable three-part division of image or metaphor in the first twelve lines here as in "Sonnet 100," and show that the three units cannot have their order shifted.

c. Is the three-part division of the first twelve lines emphasized more or less than in "Sonnet 73"? What are the structural elements involved?

d. Is the division between the first twelve lines and the last two sharper here or less sharp than in "Sonnet 73"? What structural elements are involved?

e. On the basis of your answers to the two preceding questions, what general statement would you make about the structure of image and idea in the poem, in comparison or contrast with "Sonnet 73"?

f. Broadly speaking, is the structure of the poem more in evidence than that of "Sonnet 73" or less? What effect would you say the structure has upon the degree of seriousness of mood of the poem?

3.

SONNET 15

When I consider everything that grows
Holds in perfection but a little moment,
That this huge stage presenteth nought but shows
Whereon the stars in secret influence comment;
When I perceive that men as plants increase,   5
Cheered and checked even by the selfsame sky,
Vaunt in their youthful sap, at height decrease,
And wear their brave state out of memory:
Then the conceit of this inconstant stay
Sets you most rich in youth before my sight,   10
Where wasteful Time debateth with Decay
To change your day of youth to sullied night;
And, all in war with Time for love of you,
As he takes from you, I ingraft you new.

—William Shakespeare

a. Compare the structural details of "Sonnet 15" and "Sonnet 73," considering rhyme, sentence use, progress of argument, and orderly relationship between image and idea.

b. Devise a rhyme scheme for the poem that would be congruent with the progress of the argument. State the effect of the overall structure in such a way as to explain why Shakespeare was content to use the present rhyme scheme.

4.

YEW-TREES

There is a Yew-tree, pride of Lorton Vale,
Which to this day stands single in the midst
Of its own darkness, as it stood of yore:
Not loth to furnish weapons for the bands
Of Umfraville or Percy ere they marched   5
To Scotland's heaths; or those that crossed the sea
And drew their sounding bows at Azincour,

Perhaps at earlier Crecy, or Poictiers.
Of vast circumference and gloom profound
This solitary Tree! a living thing 10
Produced too slowly ever to decay;
Of form and aspect too magnificent
To be destroyed. But worthier still of note
Are those fraternal Four of Borrowdale,
Joined in one solemn and capacious grove; 15
Huge trunks! and each particular trunk a growth
Of intertwisted fibres serpentine
Up-coiling, and inveterately convolved;
Nor uninformed with Phantasy, and looks
That threaten the profane; a pillared shade, 20
Upon whose grassless floor of red-brown hue,
By sheddings from the pining umbrage tinged
Perennially—beneath whose sable roof
Of boughs, as if for festal purpose decked
With unrejoicing berries—ghostly Shapes 25
May meet at noontide; Fear and trembling Hope,
Silence and Foresight; Death the Skeleton
And Time the Shadow;—there to celebrate,
As in a natural temple scattered o'er
With altars undisturbed of mossy stone, 30
United worship; or in mute repose
To lie and listen to the mountain flood
Murmuring from Glaramara's inmost caves.

—*William Wordsworth*

a. Point out the similarities in structural detail between "Yew-Trees" and "There was a Boy" in rhyme and rhythm. Point out the differences in stanza use and narrative.

b. What parts of the poem, if any, could be omitted or interchanged without disrupting the character of the poem? Justify your answer. What structural principle or principles would account for the present ordering and development of material within the single stanza? (Observe the elements of description, history, and imaginative reflection in the poem.)

c. Summarize the structural character of the poem and show its connection to the ideas expressed in the last ten lines.

ADDITIONAL EXERCISES

1. Compare and contrast the structures of Sir Thomas Wyatt, "Who So List to Hunt," p. 190; Sir Philip Sidney, "Sonnet 1" (*Astrophel and Stella*), p. 17; William Shakespeare, "Sonnet 129," p. 62; and William Wordsworth, "Surprised by Joy," p. 243.

2. Compare and contrast the structures of John Keats, "Ode on a Grecian Urn," p. 260, and William Butler Yeats, "Lapis Lazuli," p. 304.

3. Compare and contrast the structures of Lord Byron, "The Dream," p. 248, and Robert Browning, "Childe Roland to the Dark Tower Came," p. 267.

9

TONE

D. H. Lawrence was the son of a coal miner. He was poor most of his life, and sometimes lived on the gifts of friends. Novels and paintings of his were banned as being indecent. Imagine him writing the following poem.

TO BE SUPERIOR

> How nice it is to be superior!
> Because really, it's no use pretending, one *is* superior, isn't one?
> I mean people like you and me.—
>
> Quite! I quite agree.
> The trouble is, everybody thinks they're just as superior   5
> as we are; just as superior.—
>
> That's what's so boring! people are so boring.
> But they can't really think it, do you think?
> At the bottom, they must *know* we are really superior
> don't you think?   10
> Don't you think, *really*, they *know* we're their superiors?—
> I couldn't say.
> I've never got to the bottom of superiority.
> I should like to.

The most notorious fact of Lawrence's private life was his elopement with an already married woman. Imagine him celebrating his happiness with the following poem.

THE SONG OF A MAN WHO HAS COME THROUGH

> Not I, not I, but the wind that blows through me!
> A fine wind is blowing the new direction of Time.

If only I let it bear me, carry me, if only it carry me!
If only I am sensitive, subtle, oh, delicate, a winged gift!
If only, most lovely of all, I yield myself and am borrowed   5
By the fine, fine wind that takes its course through the
     chaos of the world
Like a fine, an exquisite chisel, a wedge-blade inserted;
If only I am keen and hard like the sheer tip of a wedge
Driven by invisible blows,
The rock will split, we shall come at the wonder, we shall   10
     find the Hesperides.

Oh, for the wonder that bubbles into my soul,
I would be a good fountain, a good well-head,
Would blur no whisper, spoil no expression.

What is the knocking?
What is the knocking at the door in the night?   15
It is somebody wants to do us harm.

No, no, it is the three strange angels.
Admit them, admit them.

The differences between the two poems are striking, and perhaps most
striking are the differences in tone.

Tone in poetry can be thought of as the inferred tone of voice in
which a passage or whole poem is to be spoken. When a person talks,
his voice exhibits a tone—hard, cynical, gay, light, savage, or something else, or a combination of things. Recognizing his tone is a necessary part of understanding what he is and what he is saying. Suppose he says, *I am a coward*. He might say it in a squeaky, nervous
tone that could make you feel him sweating beneath his shirt. He might
say it slowly, emphasizing *I* and raising the note of *coward* into a hard
question, so that you yourself might begin sweating if you had been
the one to accuse him. He might say it flatly and lightly, as though he
were shrugging his shoulders at the absurd notion of heroism. In each
case, both the meaning of the phrase and the character of the speaker
would be caught in the tone. So it is with poetry, except that a poem
cannot give clues by speaking squeakily or by raising its voice. Some
of the clues are the same as in ordinary speech: the sort of language
that is used, whether colloquial or formal, plain or metaphorical, abstract or elegant, harsh or mellifluous. Some are the conventional written clues of question marks and exclamation points that substitute for
raised inflection and stress. Some are the clues of rhythm, in which both
the rhythms of speech and the rhythms peculiar to poetry mingle.

Hearing the tone of a poem or passage will precede analyzing it. The tone of "To Be Superior" is conversational, intimate, polite, light. That of "The Song of a Man Who Has Come Through" is elevated and passionate. The one seems to be the tone of English ladies talking as they sip their tea—or of effeminate English gentlemen doing the same. The other is the tone of a romantic enthusiast. It would embarrass the ladies and upset the teacups. How does Lawrence achieve the differences? The vocabulary of "To Be Superior" is the ordinary vocabulary of polite speech: *nice, really, quite,* the contractions such as *isn't.* The phrasing is the same, short and colloquial, but never abrupt or vulgar: *because really, I mean, don't you think.* Above all, the rhythm is the nonmetrical rhythm of speech, lacking a regular beat; and the repeated phrasing, as with *that's what's so boring! people are so boring,* suggests the particular rippling rhythm of polite conversation, in which it is necessary that there be no awkward silences, and so the speaker vivaciously repeats his trivial phrase. At a glance, "The Song of a Man Who Has Come Through" is similar: except for *Hesperides,* the vocabulary is not exotic; the phrasing is repetitious; and the rhythm is nonmetrical with a continuous forward movement. But while two women over tea might speak of someone's exquisitely chiselled features, they would be unlikely to speak of an *exquisite chisel* or of a wind that is like an exquisite chisel, and their chatter would not allow for the sustained formal phrasing of *I yield myself and am borrowed by the fine, fine wind that takes its course through the chaos of the world like a fine, an exquisite chisel, a wedge-blade inserted.* They might mention an angelic young man who knocks at their door of an evening, but their lightness and gaiety would have nothing to do with strange angels seen in a revelation. In sum, the language of "The Song of a Man Who Has Come Through" is vividly metaphorical, symbolic; the phrasing is elaborate; the rhythm is full and often intense. (See page 70 for a more detailed discussion of the rhythm of the poem.)

Recognizing the tones of the two poems is essential to understanding them. The tone of the first one tells us who the people are and makes their assertions the frivolous conceit of polite speech. The tone of "The Song of a Man Who Has Come Through" asks that what is said be taken seriously. Even if we object to the ideas and emotion of the poem, we cannot escape the intention that the tone proclaims. Ultimately it may seem that in "To Be Superior" Lawrence is indulging in an artful piece of mimicry, whereas in "The Song of a Man Who Has Come Through" his tone is his own. This questionable inference will be considered in the next chapter.

One of the distinctive means of establishing a tone is the device known as *verbal irony*. There are several sorts of irony in the world, and some of them have nothing directly to do with tone. One of these can be found in the *Glossary* on page 171. Verbal irony consists of saying one thing and meaning another, perhaps the reverse, perhaps something more, perhaps something less.

ON HEARING THAT THE STUDENTS OF OUR NEW UNIVERSITY HAVE JOINED THE AGITATION AGAINST IMMORAL LITERATURE

> Where, where but here have Pride and Truth,
> That long to give themselves for wage,
> To shake their wicked sides at youth
> Restraining reckless middle-age?

> *—William Butler Yeats*

(Here at the university those prostitutes Pride and Truth are having a good time laughing at the young students who are trying to prohibit the immoral work of some middle-aged writers.) The question is: whose side is the speaker of the poem on, the students' or the writers'? The answer is easy to guess from the fact that Yeats is a writer himself, but such a guess lies outside the evidence of the poem, and Yeats is not the speaker. In the poem itself the speaker attacks the writers as *reckless*. Why should we not believe that fact? The chief clue is the personification of Pride and Truth as wicked, money-grubbing figures. The terms are contradictory. Another contradiction is that Pride and Truth seem to be on the side of immoral literature insofar as they ridicule the attempts to restrain it. Thus by the time the reader reaches *reckless,* he knows that something is wrong, and the phrase *reckless middle-age* gives him one more contradiction—for middle-age is customarily associated with caution. If the contradictions are meant, the four lines become absurd. If the contradictions are not meant, the lines become ironical. Paraphrase the poem, translating the irony: Here at the university anyone who is interested in literature (which at its best exhibits pride and truth) may be amused by the spectacle of some misguided, immature students acting as censors.

The second question is: why should the speaker—and William Butler Yeats behind him—bother to be ironical? Why should he not say just what he means? The answer can be expressed in terms of tone, but another way may be useful first. What is achieved in the poem is not only an attack on the censors but also an expression of their viewpoint. When used non-ironically, *give themselves for wage, wicked,* and *reckless* are the terms censors apply to those whom they take to be corrupt writers and their supporters; and *pride* and *truth* are the ideals that censors often claim as their own. The poem in this respect shows some understanding of the censors, and the fact that it does not attack them directly strengthens the sense of understanding. At the same time the poem defends the writers. Irony can do two or three things for the price of one. Good irony always ends by saying just what it complexly means.

The use of irony so affects tone that we speak of an *ironical tone.* Suppose Yeats had let his speaker make an outright attack on foolish, smug, arrogant censors, or an outright defense of wise, noble writers. The tone of his poem would have been serious, perhaps savage and vindictive, or perhaps indignant and lofty. The irony, though, plays a game. It lightens the tone in a peculiar way, not to the point of frivolousness but to a point of wittiness and ease. The seriousness becomes restrained, disengaged. In other poems, made of other material, the tonal effects of irony would not be the same; and even in this poem the tone is not adequately described by saying that it is ironical. There are other contributing elements: the rather intense and artificial *where, where,* the formally elaborate sentence construction with its sustained rhythm, the diction that except in the title and in the last line tends to be monosyllabic, plain, and strong (as with *pride, wage,* and *shake*) but never colloquial; the grotesque image of the prostitutes Pride and Truth shaking with laughter; the phrasing of the whole four lines as a question. All these at times contradictory elements create a tone that is forceful yet restrained, elevated yet ironical.

There are three familiar kinds of irony that are identified by special terms. *Sarcasm* (in a limited sense of the word) is praise intended as dispraise: *those students are doing a virtuous, thoughtful, impartial thing,* Yeats might have said. *Ironic invective* is a sham attack: *those writers are reckless, evil money-grubbers,* Yeats said in part. *Understatement* is saying less than one means: *I think those students are just a little upset.* Like all other devices of poetry, the device of irony is available for anyone to use; but a consistent use of irony by a poet suggests a particular complex outlook on life, at once witty, detached, and serious. Thus the fundamental answer to the question of why a poet should bother to be ironical is perhaps that he is bothering to be one sort of person rather than another. Tone, therefore, may be a key to the poet behind his speaker. That is a subject for the next chapter.

EXERCISES

1.

NEITHER OUT FAR NOR IN DEEP

The people along the sand
All turn and look one way.
They turn their back on the land.
They look at the sea all day.

As long as it takes to pass   5
A ship keeps raising its hull;
The wetter ground like glass
Reflects a standing gull.

The land may vary more;
But wherever the truth may be—   10
The water comes ashore,
And the people look at the sea.

They cannot look out far.
They cannot look in deep.
But when was that ever a bar   15
To any watch they keep?

—*Robert Frost*

a. Analyze the diction, and characterize it as plain or elaborate, blunt or restrained, nonmetaphorical or metaphorical, colloquial or informal or formal (see the distinctions on p. 28).

b. Analyze the rhythm, and characterize it as fast or slow, regular or irregular, smooth or rough, intense or calm.

c. On the basis of the preceding answers, characterize the tone of the poem.

d. Here are two interpretations of the poem: (1) Frost is commenting on the fact that the human race stupidly contemplates what it cannot understand; (2) Frost is saying that mankind is perennially attracted to the marvelous source of its existence. Does the tone of the poem support both, one, three-quarters of one, or neither of the interpretations? Explain.

2.

"HUMANITY I LOVE YOU"

Humanity i love you
because you would rather black the boots of
success than inquire whose soul dangles from his
watch-chain which would be embarrassing for both

parties and because you   5
unflinchingly applaud all
songs containing the words country home and
mother when sung at the old howard

Humanity i love you because
when you're hard up you pawn your   10
intelligence to buy a drink and when
you're flush pride keeps

you from the pawnshop and
because you are continually committing
nuisances but more   15
especially in your own house

Humanity i love you because you
are perpetually putting the secret of
life in your pants and forgetting
it's there and sitting down   20

on it
and because you are
forever making poems in the lap
of death Humanity

i hate you   25

—*e. e. cummings*

a. Identify the most apparent contradiction in the poem that indicates irony.

b. Identify several contradictions subordinate to the main contradiction.

c. Explain what Cummings is referring to when he says that humanity is *continually committing nuisances in* . . . [*its*] *own house*. Is his irony here sarcasm, ironic invective, or understatement?

d. Is sarcasm or ironic invective the chief ironic mode in the poem? Explain how you know.

e. If the last line were removed, would the irony of the poem be lost or blunted? Use your answer to discuss the effectiveness of the irony in the poem.

f. Discuss what contribution is made to the tone of the poem by the general rhythm, the absence of punctuation, and the small *i*. Is the presence of the last line of the poem (see Question "e") consonant with the tone of the poem as suggested by these three elements?

3.

EPITAPH ON AN ARMY OF MERCENARIES

These, in the day when heaven was falling,
    The hour when earth's foundations fled,
Followed their mercenary calling
    And took their wages and are dead.

Their shoulders held the sky suspended;   5
    They stood, and earth's foundations stay;
What God abandoned, these defended,
    And saved the sum of things for pay.

                    —*A. E. Housman*

a. Compare the diction of the poem point by point with that of "Neither out Far Nor in Deep," Question 1.

b. Analyze the rhythm of the poem and characterize it along the lines suggested in Question 1.

c. *Epitaph* and *mercenaries* in the title and *mercenary* and *calling* in the third line provide two contradictions that suggest verbal irony. Explain, indicating which word in each pair is to be taken ironically. Or are both words?

d. The fifth line exaggerates. Would you call it ironical? Explain.

e. Characterize the tone of the poem, with special attention to its degree of irony, and compare the tone with that of Yeats' poem on page 123.

4.

SONNET 71

No longer mourn for me when I am dead
Than you shall hear the surly sullen bell
Give warning to the world that I am fled
From this vile world, with vilest worms to dwell:
Nay, if you read this line, remember not   5
The hand that writ it; for I love you so,
That I in your sweet thoughts would be forgot,

If thinking on me then should make you woe.
O, if, I say, you look upon this verse
When I perhaps compounded am with clay,   10
Do not so much as my poor name rehearse,
But let your love even with my life decay;
Lest the wise world should look into your moan,
And mock you with me after I am gone.

—William Shakespeare

SONNET 73

That time of year thou mayst in me behold
When yellow leaves, or none, or few, do hang
Upon those boughs which shake against the cold,
Bare ruined choirs, where late the sweet birds sang.
In me thou see'st the twilight of such day   5
As after sunset fadeth in the west;
Which by and by black night doth take away,
Death's second self, that seals up all in rest.
In me thou see'st the glowing of such fire,
That on the ashes of his youth doth lie,   10
As the deathbed whereon it must expire,
Consumed with that which it was nourished by.
This thou perceiv'st, which makes thy love more strong,
To love that well which thou must leave ere long.

—William Shakespeare

a. Discuss what contribution the following vowel and consonant sounds make to the tone of the first lines of "Sonnet 71": *long, er, our, or* in line 1; *ear, surl, sull* in line 2; *war, worl* in line 3; *vile, worl, vile, wor* in line 4. What contrasting statement must be made about the vowel and consonant sounds of the first four lines of "Sonnet 73"?

b. Analyze the rhythm of the first four lines in each sonnet, comparing first the regularity of metrical pattern and secondly the units of grammatical phrasing and the overall sentence movement. Then state the tonal effect of the rhythm in each case.

c. The first twelve lines of each poem make the same point three times, "Sonnet 71" by explicit statement assisted by metaphors, "Sonnet 73" largely by images. Discuss the consequent tonal differences.

d. "Sonnet 71" says *do not mourn for me when I am dead.* How strongly does the tone of the poem support the point? State the meaning of the poem that the tone implies. "Sonnet 73" says three times that the speaker is growing old. Does the tone of the poem suggest he is taking the fact bitterly, gloomily, resignedly, stoically, or what?

5. "To be Superior," as analyzed on p. 120, is not ironical in the sense in which irony has been discussed in the chapter. Distinguish the sense in which it is ironical, and discuss whether Yeats' poem, p. 123, is ironical in that sense as well. Discuss whether the last three lines in "To be Superior" mark a shift in tone that makes them ironical in the sense discussed in the chapter.

6. Irony consists of saying one thing and meaning another, and metaphor consists of identifying one thing with another. Are the two devices related to each other? Write an essay discussing the matter, relying mainly upon an analysis of "Epitaph on an Army of Mercenaries" above. Include in your remarks some comment on whether there can be metaphor without irony and irony without metaphor. One or another of the questions on Housman's poem may be helpful.

ADDITIONAL EXERCISES

1. Analyze the function of the tone in Lawrence Durrell's "Nemea," p. 339.

2. Discuss whether the irony in A. E. Housman's "1887," p. 296, makes the poem antimonarchical, relying upon an analysis of the general tone of the poem for your answer.

3. Discuss the relationship of the tone of the last two lines of "Stopping by Woods on a Snowy Evening," p. 105, to the meaning of the two lines. A review of the questions on the poem on p. 106 may help.

4. Trace the shift in tone in John Donne's "The Canonization," p. 203, and show its congruence with the meaning of the poem.

5. Discuss the irony of W. H. Auden's "Sext," p. 335, in relation to the overall tone of the poem.

10

PERSONA, CHARACTER, AND VOICE

When Robert Browning writes a monologue beginning *That's my last Duchess painted on the wall,* we say that the speaker of the poem is a duke, but we know the ultimate source of his speech. When Shakespeare writes a sonnet that begins, *Shall I compare thee to a summer's day,* we say that the speaker is a lover; and if we happen to guess that the beloved person is a man, are we then permitted to feel that the speaker is Shakespeare disguised as a woman? When John Donne writes, *Batter my heart, three-personed God,* we say that the speaker is a man in religious agony, but the expression seems so direct and intense that we may be inclined to assume that the speaker is John Donne, undisguised. The notions of persona, character, and voice are useful in illuminating these and other matters.

Persona (plural *personae*) refers to the speaker of a poem and to any speaking person in a poem. *Character* is used in its familiar meanings, referring to any person of a poem, speaking or not, and also referring to the mental quality of any of those persons. *Voice* refers to the inferred quality of voice of any of the speaking persons. Consider the following poem.

LEDA AND THE SWAN

A sudden blow: the great wings beating still
Above the staggering girl, her thighs caressed
By the dark webs, her nape caught in his bill,
He holds her helpless breast upon his breast.

How can those terrified vague fingers push   5
The feathered glory from her loosening thighs?

And how can body, laid in that white rush,
But feel the strange heart beating where it lies?

A shudder in the loins engenders there
The broken wall, the burning roof and tower   10
And Agamemnon dead.
                              Being so caught up,
So mastered by the brute blood of the air,
Did she put on his knowledge with his power
Before the indifferent beak could let her drop?

—*William Butler Yeats*

(See the footnote below if the legend that the poem deals with is not known.) * The poem has a single persona, the unidentified speaker of all its lines. No one else speaks, no one else is a persona. There are four characters: the speaker, Leda, the swan Zeus, and Agamemnon. Since the speaker is uninvolved in action with the other characters, he is a different sort of character, and the distinction is most easily kept in mind by referring to him as the speaker or persona. Implied in the poem, of course, are other characters, such as Agamemnon's wife and all the figures of the Trojan war, but they are not properly characters of the poem itself. What are the mental qualities—the characters—of the characters? Agamemnon is nothing more than a name. In the poem he has no character. The fact that he is a leader in the Trojan war and that he appears as an important figure in Homer's *Iliad* and in Greek drama allows the knowledgeable reader to associate bravery and pride with him, but these qualities are not directly in the poem. Leda and Zeus have assignable characters. Leda is a frightened girl rather than a wanton one; at the same time she remains conscious of the rape (feels the strange heart beating), and she perhaps responds to the greatness of the godly act (did she put on his knowledge). Zeus's character is more complex. He is something nonhuman, bestial, strange; he is also an ordinary man, shuddering in the loins and indifferent afterwards; and he is a god, glorious, omnipotent, omniscient. Partly by means of these two brief characterizations, Yeats achieves an extraordinary image of human life.

* The poem describes the union of Leda, a Spartan queen, and Zeus, who appears to her in the form of a swan. The result of the union is a girl, Helen, whose beauty later instigates the Trojan war (alluded to in the tenth line). Another of Leda's daughters becomes the wife of Agamemnon, one of the leaders in the war, and on his return home she kills him. Yeats supposes that the violent union of Leda and the swan is the first cause of a tragic history.

What now of the speaker? Since he merely speaks the poem, he may seem to be without character, but a person's voice will tell something about him, and so we listen to the voice of the poem. Analyzing poetic voice is to infer from written language the sort of way it is presumably meant to be spoken, and the tools of analysis are identical with those of analyzing tone (Chapter 9). Here the speaker's vocabulary is formal rather than colloquial, without the abstractness ordinarily associated with formality: such phrasing as *thighs caressed, strange heart beating,* and *brute blood* is direct, vivid, and powerful. The rhythm of the speaker's voice has a slow intensity: the meter is broken irregularly by caesura, run-on line, and variety in sentence construction; and yet the repeated phrasing, as in *wings beating, thighs caressed,* and *nape caught,* presses the rhythm forward. There is an assurance in the voice, evidenced in the two rhetorical questions in the second stanza: the speaker knows that the girl cannot deny the god or deny her womanhood. And the question at the end, while perhaps less rhetorical, implies assurance in its suggestion that the speaker sees into the mystery of life and human history. In sum, the speaker's voice has power and dignity. Given what he has to say, his voice is the voice of a seer.

Examine persona, character, and voice in another poem by Yeats.

CRAZY JANE TALKS WITH THE BISHOP

I met the Bishop on the road
And much said he and I.
"Those breasts are flat and fallen now,
Those veins must soon be dry;
Live in a heavenly mansion,   5
Not in some foul sty."

"Fair and foul are near of kin,
And fair needs foul," I cried.
"My friends are gone, but that's a truth
Nor grave nor bed denied,   10
Learned in bodily lowliness
And in the heart's pride.

"A woman can be proud and stiff
When on love intent;
But Love has pitched his mansion in   15
The place of excrement;
For nothing can be sole or whole
That has not been rent."

The two personae of the poem, the two speakers, are Crazy Jane and the Bishop. What Crazy Jane says includes not only her response to the Bishop in the second and third stanzas but also the first two lines of the poem and *I cried* in the eighth line. The two personae are identical with the two characters of the poem, there being no one else in the poem aside from the two speaking persons. What are these characters like? Very little is revealed about either. The Bishop seems to be a conventional cleric, expressing familiar religious sentiments about putting aside the flesh and tending the spirit. Crazy Jane is identified as a crazy woman, and her outlook on life is opposed to the Bishop's: she may agree with him that sex is dirty, but she believes that the soul needs such dirt. Is she crazy? Is she a sane woman with a crazy, irreligious idea? Or is she a sane woman with a right idea? Not the reader's own moral preference but the poem itself must determine the answer. Crazy Jane is the main persona of the poem: she begins it, ends it, and has the most to say. The Bishop is present for four lines to utter a conventional view; he is used by Crazy Jane herself as a foil to make more effective her own unconventional attitude. She makes herself seem confidently wise.

The voices of the two personae comment curiously on their characters. The Bishop's language is direct and precise (*breasts, veins*), it has the flavor of Biblical allusion (*heavenly mansion*), and it is rather more formal than colloquial. The structure of his sentence is straightforward, and the rhythm in which it is couched is forceful. His inferred voice is thus vigorous, and dignified without being pretentious. Insofar as a person's voice expresses his character, the Bishop's voice either contradicts the smugly conventional character that has just been assigned to him, or it modifies how his character is seen. Assuming the first of these to be so, one can infer that Yeats was careless in his character delineation, that he was more concerned about other aspects of his poem, or that Crazy Jane distorts the Bishop's language in reporting it. The second of these perhaps makes the most sense. The Bishop is in fact barely more of a character than Agamemnon in "Leda and the Swan": he exists as a voice to utter vigorously a conventional view, in a poem that mainly aims to express vigorously a counter view. The point is that personae as well as characters in a poem are often little more than names (one reason for using the technical term *persona* rather than *person*), and voice and character (mental quality) may purposely be set at odds with each other, insofar as character can be revealed by other things than voice (by ideas, actions, etc.).

What is to be said of Crazy Jane's voice? A glance at its elements shows that she speaks in the same voice as the Bishop, perhaps more formally but hardly enough so for a distinction to be clear. To put it another way, her voice has no intimation in it of a wild, uneducated, lower class woman who lives with her lover in farm outbuildings or the woods. The poem has two personae, two characters (whose individual characters—mental qualities—are sketchy, possibly contradictory), and oddly enough a single voice that seems inappropriate to either persona.

Now compare "Crazy Jane Talks with the Bishop" with "Leda and the Swan." The personae and characters may seem on the surface to be very different, but the voices of both poems are vigorous, direct, and formal. The similar voices belong in part to two personae, two characters, who in an important way are more like than not: the speaker of "Leda and the Swan," who is a seer, and Crazy Jane, who is a wise woman. An interesting if rash inference may follow: the two voices are modulations of the voice of Yeats; the two personae are thin disguises that Yeats is wearing while he contemplates—in both poems —the union of man and woman.

Look briefly at one more of Yeats' poems.

THE SPUR

> You think it horrible that lust and rage
> Should dance attention upon my old age;
> They were not such a plague when I was young;
> What else have I to spur me into song?

It is known that Yeats wrote this poem late in his life, at a time when he underwent an operation to rejuvenate himself sexually. The persona of the poem is an old song-maker or poet of violent passion, and it is tempting to think that Yeats and the persona are one, that Yeats wrote the poem without any effort at disguise. This may be so, but art is limited and artificial, and the persona can not be the whole of Yeats if it even represents one side of him without exaggeration. Thus in talking about such a poem it is useful to consider the persona in two ways: as an artificial figure that the poet creates and as an artificial representation of himself. A root meaning of *persona* is *mask,* and the

mask that Yeats creates and wears in "The Spur" may seem transparent. He is not so recognizable behind the persona of Crazy Jane,
if he is recognizable at all or is there at all. It remains a rash inference
to say that behind the persona of Crazy Jane and behind the persona
who is the speaker of "Leda and the Swan" lurks the person Yeats;
and since he may be disguised even when he seems not to be, as in
"The Spur," it is perhaps best to say that behind the persona who is
Crazy Jane may lurk a persona (a mask) of Yeats, behind which we
may discern something of Yeats himself.

Two qualifications have to be made to the preceding paragraphs.
The notions of persona, character, and voice can be applied to all
poetry, but not always fruitfully. Some poems seem to lack voice just
as some poems yield little or nothing in the way of incidental symbol
or rhyme. The terms for analyzing poetry are metaphors to describe
an actuality, useful more or less according to the particular poem.
Secondly, the relationship of a poet to his poem is a strange thing, and
the assumption that the persona of the poet lies behind his poems is
one that many critics would say is nonsense or irrelevant or useless
to consider or useful to consider only with certain poets. The subject
is discussed further in the next chapter.

EXERCISES
1.

PUSS-PUSS!

—Oh, Auntie, isn't he a beauty! And is he a gentleman
    or a lady?

—Neither, my dear! I had him fixed. It saves him from
    so many undesirable associations.

—D. H. Lawrence

    a. Identify the personae and the characters.
    b. The characters are typical rather than individual. Identify the simi-
larities and differences between them as suggested by the sort of language
they use and their attitudes towards each other and towards sex. (Answering Question "c" may help in answering this question.)
    c. Analyze voice in the poem, discussing euphemism, colloquialism,
formality, and familiarity in diction. Does your analysis suggest two distinct voices appropriate to each character as described in Question "b," two

distinct voices inappropriate to each character, one voice appropriate to both, or something else?

2. Discuss the "questionable inference" on p. 123 in the light of the present chapter, using "Puss-puss" as well as "To Be Superior" and "The Song of a Man Who Has Come Through" in your analysis.

3.

MY LAST DUCHESS *

Ferrara

That's my last Duchess painted on the wall,
Looking as if she were alive. I call
That piece a wonder, now: Frà Pandolf's hands
Worked busily a day, and there she stands.
Will't please you sit and look at her? I said   5
"Frà Pandolf" by design, for never read
Strangers like you that pictured countenance,
The depth and passion of its earnest glance,
But to myself they turned (since none puts by
The curtain I have drawn for you, but I)   10
And seemed as they would ask me, if they durst,
How such a glance came there; so, not the first
Are you to turn and ask thus. Sir, 'twas not
Her husband's presence only, called that spot
Of joy into the Duchess' cheek: perhaps   15
Frà Pandolf chanced to say, "Her mantle laps
Over my lady's wrist too much," or "Paint
Must never hope to reproduce the faint
Half-flush that dies along her throat": such stuff
Was courtesy, she thought, and cause enough   20
For calling up that spot of joy. She had
A heart—how shall I say?—too soon made glad,
Too easily impressed: she liked whate'er
She looked on, and her looks went everywhere.
Sir, 'twas all one! My favor at her breast,   25
The dropping of the daylight in the West,
The bough of cherries some officious fool
Broke in the orchard for her, the white mule
She rode with round the terrace—all and each
Would draw from her alike the approving speech,   30
Or blush, at least. She thanked men,—good! but thanked
Somehow—I know not how—as if she ranked
My gift of a nine-hundred-years-old name
With anybody's gift. Who'd stoop to blame

* Frà Pandolf and Claus of Innsbruck are fictitious.

This sort of trifling? Even had you skill   35
In speech—(which I have not)—to make your will
Quite clear to such an one, and say, "Just this
Or that in you disgusts me; here you miss,
Or there exceed the mark"—and if she let
Herself be lessoned so, nor plainly set   40
Her wits to yours, forsooth, and made excuse,
—E'en then would be some stooping, and I choose
Never to stoop. Oh Sir, she smiled, no doubt,
Whene'er I passed her; but who passed without
Much the same smile? This grew; I gave commands;   45
Then all smiles stopped together. There she stands
As if alive. Will't please you rise? We'll meet
The company below, then. I repeat,
The Count your master's known munificence
Is ample warrant that no just pretence   50
Of mine for dowry will be disallowed;
Though his fair daughter's self, as I avowed
At starting, is my object. Nay, we'll go
Together down, sir! Notice Neptune, though,
Taming a sea-horse, thought a rarity,   55
Which Claus of Innsbruck cast in bronze for me!

—Robert Browning

a. Identify the several characters in the poem. Identify the persona. Describe the character (mental quality) of the persona, relying upon evidence of action, conduct, manners, and taste. Analyze the voice, relying upon diction and rhythm. Does the quality of voice support the mental quality of the persona as otherwise seen?

b. Which aspects of the mental quality of the persona are unattractive by conventional standards? Which are attractive? Which seem more important to his total makeup? Would you infer that Browning would be pleased to recognize himself in the persona?

c. T. S. Eliot has said that it is impossible for a poet to write a monologue such as "My Last Duchess" without speaking in his own person and voice. Assuming that he is right, what bearing does his view have upon your answer to the previous question?

d. Examine briefly the personae and voices in "Childe Roland to the Dark Tower Came" and "Prospice," pages 267–73. Do they seem fundamentally like or unlike those of "My Last Duchess"? Does your answer support Eliot's view?

e. In Eliot's opinion, the only way for a poet to create a voice truly independent from his own is to have two characters in conflict with one another. Does your answer to Question "c" on "Puss-puss" support Eliot's view? Does the analysis of "Crazy Jane Talks with the Bishop" support it? If they do not seem to, suggest an appropriate modification either of Eliot's view or of the accounts of the two poems.

4. Write a brief essay that considers the following questions: (1) assuming that Yeats' persona and voice lie behind "Crazy Jane Talks with the Bishop," what poetic value is there in our awareness of them? (2) making the same assumption, what might be the purpose in the surface deception of using Crazy Jane? (consider the process of writing as well as poetic value to the reader); (3) assuming that Yeats' persona and voice are either not present or not discernible, what purpose is served in creating a single voice in "Crazy Jane Talks with the Bishop" rather than two, and in making that voice inconsistent with the character of one persona and the probable station in life of the other?

ADDITIONAL EXERCISES

Analyze persona, character, and voice in the first poem in each of the following sets. Use the second and third poems, and perhaps additional poems by each poet, for comparison and contrast and possibly as a means of inferring the poet's persona and voice.

1. A. E. Housman, " 'Is my team ploughing?' " p. 296, "Be still, my soul, be still; the arms you bear are brittle," p. 27, "Epitaph on an Army of Mercenaries," p. 127.

2. Thomas Hardy, "His Heart," p. 291, "The Convergence of the Twain," p. 289, "The Going," p. 290.

3. John Donne, "Holy Sonnet 14," p. 78, "Song" (Go and catch a falling star), p. 201, "Song" (Sweetest love, I do not go), p. 204.

4. William Shakespeare, "Sonnet 18," "Sonnet 33," and "Sonnet 129," pp. 60, 198, and 62.

5. Robert Frost, "The Subverted Flower," p. 312, "In Divés' Dive," p. 104, and "Desert Places," p. 23.

6. T. S. Eliot, "The Love Song of J. Alfred Prufrock," p. 320, "Rhapsody on a Windy Night," p. 324. "The Hollow Men," p. 326.

11

STYLE AND THE WHOLE POEM

One of the masterpieces of English poetry is William Blake's "The Sick Rose":

THE SICK ROSE

O Rose, thou art sick!
The invisible worm
That flies in the night,
In the howling storm,

Has found out thy bed   5
Of crimson joy:
And his dark secret love
Does thy life destroy.

The poem is a vision of roses, women, women and men, sexual joy and horror, life and death. It is direct, vivid, intense, and lovely. It is a fine poem to ask questions about, as was done on page 107, and it survives the questions. Ask what *howling storm* is. As symbol it is lust, prurience, the process of death; as sense image it is a howling storm; as rhythm it is two strong beats that submerge an unaccented syllable in between; as sound it is mainly heavy and full vowels and consonants; as diction it is something else. The answers give us bits and pieces of the poem, or abstractions about bits and pieces. What we sense with any great poem is the wholeness as well as the detail. The word *style* suggests this unity.

Style refers to the way a poem is written. It applies to every choice the poet makes to speak one way rather than another, whether his choice is conscious or unconscious; and it equally applies to the sum of his choices. Such choices are or ought to be coherent in a given poem; they are likely to be coherent from poem to poem in a given poet; and they can be coherent among several poets. All the preceding chapters have been concerned with style insofar as they have suggested or shown choices. In "The Sick Rose" Blake's choice of vocabulary is relatively simple, and in this respect his style is relatively simple. His choice of rhythm is energetic and compact, and in this respect his style is energetic and compact. His imagery is vivid and has symbolic force, and so his style is vivid and symbolic. He says half a dozen things at once instead of one thing at a time, and his style is thus complex. To describe the style of the whole poem, we do not simply add these and other elements together; for at least in part we would seem to be saying that the style is incoherent: it is both simple and complex. What Blake achieves is an extraordinary union of the simple and complex. His style is a wholeness of diverse parts.

In a certain respect, the elements of style are available to everyone. Write a poem using simple diction, energetic rhythm, complex symbolism. Any poet, good or bad, relies on stylistic elements that other people have used before him. When Blake says, *O Rose,* he is relying on the stylistic device known as *apostrophe,* which poets were using two thousand years before him and with the same at once intense and formal effect. The rhyme scheme, the short line, and the four-line stanza are not his inventions. It frequently happens that at a particular time several poets will use many of the same devices, small and large, so that their overall styles will be similar, and sometimes that shared style will be given a name. During the hundred years before Blake was writing, many poets wrote poems in iambic pentameter couplets, and they handled these couplets in such a way that the general style was elegant and witty. Here is John Dryden writing in such a way in an attack upon a man whom he identifies as Zimri:

> Some of their chiefs were princes of the land:
> In the first rank of these did Zimri stand;
> A man so various, that he seemed to be
> Not one, but all mankind's epitome:
> Stiff in opinions, always in the wrong;   5
> Was everything by starts, and nothing long;
> But in the course of one revolving moon,
> Was chemist, fiddler, statesman, and buffoon:
> Then all for women, painting, rhyming, drinking,
> Besides ten thousand freaks that died in thinking.   10
>
> —from *Absalom and Achitophel*

Here is Alexander Pope writing in the same way in an attack upon another man:

> Damn with faint praise, assent with civil leer,
> And without sneering, teach the rest to sneer;
> Willing to wound, and yet afraid to strike,
> Just hint a fault, and hesitate dislike;
> Alike reserved to blame or to commend,   5
> A timorous foe, and a suspicious friend . . .

> —from *Epistle to Dr. Arbuthnot*

Blake himself occasionally shows traces of such a style, but he preferred the more natural and lyrical style that writers two hundred years before him often practised, and "The Sick Rose" is closer to a poem of that time by Thomas Lodge:

A FANCY

> When I admire the rose
> That nature made repose
> In you the best of many,
> More fair and blest than any,
> And see how curious art   5
> Hath deckéd every part,
> I think, with doubtful view,
> Whether you be the rose, or the rose is you.

Of course the striking fact about "The Sick Rose" stylistically is that it is most like itself, or most like a few other poems by Blake:

THE TIGER

> Tiger! Tiger! burning bright
> In the forests of the night,
> What immortal hand or eye
> Could frame thy fearful symmetry?

> In what distant deeps or skies   5
> Burnt the fire of thine eyes?
> On what wings dare he aspire?
> What the hand dare seize the fire?

> And what shoulder, and what art,
> Could twist the sinews of thy heart?   10
> And when thy heart began to beat,
> What dread hand? and what dread feet?

What the hammer? what the chain?
In what furnace was thy brain?
What the anvil? what dread grasp   15
Dare its deadly terrors clasp?

When the stars threw down their spears,
And watered heaven with their tears,
Did he smile his work to see?
Did he who made the Lamb make thee?   20

Tiger! Tiger! burning bright
In the forests of the night,
What immortal hand or eye,
Dare frame thy fearful symmetry?

Here are the same vividness and energy of "The Sick Rose," the same
visionary clarity and complexity. The fact illustrates a point upon
which critics are generally agreed: the great poem of a great poet bears
the stamp of his own style. Though all his poems will show indebted-
ness to the writings of others, his great work will display an original
style. So apparent is this fact that some poets search for original styles
as the stepping stone to greatness. And so awkward is the fact that
critics do not know what to make of it. Is originality of style a synonym
for greatness? Is it an incidental accompaniment of greatness? Is it
technical virtuosity carried to one extreme? Is it the inevitably distinct
mark of a unique mind?

    Blake's poems are not all like "The Sick Rose" and "The Tiger."
Even some of the other great ones are sufficiently different to provide
problems in defining his style. Here are two small pieces of his writing.
Great or not, do they bear something of his stylistic signature? The
first of them is addressed to a friend who regarded Blake's outlook on
life as eccentric.

        I mock thee not, though I by thee am mockéd;
        Thou call'st me madman, but I call thee blockhead.
        ————————
        When a man has married a wife, he finds out whether
        Her knees and elbows are only glued together.

The obvious fact about these two epigrams is that their knees and
elbows are glued together. They have none of the intensity and vividness of "The Sick Rose" and "The Tiger." Their rhythms are halting
and slow. Their meanings are exhausted in a moment. Yet if one

thinks of them in comparison with the couplets of Dryden and Pope, they may seem Blakian. They are not elegant and witty, but direct and simple. Their humor is earnest rather than clever. *I mock thee not* goes as simply to the point as *O Rose, thou art sick!,* and *blockhead* seems less artful or awkward than it seems solid, like *what the hammer* in "The Tiger." The epigrams suggest that in analyzing and defining the style of a writer, one must distinguish between superficial and fundamental similarities and differences. The task is not easy. A poet's style changes and develops; floating in it, affecting it, and inseparable from it, are all those conventional stylistic elements; and the individual poem requires and provides its special stylistic color. Are the two epigrams in fact more like "The Sick Rose" and "The Tiger" than unlike? If we did not know they were Blake's, would we ever suspect it? The answer will not come by a mechanical process. It will always be questionable except to the reader's awareness.

What is the significance of style? Among several possible answers, two are perhaps most relevant here. The first is that style is a symbol of the writer. This implies not only that the individual great poet has an original style but also that he is revealed in his style. His mind and character go into his style, and the reader reads backwards and obtains through the style a glimpse into him. This view would seem to fly in the face of the fact that style is inherited and borrowed as well as original. But a defender of the view would say: a man derives his personality from his parents, from his experience, from his cultural inheritance, and yet his personality is finally his own; why should not the same be true of style? The evidence is perhaps clearest in the stylistic elements of tone, voice, and persona. The discussions of these elements in the two previous chapters suggest that they provide ways in which the reader meets the poet's mind.

Less questionable is the view that style provides meaning. Whether a poet's style is his by accident or design, whether it displays his mind or not, it is a bundle of choices to write one way rather than another, and in each choice there is meaning. This viewpoint has been argued in every chapter of this book, in the discussions of meaning in rhythm and structure as well as in diction. It implies that the whole meaning of a poem is not to be had unless every element of the way it is put together has been grasped: sentence structure, rhythm, imagery, symbol, and so forth.

The two views can be thought of as complementary rather than opposed. The first sees through the poem to its creator, emphasizing the poem as a means of expression; the second focuses upon the poem, regarding it as a meaningful object. Together the two views suggest the subtlety and immediacy of the perception of style. Such perception gives the reader the whole poem.

EXERCISES

1. Show that the rhythms of Emily Dickinson's poems, pp. 283–84, are essentially similar, and characterize their overall quality.

2. The discussions of the structure and metaphors of "Dust of Snow," pp. 109–10 and 83, indicate that these two elements are consistent with one another stylistically. Show that the rhythm and symbolism of the poem are likewise consistent, and characterize the overall style of the poem. (It may be helpful to review the questions on the rhythm of the poem on p. 56 and to review the comments on the symbolism in Frost's "The Pasture" on pp. 98–100.)

3. Dylan Thomas was influenced by the poetry of Gerard Manley Hopkins. Compare "A Refusal to Mourn the Death, by Fire, of a Child in London," p. 18, and "The Force That Through the Green Fuse Drives the Flower," p. 339, with "The Windhover," p. 295, to see what the influence might have been.

4. John Keats is remarkable for his organic imagery. Make a brief survey of his poems on pp. 93, and 258–63, and show that this is so, noting in which poem the organic imagery seems strongest and in which weakest.

5. Wilfred Owen's poetry shows some Keatsian traces. Using the "Ode on a Grecian Urn," p. 260, as a standard, eliminate at a glance the Owen poems, pp. 24 and 329–32, that show little or no Keatsian quality; and of the one or two remaining, isolate the main similarities.

6. Sum up the stylistic elements that make "The Song of a Man Who Has Come Through," p. 120, and "Bavarian Gentians," p. 159, like one another. Sum up the elements that make "To Be Superior," p. 120, and "The English are so Nice," p. 39, alike. Discuss whether there seem to be any significant stylistic similarities between the two groups. Your analysis should at one point or another consider rhythm, voice, and structure.

7. Discuss whether T. S. Eliot's "The Love Song of J. Alfred Prufrock," p. 320, is closer to Tennyson's "Tithonus," p. 265, or to Browning's "My Last Duchess," p. 136, stylistically. Consider the following elements: diction, metaphorical language, rhythm, and voice.

8. Relying upon tone, divide the following poems by Robert Frost into two or three groups, defining the dominant tone of each group. Then relying upon voice, discuss the similarities among the groups. "The Pasture,"

p. 98; "Acquainted with the Night," p. 311; "Desert Places," p. 23; "It Bids Pretty Fair," p. 313; "Not all There," p. 27; and "In Divés' Dive," p. 104.

9. Over the course of years, the poetry of William Butler Yeats exhibited several changes. Characterize each of the following poems stylistically, emphasizing its difference from the others. The date of publication of each poem is given in parentheses after it. "When You are Old" (1892), p. 299; "No Second Troy" (1910), p. 299; "Leda and the Swan" (1924), p. 130; and "Crazy Jane Talks with the Bishop" (1932), p. 132. State whether these differences seem more fundamental to you than the similarities between the last two poems pointed out on pp. 130–34.

10. The poem below is by William Butler Yeats or Robert Frost. Can you guess whose it is, and will a stylistic analysis help? Questions 8 and 9 may indicate the possibility or impossibility. The poem is addressed to a squirrel.

> Come play with me;
>   Why should you run
> Through the shaking tree
>   As though I'd a gun
> To strike you dead?   5
>   When all I would do
> Is to scratch your head
> And let you go.

11. Look up the definitions of *classical, romantic,* and *metaphysical* in the *Glossary.* Review the poets who are said to illustrate the three modes. Then examine two of the following poems, and discuss where you would place them stylistically. (Keep in mind that the three terms are not entirely distinct from one another, that they are invented and rough labels to classify great masses of individually different works, and that they are sometimes defined differently from the way they are defined here.) T. S. Eliot, "The Love Song of J. Alfred Prufrock," p. 320; Robert Browning, "Childe Roland to the Dark Tower Came," p. 267; William Wordsworth, "Lines Composed a Few Miles Above Tintern Abbey," p. 239; John Milton, "Lycidas," p. 214; Edmund Spenser, "Prothalamion," p. 192.

PART TWO

The Poet Writing His Poem

How does a poet write a poem, and how does he know when it is finished? Thomas Hardy often wrote his poems first as prose, which he then fitted out with rhymes and rhythms. Shelley sometimes began with a rhythm, and fitted it out with words. Byron would write a line of verse, and strike it out and try another whole line. Keats would worry over individual words. And Housman drank a pint of beer and let complete stanzas come full-blown into his head. There are as many ways to write poetry as there are individual talents to write it. And there is no guarantee of success. Housman's pint of beer failed him more often than not. Wordsworth wrote great poetry for several years, and then for the next thirty or more years wrote nothing to equal it, though presumably he knew as much technically about his craft as before. All of this can be called the mystery of genius and art; and until the mystery is solved, there will not be electronic computers either to write great poems or to judge them. In the meantime, it is possible to speculate with some sense about the substance of a poem; and because poets have left drafts and revisions of their poems, it is possible to see something of the process of writing.

When Robert Frost published "Canis Major" in *West-Running Brook* in 1928, it appeared thus:

> The great Overdog,
> That heavenly beast
> With a star in one eye,
> Gives a leap in the east.
>
> He dances upright
> All the way to the west

5

And never once drops
On his forefeet to rest.

I'm a poor underdog,
But tonight I will bark   10
With the great Overdog
That roams through the dark.

Twenty-one years later it was published in his *Complete Poems* with
two small changes:

The great Overdog.
That heavenly beast
With a star in one eye,
Gives a leap in the east.

He dances upright   5
All the way to the west
And never once drops
On his forefeet to rest.

I'm a poor underdog,
But tonight I will bark   10
With the great Overdog
That romps through the dark.

The period instead of the comma at the end of the first line may at
first seem a mistake: the neatly balanced four-line sentence of the first
version becomes an abrupt first sentence and an unbalanced second
sentence. But then one sees that Frost wants the unbalance, so that the
reader will not come tamely to the end of the first stanza but be
thrown forward—in motion like the leaping dog. The change from
roams to *romps* in the last line is of the same sort: his dog in the sky
is not a roaming, sniffing dog but a romping, dancing, leaping dog.
The small changes increase the energy of the image of the dog and
imply the energy of response of the speaker of the poem.

John Keats' poem "La Belle Dame Sans Merci" made its first public
appearance in the following form in a letter to his brother and sister-
in-law.

LA BELLE DAME SANS MERCI

O what can ail thee, Knight at arms,
Alone and palely loitering?

The sedge has withered from the Lake
    And no birds sing!

O what can ail thee, Knight at arms,   5
    So haggard, and so woebegone?
The squirrel's granary is full
    And the harvest's done.

I see a lily on thy brow
    With anguish moist and fever dew,   10
And on thy cheeks a fading rose
    Fast withereth too.

I met a Lady in the Meads,
    Full beautiful, a faery's child,
Her hair was long, her foot was light   15
    And her eyes were wild.

I made a Garland for her head,
    And bracelets too, and fragrant Zone;
She looked at me as she did love
    And made sweet moan.   20

I set her on my pacing steed
    And nothing else saw all day long,
For sidelong would she bend and sing
    A faery's song.

She found me roots of relish sweet,   25
    And honey wild, and manna dew,
And sure in language strange she said
    "I love thee true."

She took me to her elfin grot
    And there she wept and sighed full sore,   30
And there I shut her wild wild eyes
    With kisses four.

And there she lulléd me asleep,
    And there I dreamed, Ah Woe betide!
The latest dream I ever dreamt   35
    On the cold hill side.

I saw pale Kings, and Princes too,
    Pale warriors, death-pale were they all;
They cried, "La belle dame sans merci
    Thee hath in thrall!"   40

I saw their starved lips in the gloam
    With horrid warning gapéd wide,

> And I awoke, and found me here
>   On the cold hill's side.
>
> And this is why I sojourn here,   45
>   Alone and palely loitering;
> Though the sedge is withered from the Lake
>   And no birds sing.

Keats remarked to his brother and sister-in-law about the eighth stanza: "Why four Kisses—you will say—why four because I wish to restrain the headlong impetuosity of my Muse—she would have fain said 'score' without hurting the rhyme—but we must temper the Imagination as the Critics say with Judgment. I was obliged to choose an even number that both eyes might have fair play: and to speak truly I think two a piece quite sufficient." Later he played the critic less playfully, and revised the eighth and ninth stanzas thus:

> She took me to her elfin grot
>   And there she gazed and sighéd deep,
> And there I shut her wild sad eyes
>   So kissed to sleep.
>
> And there we slumbered on the moss,
>   And there I dreamed, Ah Woe betide!
> The latest dream I ever dreamt
>   On the cold hill side.

He also changed the opening line of the first two stanzas to read *Ah! what can ail thee, wretched wight,* and made a few other minor revisions. The reasons for the changes might have been these. The speaker of the main portion of the poem, from stanza 4 onward, is its most important figure, and attention must be kept fairly steadily upon him. The first version of the eighth stanza emphasizes too greatly the Lady's condition, makes it too mysteriously interesting, and detracts from the climax that should come with the man's dream. Furthermore, the first version makes the Lady's condition the same anguished condition as the man's, and again lessens its special importance. Keats' revision of the first line of the first two stanzas suggests an attempt to emphasize at the outset the man's anguished condition as the most important element of the poem.

Such explanations of the changes made in "La Belle Dame Sans Merci" and "Canis Major" are educated guesses. They become more respectable when supported by evidence from other poems by each poet. They also assume that a poet knows what he is doing when he revises a poem and that his revisions are better than his first attempts. By and large the assumption is valid: it is hardly likely that the writing of a good or great poem has not involved a thousand and one unsatisfactory or muddled preliminary thoughts, even if only in the recesses of the poet's mind before he drinks his pint of beer. But just as Wordsworth was unable late in life to write the great poetry of his earlier years, so another poet is privileged to make mistakes in revising a great poem. Most critics agree that Keats did just this in revising "La Belle Dame Sans Merci." They say that the original version is not only a better poem but also a more Keatsian poem: the qualities he gave up in revising it are the qualities he usually sought in revising other poems. Had he lived more than a year afterwards, presumably he would have changed the poem back again. What would have been his reasoning? Would he have said: I am painting a harsh scene, and *Knight at arms* has a harsher sound than *wretched wight?* Would he have said: any woman who takes a man to her elfin grot has reason to weep? There is bad reasoning for good changes as well as good reasoning for bad changes. Perhaps Keats' thoughts would have been in the following vein. *Knight at arms* is an attractive image and a lovely sound, and is more suitable than the harshness of *wretched wight* to a poem that tries to cast a strange beauty over its partly bleak scene. The image of the weeping Lady with wild wild eyes increases the strange beauty of the scene, which is more important than single focus and climax. The phrase *kisses four* has a sensuousness, a magical reality, unmatched by *kissed to sleep.*

To many critics, the original version of "La Belle Dame Sans Merci" is a perfect poem. Having achieved perfection, could Keats have done anything but mar it? And having marred it, could he have done anything better than go back to the original? Perhaps. A poet writing a poem sometimes does unimaginable things. A critic can only second-guess.

EXERCISES

Three of the following poems, E. A. Robinson's "The House on the Hill" and D. H. Lawrence's "Glory of Darkness" and "Bavarian Gentians," are shown in two versions apiece. The first version of each may have satisfied its author for a time. The second version of "Glory of Darkness" was not final: Lawrence transformed it into the first version of "Bavarian Gentians." The other poems, "The Tiger" and "Anthem for Doomed Youth," are shown in stages of development from unsatisfactory to satisfactory form. Some minor changes in "The Tiger" are not shown.

The basic task with each poem is to isolate the changes that the poet makes and to try to see how the changes serve the overall quality of the final version or draft of his poem. With "The House on the Hill," "Glory of Darkness," and "Bavarian Gentians" the second versions may not seem better than the first but only different, and the explanations need only describe the different effects achieved. If one or another second version does seem better, explain how the changes help.

1. [First version]

THE HOUSE ON THE HILL

They are all gone away,
   The house is shut and still:
There is nothing more to say.

Malign them as we may,
   We cannot do them ill: 5
They are all gone away.

Are we more fit than they
   To meet the Master's will?—
There is nothing more to say.

What matters it who stray   10
   Around the sunken sill?—
They are all gone away,

And our poor fancy play
   For them is wasted skill:
There is nothing more to say.   15

There is ruin and decay
   In the House on the Hill:
They are all gone away,
There is nothing more to say. . . .

[Second version]

THE HOUSE ON THE HILL

They are all gone away,
   The house is shut and still:
There is nothing more to say.

Through broken walls and gray
   The wind blows bleak and shrill: 5
They are all gone away.

Nor is there one today
   To speak them good or ill:
There is nothing more to say.

Why is it then we stray   10
   Around that sunken sill?
They are all gone away,

And our poor fancy play
   For them is wasted skill:
There is nothing more to say.   15

There is ruin and decay
   In the House on the Hill:
They are all gone away,
There is nothing more to say.
          —E. A. Robinson

2. [First draft]

THE TIGER

Tiger Tiger burning bright
In the forests of the night
What immortal hand or eye
Dare frame thy fearful symmetry

In what distant deeps or skies   5
The cruel fire of thine eyes
On what wings dare he aspire
What the hand dare seize the fire

And what shoulder and what art
Could twist the sinews of thy heart   10
And when thy heart began to beat
What dread hand and what dread feet

Could fetch it from the furnace deep
And in thy horrid ribs dare steep
In the well of sanguine woe   15
In what clay and in what mold
Were thy eyes of fury rolled

Where the hammer where the chain
In what furnace was thy brain
What the anvil what dread grasp   20
Dare its deadly terrors clasp

Tiger Tiger burning bright
In the forests of the night
What immortal hand and eye
Dare frame thy fearful symmetry   25

[Second draft]

THE TIGER

Tiger Tiger burning bright
In the forests of the night
What Immortal hand and eye
Dare frame thy fearful symmetry

And what shoulder and what art   5
Could twist the sinews of thy heart
And when thy heart began to beat
What dread hand and what dread feet

When the stars threw down their spears
And watered heaven with their tears   10
Did he smile his work to see
Did he who made the lamb make thee

Tiger Tiger burning bright
In the forests of the night
What immortal hand and eye   15
Dare frame thy fearful symmetry

[Third draft]

THE TIGER

Tiger! Tiger! burning bright
In the forests of the night,
What immortal hand or eye
Could frame thy fearful symmetry?

In what distant deeps or skies   5
Burnt the fire of thine eyes?
On what wings dare he aspire?
What the hand dare seize the fire?

And what shoulder, and what art,
Could twist the sinews of thy heart?   10
And when thy heart began to beat,
What dread hand? and what dread feet?

What the hammer? what the chain?
In what furnace was thy brain?
What the anvil? what dread grasp   15
Dare its deadly terrors clasp?

When the stars threw down their spears,
And watered heaven with their tears,

Did he smile his work to see?
Did he who made the Lamb make thee?   20

Tiger! Tiger! burning bright
In the forests of the night,
What immortal hand or eye,
Dare frame thy fearful symmetry?

—*William Blake*

3. [First version]

GLORY OF DARKNESS

Blue and dark
Oh Bavarian gentians, tall ones
make a dark-blue gloom
in the sunny room

They have added blueness to blueness, until   5
it is dark: beauty
blue joy of my soul
Bavarian gentians
your dark blue gloom is so noble!

How deep I have gone   10
dark gentians
since I embarked on your dark blue fringes
how deep, how deep, how happy!

What a journey for my soul
in the dark blue gloom   15
of gentians here in the sunny room!

[Second version]

GLORY OF DARKNESS

. . . .
it is dark
and the door is open
to the depths

it is so blue, it is so dark   5
in the dark doorway
and the way is open
to Hades.

Oh, I know—
Persephone has just gone back   10

down the thickening thickening gloom
of dark-blue gentians to Pluto
to her bridegroom in the dark
and all the dead
and all the dark great ones of the underworld   15
down there, down there
down the blue depths of mountain gentian flowers
cold, cold
are gathering to a wedding in the [winter] dark
down the dark blue path   20

What a dark-blue gloom
of gentians here in the sunny room!

—*D. H. Lawrence*

4. [First version]

BAVARIAN GENTIANS

Not every man has gentians in his house
In soft September, at slow, sad Michaelmas.

Bavarian gentians, tall and dark, but dark
Darkening the daytime torch-like with the smoking blueness of Pluto's
    gloom,
ribbed hellish flowers erect, with their blaze of darkness spread blue,   5
blown flat into points, by the heavy white draught of the day.

Torch-flowers of the blue-smoking darkness, Pluto's dark-blue blaze
black lamps from the halls of Dis, smoking dark blue
giving off darkness, blue darkness, upon Demeter's yellow-pale day
whom have you come for, here in the white-cast day?   10

Reach me a gentian, give me a torch!
let me guide myself with the blue, forked torch of a flower
down the darker and darker stairs, where blue is darkened on blueness
down the way Persephone goes, just now, in first-frosted September.
to the sightless realm where darkness is married to dark   15
and Persephone herself is but a voice, as a bride,
a gloom invisible enfolded in the deeper dark
of the arms of Pluto as he ravishes her once again
and pierces her once more with his passion of the utter dark
among the splendor of black-blue torches, shedding fathomless darkness
    on the nuptials.   20

Give me a flower on a tall stem, and three dark flames,
for I will go to the wedding, and be wedding-guest
at the marriage of the living dark.

[Second version]

BAVARIAN GENTIANS

Not every man has gentians in his house
in Soft September, at slow, sad Michaelmas.

Bavarian gentians, big and dark, only dark
darkening the day-time, torch-like with the smoking blueness of Pluto's
    gloom,
ribbed and torch-like, with their blaze of darkness spread blue   5
down flattening into points, flattened under the sweep of white day
torch-flower of the blue-smoking darkness, Pluto's dark-blue daze,
black lamps from the halls of Dis, burning dark blue,
giving off darkness, blue darkness, as Demeter's pale lamps give off light,
lead me then, lead the way.   10

Reach me a gentian, give me a torch!
let me guide myself with the blue, forked torch of this flower
down the darker and darker stairs, where blue is darkened on blueness
even where Persephone goes, just now, from the frosted September
to the sightless realm where darkness is awake upon the dark   15
and Persephone herself is but a voice
or a darkness invisible enfolded in the deeper dark
of the arms Plutonic, and pierced with the passion of dense gloom,
among the splendor of torches of darkness, shedding darkness on the lost
    bride and her groom.

                      —*D. H. Lawrence*

5. [First draft]

ANTHEM FOR DEAD YOUTH *

    passing
What ~~minute~~ bells for these who die so fast?

      ~~solemn~~   *the*
—Only the monstrous anger of ~~our~~ guns.

   blind insolence   *iron*
Let the ~~majestic insults~~ of ~~their iron~~ mouths

     requiem
Be as the ~~priest word~~ of their ~~burials.~~
         requiem

Of choristers and holy music, none;   5

   Nor any voice of mourning, save the wail

* Amendments made by Siegfried Sassoon rather than by Wilfred Owen are italicized.
Two or three unreadable trial phrases have been omitted here.

And the   *hiss*   *lonely*
The long ~~drawn wail~~ of ~~high far~~ sailing shells.

                      to light
What candles may we hold ~~for~~ these lost? ~~souls?~~

—Not in the hands of boys, but in their eyes,

      shine the ~~tapers~~   No holy ~~tapers~~ candles
Shall ∧ many   ~~candles~~; flames: shine; ~~and will light them.~~   10
        ~~holy~~   to

And Women's wide-spread~~ed~~ arms shall be their wreaths,

And pallor of girls' cheeks shall be their palls.

                    mortal
Their flowers, the tenderness of ~~all men's~~ minds,
                    ~~comrades'~~
                    rough men's

      each slow
And ~~every~~ Dusk, a drawing-down of blinds.

[Second draft]

FOR
ANTHEM TO DEAD YOUTH

What passing-bells for you who die in herds?

                              the
—Only the monstrous anger of ~~more~~ guns!

—Only the stuttering rifles' rattled words

Can patter out your hasty orisons.

                       choirs
No chants for you, nor balms, nor wreaths, nor bells,   5
                       shells

Nor any voice of mourning, save the choirs,

And long-drawn sighs
~~The shrill demented choirs~~ of wailing shells;

And bugles calling for you from sad shires.

What candles may we hold to speed you all?

Not in the hands of boys, but in their eyes   10

Shall   ~~and gleams~~ our
~~Shall~~ shine the holy lights ∧ of ~~long~~ goodbyes.

           must
The pallor of girls' brows ~~shall~~ be your pall;

             ~~broken simple frail mortal~~ comrades'
Your flowers, the tenderness of ~~mortal minds,~~
                ~~pain white~~
                ~~grief torment~~

And each slow dusk, a drawing-down of blinds.

[Third draft]

[no title]

What passing-bells for these ~~po~~ dumb-dying cattle?
    —Only the monstrous anger of more guns!
Only the stuttering rifles' rapid rattle
    Can patter out their hasty orisons.
No chants for them, nor wreaths, nor asphodels,   5
    Nor any voice of mourning save the choirs
The shrill demented choirs of wailing shells;
    And bugles calling for them from sad shires.

What candles may we hold to speed them all?
    Not in the hands of boys, but in their eyes   10
Shall shine the holy gleams of their goodbyes.
    The pallor of girls' cheeks shall be their pall.
Their flowers the tenderness of silent minds
And each slow dusk a drawing-down of blinds.

[Fourth draft]

DOOMED
ANTHEM FOR DEAD YOUTH *

What passing-bells for these who die as cattle?

    —Only the monstrous anger of the guns.

    Only the stuttering rifles' rapid rattle

Can patter out their hasty orisons.

    ~~music for all them~~   ~~not~~ no   nor
No mockeries for them; from prayers ~~or~~ bells,   5
      now

* Sassoon's amendments are italicized. One unreadable trial phrase has been omitted.

Nor any voice of mourning save the choirs,—

        ented
The shrill demonic choirs of wailing shells;

And bugles calling ~~sad across the~~ shires.
        for them from sad

What candles may be held to speed them all?

Not in the hands of boys, but in their eyes   10

Shall shine the holy glimmers of goodbyes.

And The pallor of girls' brows shall be their pall;

        patient
Their flowers the tenderness of ~~silent~~ minds,
        ~~sweet white~~

And each slow dusk a drawing-down of blinds.

        —*Wilfred Owen*

ADDITIONAL EXERCISES

Examining the drafts of a single poem in isolation from all other evidence means that the explanation for changes cannot be wholly convincing. For an example of a different approach, read Martin Nurmi, "Blake's Revisions of 'The Tiger,' " *PMLA*, LXXI (September 1956), 669–685. (1) Summarize Nurmi's argument. (2) Try to abstract the theoretical basis of Nurmi's article; that is, try to discern the sort of thinking he applies to the poem and presumably could bring to bear upon any poem. (3) Decide whether his and your interpretations complement each other or clash. If they clash, does the clash seem an inevitable consequence of difference in approach? Which explanation seems more satisfactory?

PART THREE

Glossary

ABSTRACT DICTION Language that is nonsensuous and general, as in the line, *Know then thyself, presume not God to scan,* the opposite of concrete diction, which is sensuous and specific, as in the line *She took the dappled partridge flecked with blood.* The dividing line is not always sharp; and in other contexts such a word as *scan* would be concrete.

ACCENT The greater emphasis given to one syllable over surrounding syllables. In the word *country,* the first syllable, *coun* is normally accented. Occasionally a poet wrenches normal accent, as has often been done with *country,* forcing the accent upon the second syllable. See Chapter 4 for further discussion.

AFFECTIVE FALLACY The mistaken notion, according to one critical viewpoint, of judging a poem by its emotional effect upon the reader. See also *Intentional fallacy.*

ALEXANDRINE A line with six iambic feet. On kinds and number of feet, see p. 59. The last line in the Spenserian stanza (see below) is an Alexandrine.

ALLEGORY The word is variously defined. Commonly it refers to a narrative whose characters and actions are no more important for themselves than for an abstract viewpoint or conception that they exemplify. "Childe Roland to the Dark Tower Came," pp. 267–72, is an allegorical narrative in which the adventure of the hero may be seen, in one interpretation, to be a description of the mind. See *Myth* and *Realism.*

ALLITERATION Repetition of consonantal sounds. The word is sometimes restricted—but not in the present text—to such repetition when it comes in accented syllables or at the beginnings of words. See p. 43 for illustration. See also *Assonance, Consonance,* and *Internal rhyme.*

ALLUSION Brief, unexplained reference to persons, places, events, etc., the poet expecting the reader to be knowledgeable. Yeats' "Leda and the Swan" alludes in its title to the tale of a Spartan queen who was raped by the god Zeus in the form of a swan. See p. 130 for the poem and for other allusions in it.

AMBIGUITY See p. 9.

AMPHIBRACH A three-syllable foot, with the accent on the middle syllable, as in *behāvior*. On kinds of feet, see p. 59.

ANAPEST A three-syllable foot, with the accent on the last syllable, as in *interfēre*. On kinds of feet, see p. 59.

ANTISTROPHE See *Ode*.

APOSTROPHE An eloquent turning to address directly a person, place, or thing, as in the first line of Blake's "The Sick Rose": "O Rose, thou art sick," p. 139. See also *Invocation*.

APPROXIMATE RHYME Imperfect rhyme, as in *shall-shell*. Also called *false, near, off, partial,* and *slant* rhyme. On its uses, see Question 4, p. 49. See also *Eye Rhyme*.

ARCHAISM Language once standard, but now used rarely and with a sense of artifice, as with the word *ere*. See further, p. 28.

ARCHETYPE The terms *archetypal image* and *archetypal pattern,* derived from Jungian psychology, are used by some critics to describe certain recurrent images and patterns in poems. These images and patterns are believed to reflect fundamental experience throughout human history, and their presence in poems to elicit profound response in the reader. Milton's "Lycidas," p. 214, and Whitman's "When Lilacs Last in the Dooryard Bloomed," p. 273, have a death-rebirth pattern, both poems moving in focus from a contemplation of death to a sense of new life.

ASSONANCE Repetition of vowel sounds. The word is sometimes restricted —but not in the present text—to such repetition when it comes in accented syllables or at the beginnings of words. See p. 43 for examples. See also *Alliteration, Consonance,* and *Internal rhyme.*

BALLAD A short dramatic narrative poem, originally sung. Many such poems have a characteristic stanzaic form: four lines of alternating four and three accents and a rhyme scheme of *abcb*. "Sir Patrick Spens," p. 183, is an example. Some ballads employ *refrain* (see below) and *incremental repetition* (see below). *Folk ballads* (or *popular ballads*) have been composed and sung over many centuries by ordinary people, and handed down by memory among them. "Sir Patrick Spens" is a folk ballad composed perhaps in the 13th century. It is printed here without its music. *Literary ballads* are conscious imitations of folk ballads, but composed without music. Keats' "La Belle Dame Sans Merci," p. 150, is a literary ballad written in 1819.

BLANK VERSE Unrhymed iambic pentameter, as in Wordsworth's "Lines Composed a Few Miles Above Tintern Abbey," p. 239. On iambs and pentameter, see p. 59.

CACAPHONY Harsh, unpleasant sound, as in the first lines of Hardy's "The Wound," analyzed on p. 44. See also *Euphony.*

CAESURA Internal breaks in the rhythm of a line, caused by phrasal pauses and punctuation. Slight caesura occurs in almost every line of four feet or more. Frequently—but not in the present text—the term is restricted to the single most important break in a line. See p. 65 for illustration.

CHARACTER The persons in a poem, also the qualities of mind of those persons. See Chapter 10.

CLASSICAL The term is variously used. A familiar usage implies order, adherence to convention, controlled emotion, and objectivity. Some of the best Greek and Roman art of antiquity exhibits such qualities, and Greek and Roman art generally are given the label *classical.* Other arts of other societies are called classical when they exhibit such qualities, or *neoclassical* when they consciously imitate or rely on classical models. English poetry of the late seventeenth century and most of the eighteenth is called neoclassical. Alexander Pope's poetry, as in his "Essay on Man," p. 225, is the most brilliant example. See also *Realistic* and *Romantic.*

CLICHÉ A worn-out expression such as *sharp as a tack* or *whispering wind.*

CLOSED COUPLET See *Couplet.*

COLLOQUIAL DICTION The special language of familiar speech, as against the language of ordinary or formal speech or writing. See p. 28.

CONCEIT A term usually applied to an elaborate and extravagant simile or metaphor, as in the first lines of Wyatt's "They Flee from Me," p. 190, in which women are likened to tame and wild deer. The so-called *metaphysical conceit* is one which has an especially harsh, incongruous, or scientific color, as in Crashaw's "Upon the Body of our Blessed Lord, Naked and Bloody," p. 219, in which Christ's body and blood are likened to a wardrobe and its garments.

CONCRETE DICTION See *Abstract diction.*

CONNOTATION Overtone of meaning in a word. See p. 30 for illustration, and Question 7, p. 34, on the difficulties of distinguishing between connotation and denotation, the basic meaning of a word.

CONSONANCE A term sometimes used as a synonym for all alliteration and sometimes reserved for elaborately patterned alliteration. The term alliteration is alone used in the present text. See p. 43 for examples. The two lines from Swinburne beginning *the lilies and languors,* p. 46, are elaborately patterned alliteration. See also *Assonance.*

CONVENTION Any long-familiar or established device, method, or outlook that a poet relies on. Sometimes conventions are precise rules, such as those for writing sonnets; sometimes they are tacitly accepted notions, such as the view that the language of poetry should be beautiful. The history of poetry is in part a history of conventions developing and dissolving.

COUPLET   Two consecutive lines of the same length rhyming. When the second of the two lines closes a thought or a segment thereof, the couplet is said to be *closed;* otherwise it is *open.* The Pope quotation, pp. 46–47, is in closed couplets, though line 6 only momentarily closes. The Browning quotation, p. 47, is open. When closed couplets are in iambic pentameter, they are known as *heroic couplets.* The Pope couplets are heroic, being both closed and in iambic pentameter; the Browning couplets are not, since although they are in iambic pentameter too, they are open. On iambs and pentameter, see p. 59.

DACTYL   A three-syllable foot, with the accent on the first syllable, as in *hŏrrible.* On kinds of feet, see p. 59.

DEAD METAPHOR   See p. 81.

DECORUM   Appropriateness of language to the speaker and subject, dignified language being appropriate to a prince and to tragedy, ordinary language to an average person in familiar conversation, and so forth.

DENOTATION   The basic meaning of a word. See p. 30 for illustration, and Question 7, p. 34, on the difficulties of distinguishing between denotation and connotation, the overtone of meaning in a word.

DICTION   Choice of language. See p. 27. See also *Decorum* and *Poetic diction.*

DIDACTIC   Verse that openly intends to instruct. Pope's "Essay on Man," p. 225, is didactic.

DIMETER   A line of two feet. See p. 59 on meter and feet.

DOUBLE RHYME   End rhyme involving two vowel sounds and intermediate and succeeding consonants. See p. 45.

DRAMATIC MONOLOGUE   A poem having something of a narrative and dramatic element, with one character speaking all its lines and the poem focusing upon him. Browning's "My Last Duchess," p. 136, is a dramatic monologue. Such a poem as Yeats' "Leda and the Swan," p. 130, is spoken by a single person, but it lacks in various degree the other elements of a dramatic monologue.

ELEGY   A lament for the dead, such as Milton's "Lycidas," p. 214.

END RHYME   Rhyme at the end of the line. See Chapter 3. See also *Internal rhyme.*

END-STOPPED LINE   A line that comes to a phrasal pause at the end. See pp. 67–70 for illustration. See also *Run-on line.*

ENGLISH SONNET   See *Shakespearian sonnet.*

ENJAMBEMENT   The same as *Run-on line.*

EPIC   A long narrative poem usually treating of tribal, national, or larger-scale action and usually focusing upon a hero. *Beowulf* describes the hero Beowulf's defense of a Danish tribe and then of his own tribe against the onslaughts of monstrous creatures. Milton's Christian epic, *Paradise Lost,* describes the creation and fall of man. The term *folk epic* is applied to poems such as *Beowulf* which evolve from and celebrate the triumphs and disasters of primitive societies. *Literary epic* applies to the more deliberately and more artificially conceived production of a writer in a sophisticated, literate society. *Beowulf* was probably composed in the 8th century, developing from brief oral accounts of events of two centuries before. Milton's literary epic was written in the 1660's. By analogy the term epic is applied to any other large-scale art work. The term *mock epic* refers to a literary epic that caricatures the type, usually by treating a trivial subject as though it were serious. Byron's *Don Juan* shows a young man whose first heroic episode ends with his fleeing unclothed into the street from a married woman's bed. One of the minor characteristic devices of the epic is the *epic simile,* an elaborate comparison sustained over several lines. In *Paradise Lost* Milton describes Satan lying in Hell as a huge sea creature lying off the coast of Norway.

EPIGRAM   A brief, neat, and usually witty poem, such as Byron's poems on Castlereagh, p. 253.

EPITHALAMION   A poem to celebrate a marriage. Spenser's "Prothalamion" (the two words mean approximately the same thing: at the bridal chamber), p. 192, is an example.

EPODE   See *Ode.*

EUPHEMISM   A polite term to substitute for another that might seem unpleasant or blunt. John Donne indulges in a witty euphemism when he says that two lovers' hands *were firmly cemented with a fast balm,* meaning that they were sticking together with sweat.

EUPHONY   Pleasant, musical sound. Most poetry in the past has attempted to be at least fairly euphonious. *Thou still unravished bride of quietness* is euphonious; *Gr-r-r—there go, my heart's abhorrence!* is cacaphonous (harsh sounding) in its opening syllable, euphonious in the rest.

EUPHUISM   Not a poetic term, it refers to an elaborately balanced prose style fashionable in the late 16th century.

EYE RHYME   End syllables that do not rhyme perfectly but whose spellings are the same and suggest perfect rhyme, as with *y* in lines 7 and 8 of Herrick's "Delight in Disorder," p. 8: *thereby—confusedly.* Eye rhyme is thus a form of *approximate rhyme* (see above). Because of changes in pronunciation, what may seem eye rhyme to a modern reader may not have been to the composing poet. At the end of the first stanza of Donne's "Song" (Go and catch a falling star), p. 201, the word *wind* (as in north wind) was meant to rhyme perfectly with *find* and *mind,* and should be so pronounced.

FALSE RHYME   See *Approximate rhyme.*

FEMININE ENDING   A line in which the last syllable is unaccented. See also *Feminine rhyme.*

FEMININE RHYME Double rhyme in which the second syllable is unaccented, as in *lŏver—cŏver*. See also *Masculine rhyme*.

FIGURATIVE LANGUAGE Language which goes beyond ordinary literal meaning. When the poet says his *love's like a red, red rose*, he does not mean so literally. See *Metaphor, Paradox, Irony*, and *Hyperbole*, which are various kinds of figurative language. The term *figure of speech* refers to an instance of such language.

FOOT The unit of meter. See p. 58.

FORMAL DICTION Language appropriate for formal occasions. See p. 28.

FREE VERSE Poetry whose basic rhythm is nonmetrical. See pp. 70–73 for discussion and illustration.

GENRE Literary type. The genres—types—of poetry include among them the following, which are described elsewhere in these pages: dramatic monologue, elegy, epic, epigram, lyric, pastoral, romance. Definitions of the types are not entirely agreed upon, and the types often overlap. Milton's "Lycidas" is both pastoral and elegy—a pastoral elegy; Whitman's "When Lilacs Last in the Dooryard Bloomed" is both lyric and elegy.

HEPTAMETER A line of seven feet. See p. 59 on feet.

HEROIC COUPLET See *Couplet*.

HEXAMETER A line of six feet. See p. 59 on feet.

HYPERBOLE Exaggerated statement, as when a lover in a Donne poem says, *She is all states, and all princes, I*. See also *Understatement*.

IAMB A two-syllable foot, with the accent on the second syllable, as in *concĕit*. See p. 59 on kinds of feet.

IMAGE A term used variously to refer to metaphor, visual description, and the effects of alliteration, assonance, and onomatopoeia. (See these terms elsewhere in these pages.) In Chapter 6 the term is used to identify what is sometimes called *free sense imagery*: the imaginative appeal of the meanings of words to the several senses.

IMAGISM A poetic movement of the early twentieth century that emphasized, among other things, the importance of visual and other sense imagery, as in Stevens' "Domination of Black," p. 314.

IMPERFECT RHYME See *Approximate rhyme*.

INCREMENTAL REPETITION In ballads, the repetition of a line or stanza with a variation that advances the narrative. See Edward's responses in the ballad of that name, p. 183.

INFORMAL DICTION The language of ordinary speech and writing, as against *colloquial diction* (see above) and *formal diction* (see above). See the general discussion of diction, pp. 27–30.

INTENTIONAL FALLACY A term applied to the mistaken notion that to know a poet's intention in writing his poem is to know what his poem is about. The poet may or may not understand what he is achieving. See also *Affective fallacy*.

INTERNAL RHYME   Rhyme within the line, as in the first and third lines following.

> The fair breeze *blew,* the white foam *flew,*
> The furrow followed free;
> We were the *first* that ever *burst*
> Into that silent sea.
>
> *—Samuel Taylor Coleridge*

The repeated *f*'s, *b*'s, *r*'s, and *s*'s elsewhere in the lines are a kind of internal rhyme too, but they are usually identified by the word *alliteration* (see above). See also *Assonance.*

INVECTIVE   Language of attack and abuse. See *ironic invective,* p. 124.

INVERSION   Reversal of normal word order, as when Milton says, *ever-burning sulphur unconsumed* instead of *ever-burning, unconsumed sulphur.*

INVOCATION   An address to a deity to assist in poetic composition, as when at the beginning of *Paradise Lost* Milton says, *And chiefly thou, O Spirit . . . , instruct me.*

IRONY   Verbal irony, which is saying one thing and meaning another, is discussed on pp. 123–25. Three forms of verbal irony—*sarcasm, understatement,* and *ironic invective*—are identified on p. 124. See also the comment on sarcasm on p. 175. Another kind of irony is *irony of fate* (or *irony of circumstance*), which refers to a least expected or least desired turn of events, as when the beautiful and loved woman in Byron's "The Dream," pp. 248–52, ends her life in madness and without love.

LIGHT VERSE   Verse of small size and small pretensions such as the limericks on pp. 52 and 55.

LIMERICK   A familiar form of light verse in five lines, rhyming aabba, and having a typical metrical pattern, illustrated on pp. 52–53.

LITOTES   The same as *Negative understatement.* See below.

LOCALISM   Diction peculiar to an area. See Question 3, p. 31.

LYRIC POETRY   Poetry of a personal, emotional, reflective character, usually short, usually relying upon a single speaker, and usually lacking a narrative element. Shakespeare's sonnets, pp. 197–200, are lyric poems. The ballad "Edward," p. 183, a brief impersonal narrative involving two speakers, is not. See *Ode* and *Narrative poetry.*

MASCULINE ENDING   A line in which the last syllable is accented. See also *Masculine rhyme* and *Feminine rhyme.*

MASCULINE RHYME   Ordinary single rhyme, with the rhyming syllables accented. See further p. 45.

METAPHOR   See Chapter 5 and *Metonymy, Mixed metaphor,* and *Synecdoche.*

METAPHYSICAL CONCEIT   See *Conceit.*

METAPHYSICAL POETRY   Poetry that is personal, passionate, witty, harsh, and knotty. The *metaphysical conceit* (see under *Conceit*) is its hallmark. The term is most often used in reference to a small group of seventeenth-century poets, notably John Donne and Andrew Marvell, whose poems often exhibit such qualities. It is occasionally applied to any similar poetry of another time, such as that of Gerard Manley Hopkins.

METER   Regular rhythm. See Chapter 4.

METONYMY   Figurature language (see the definition above) in which a closely related thing stands for that thing, as in the phrase *town and gown* the word *gown* stands for the academic community. See also *Synecdoche*.

MIXED METAPHOR   A bad or ludicrous mixture of metaphors, as in the phrase *her heart was like putty in the furnace of his desire.*

MOCK EPIC   See *Epic*.

MONOMETER   A line of one foot. See p. 59 on meter and feet.

MYTH   The word is used variously. It most commonly refers to unbelieved tales of gods and goddesses. By analogy it applies loosely to any fanciful story, especially one of some scope or concerned with an important figure, such as the myth of George Washington and the cherry tree. The word is also used to apply to a belief held among a large number of people, with sometimes but not always the implication that the belief is false, as when someone refers to the myth that all men are created equal. In modern poetry criticism, the term is used to refer to a narrative whose characters and action loom larger than the immediate life they portray, so that they seem to epitomize their tribe, nation, or culture, or assume fabulous, profound importance. Beowulf (who is described briefly under *Epic*) is such a mythic figure. Childe Roland, the hero of the poem of that name on p. 267, is perhaps one. The dividing line between myth and *Allegory* is not always sharp, and a figure such as Childe Roland (described under *Allegory*) can be said to be both mythic and allegorical.

NARRATIVE POETRY   Poetry in which plot, action, and sometimes character are stressed rather than personal thought and feeling. Ballads such as "Edward," p. 183, are brief narratives. See also *Lyric poetry*.

NEAR RHYME   See *Approximate rhyme*.

NEGATIVE CAPABILITY   A term used by John Keats to describe what he thought to be an important poetic faculty, an ability to rest in "uncertainties, mysteries, doubts, without any irritable reaching after fact and reason." Keats connected this faculty to the sense of beauty. See *Didactic* for an opposing view of poetry.

NEGATIVE UNDERSTATEMENT   To say *he doesn't play a bad game* and mean *he plays a good game*. See the comments on ordinary understatement on p. 124. Negative understatement was common in Middle English poetry, as when the poet would say of someone, *He was a not unworthy warrior.*

NEOCLASSICAL   See *Classical*.

OBJECTIVE CORRELATIVE   A term introduced by T. S. Eliot and quarrelled over by critics ever since. It is sometimes understood to mean the words, situation, and action by which an emotion is conveyed to the reader or playgoer. The words, situation, and action can thus be regarded as a kind of equivalent to, an objectification of, the emotion.

OCCASIONAL POETRY   Poetry written in mark of a particular occasion. Milton's "Lycidas," p. 214, was written on the death of the young man whom the poem celebrates.

OCTAMETER   A line of eight feet. See p. 59 on meter and feet.

OCTAVE   A stanza of eight lines; also the first eight lines of a sonnet, especially when those lines form a unit in rhyme or thought.

ODE   A long, serious lyric poem (see *Lyric*), usually in several stanzas. See Keats' odes, pp. 259–63. The terms *strophe, antistrophe,* and *epode* were drawn from Greek drama to describe a pattern of three stanzas used in some odes, *strophe* and *antistrophe* identifying the first two stanzas, written in the same form, and *epode* identifying the third stanza, written in another form.

OFF RHYME   See *Approximate rhyme.*

ONOMATOPOEIA   The sound of a word or group of words that suggests their sense, as in Tennyson's line *And murmur of innumerable bees.*

ORGANIC   The word has various uses. It can refer to a type of imagery that suggests sensation of the organs of the body, as discussed on p. 91. It is also used to suggest an internal principle of growth that determines the shape of a poem, or to suggest an unmechanical, indivisible wholeness of some aspect of a poem. The analysis of the structure of Wordsworth's "There Was a Boy," p. 112, shows it to be organic in its growth and wholeness. Such internally developed shape and wholeness is often thought of as the essential characteristic of great poetry.

OTTAVA RIMA   An eight-line stanza in iambic pentameter rhyming *abababcc.*

PARADOX   A self-contradictory statement or one seemingly illogical, as with Keats' phrase *Beauty is truth, truth beauty.*

PARODY   A consciously exaggerated and usually humorous imitation of a work.

PARTIAL RHYME   See *Approximate rhyme.*

PASTORAL   Poetry depicting rural life, especially poetry which follows a set of conventions in describing an idyllic existence among shepherds and shepherdesses. Robert Frost's poems about rural New England are pastoral in the broad sense, Milton's "Lycidas," p. 214, in the narrow sense. In "Lycidas" the speaker and his dead friend are described as once being shepherds together tending their flocks. As a lament for the dead friend, the poem is a *pastoral elegy.*

PATHETIC FALLACY   Giving human qualities to inanimate things, as in Andrew Marvell's phrase *the seas ruled.* The term was originally used in a derogatory sense, but is now used neutrally. It is allied to *personification* (see below), but is used to refer to less formal and less obvious humanization.

PENTAMETER   A line of five feet. See p. 59 on meter and feet.

PERIODIC SENTENCE   A sentence whose essential grammatical parts are held incomplete until nearly the end, as in lines 3–14 of "Delight in Disorder" as analyzed on p. 13.

PERSONA   The speaker of the whole poem or any speaking figure within the poem. See Chapter 10.

PERSONIFICATION   Giving human attributes to inanimate and abstract things, as when Keats calls his Grecian urn an *unravished bride*. See p. 85 for other illustration. See also *Pathetic fallacy*.

PETRARCHAN SONNET   A sonnet consisting of eight lines rhyming *abbaabba,* followed by six lines rhyming in another pattern, frequently *cdcdcd* or *cdecde*. Wyatt's "Who So List to Hunt," p. 190, is an example. See also *Shakespearian sonnet* and *Sonnet*.

POETIC DICTION   Language of an elevated sort once thought to be appropriate to poetry. A line of poetic diction by Thomas Gray to describe a brilliant sunrise, *And reddening Phoebus lifts his golden fire,* was attacked by a later poet, Wordsworth, who thought that the language of poetry should derive from ordinary speech. See also *Diction*.

POETIC JUSTICE   A term mainly used in drama to describe an ending in which the playwright gives every character his just reward or punishment for his conduct.

POETIC LICENSE   The freedom the poet has to speak in uncommon language, to distort fact, etc., in the interest of poetic excellence.

PROSODY   The study of versification.

PROTHALAMION   A poem to celebrate a marriage, as does Spenser's poem of this name on p. 192. See also *Epithalamion*.

PUN   A play on words, as when in Sonnet 33, p. 198, Shakespeare uses the word *sun* to allude at once to the sun in the sky and to a young man, a son.

PYRRHIC   A two-syllable foot with neither syllable accented. The foot appears only as an isolated exception to the normal pattern of feet in the line in which it appears. See p. 61 for illustration. See also p. 59 on meter and feet.

QUADRUPLE RHYME   End rhyme involving four vowel sounds and intermediate and succeeding consonants. See p. 43 for illustration.

QUATRAIN   A four-line stanza.

REALISTIC   The term is used variously. Commonly it refers to the depicture of ordinary life, without attempting to idealize speech, manners, character, or anything else, and without imposing obvious artificialities of artistic form upon the material. Sometimes the term is applied to the description of the unpleasant side of ordinary life. Of the poems in this text, Wilfred Owen's "A Terre," p. 331, is perhaps most realistic in both senses of the word. The term is more often used in describing prose fiction than poetry. See also *Classical* and *Romantic*.

REFRAIN   A line or stanza repeated at intervals, as with the phrase *to be a pilgrim* in Bunyan's poem on p. 222.

RHETORICAL QUESTION   A question so phrased that the answer is understood, as in Shelley's lines *O Wind, / If Winter comes, can Spring be far behind?*

RHYME   See Chapter 3.

RHYME ROYAL   A seven-line stanza in iambic pentameter rhyming *ababbcc*.

RHYTHM   See Chapter 4.

ROMANCE   A long narrative poem or prose work dealing with the life of feudal courts and knighthood. Love and supernatural incidents are frequent elements. The most famous English romances are those dealing with King Arthur and the Knights of the Round Table.

ROMANTIC   The term is used variously. Perhaps most often it refers to poetry or other art that is deliberately personal, expressive, and imaginative rather than objective and restrained. Romantic art characteristically gives less attention to orderliness and conventional rule than does classical; it characteristically gives less attention to description of the externals of ordinary life than does realistic. The term *romantic movement* is applied to the dominant English poetry of the early 19th century, represented mainly by the work of Wordsworth, Coleridge, Byron, Shelley, and Keats. Most of their poems display romantic qualities to a high degree. See *Classical* and *Realistic*.

RONDEAU (RONDEL)   A short poem, frequently of fifteen lines, having only two rhymes and using the opening words of the first line as a refrain.

RUN-ON LINE   See pp. 67–70. See also *End-stopped line*.

SARCASM   The word is commonly used to refer to a broad or obvious attack on supposed weakness or vice. E. E. Cummings' "Humanity i love you," p. 126, is an example. The word is sometimes used in a more restricted sense to denote a kind of *irony* (see above) in which praise is intended as dispraise. Much of Cummings' poem is sarcastic in this sense, as when his speaker says that he loves humanity for being a bootlicker; but the last lines, in which he says, "Humanity i hate you," cannot be included, since they do not praise.

SATIRE   A work or passage that attacks supposed weakness or vice. It includes the obvious form of attack known as *sarcasm* (see above), as illustrated in E. E. Cummings' "Humanity i love you," p. 126, and the more subtle form of attack such as is illustrated in Robert Graves' "The Philosopher," p. 16. *Irony* (see above) is frequently used in satire.

SCANSION   Metrical analysis. See Chapter 4.

SENSE IMAGERY   See Chapter 6.

SESTET   A six-line stanza; also the last six lines of a sonnet, especially when those lines are set off by rhyme or idea from the preceding lines.

SESTINA   A poem of six six-line stanzas and a concluding stanza (an envoy), with the six end-words of the first stanza repeated in varying order in the other five.

SHAKESPEARIAN SONNET   A form of the sonnet used to greatest effect by Shakespeare. The rhyme scheme is *ababcdcdefefgg.* The last two lines are usually treated as a closed couplet that sums up the idea of the poem, and the rhyme scheme also tends to divide the first twelve lines into three quatrains. See "Sonnet 73," p. 110, as illustration, and see other of the sonnets, pp. 197–200, for variations.

SIMILE   See p. 80. For epic simile see *Epic.*

SINGLE RHYME   End rhyme involving a single vowel sound and any suceeding consonant sounds, as in *no—go, by—high,* or *scan—man.*

SLANG   Newly coined and usually short-lived language of speech. See p. 30.

SLANT RHYME   See *Approximate rhyme.* .

SONNET   The term is usually applied to a fourteen-line poem in iambic pentameter, rhymed. See *Petrarchan sonnet* and *Shakespearian sonnet.* George Meredith's poems, p. 281, are sixteen-line sonnets.

SPENSERIAN STANZA   A nine-line stanza invented by Edmund Spenser, rhyming *ababbcbcc,* with the first eight lines iambic pentameter and the last line iambic hexameter (Alexandrine).

SPONDEE   A two-syllable foot with both syllables accented, as with *hārdshīp.* On kinds of feet, see p. 59.

SPRUNG RHYTHM   A term used by G. M. Hopkins to describe the special rhythm he used. Critics disagree as to what the characteristics are. In one view the two major characteristics are (1) a piling together of accented syllables which violates normal metrical alternation between accented and unaccented syllables, and (2) more than usual irregularity in number of syllables per line. See "The Windhover," p. 295, for illustration. See also Question 4, p. 79.

STANZA   The divided parts of a poem, such as the five stanzas of Keats' "Ode on a Grecian Urn," p. 260. Stanzaic division is usually but not always regular. See also *Verse paragraph.*

STRESS   In conventional metrical analysis, the same as *Accent.*

STROPHE   See *Ode.*

STRUCTURE   See Chapter 8.

STYLE   See Chapter 11.

SYMBOL   See Chapter 7.

SYNECDOCHE   Figurative language (see the definition above) in which a part is made to stand for the whole, as when in the phrase *lend a hand* the word hand refers to the whole body. See also the final paragraph of the discussion of metaphor, p. 84.

TENOR   See pp. 81–82.

TERCET   A three-line stanza, usually of a single rhyme.

TERZA RIMA   A three-line stanza pattern with an interlocking rhyme scheme, *aba bcb cdc* etc., with the last stanza a couplet. Shelley's "Ode to the West Wind," p. 255, is the most notable example in the English language.

TETRAMETER   A line of four feet. See p. 59 on meter and feet.

THEME   The idea of a poem or other composition; likewise a distinct part of the idea, or the idea of a certain portion of the poem.

TONE   See Chapter 9.

TRIMETER   A line of three feet. See p. 59 on meter and feet.

TRIOLET   An eight-line stanza with two rhymes and the first and second lines repeated, the first line as the fourth and seventh, the second as the eighth.

TRIPLE RHYME   End rhyme involving three vowel sounds and intermediate and succeeding consonants, as in *gunnery—nunnery.*

TRIPLET   The same as *Tercet.*

TROCHEE   A two-syllable foot, with the first syllable accented, as in *bārgain.* See p. 59 on kinds of feet.

TROPE   A general term that covers such figurative language as metaphor, paradox, irony, and hyperbole. See all of these terms elsewhere.

UNDERSTATEMENT   A form of irony. See p. 124.

VEHICLE   See pp. 81–82.

VERS DE SOCIÉTÉ   A form of *light verse* (see above) that treats of social manners.

VERSE   Poetry; also a stanza of poetry; also a single line of poetry; also inconsequential poetry as distinct from serious poetry.

VERSE PARAGRAPH   Division of a poem in the manner of prose paragraphing rather than into regular stanzas. Wordsworth's "Lines Composed a Few Miles Above Tintern Abbey," p. 239, is an example. See also the discussion of "There was a Boy," p. 112.

VILLANELLE   A poem of five three-line stanzas and a concluding stanza of four lines, with two rhymes used throughout. E. A. Robinson's "The House on the Hill," p. 154, is an example.

VOICE   See Chapter 10.

WRENCHED ACCENT   See *Accent.*

PART FOUR

Anthology

The following is a simplified guide to pronouncing the six Middle English poems and fragments given below.

1. Word-endings *e, ed,* and *es* that are normally silent in modern English are often pronounced as a syllable in Middle English poetry. They are marked here with an accent: *sonné, nyghtés.*

2. Consonants.

a. Pronounce all initial *k*'s and *g*'s: *knicht, gnaw.*

b. Pronounce medial *gh* as though it were the *ch* in German *ich,* a breathed *k* sound: *thought.*

c. Roll *r*'s, softly in the Chaucer fragments, more vibrantly in the other poems.

3. Vowels and diphthongs.

a. Pronounce *a* and *aa* as the *a* in modern *father: and, maad.*

b. When *e* endings are pronounced, pronounce them as the *a* in modern *about: sonné.*

c. Pronounce initial and internal long *e* as the *a* in modern *fate: he, ech.*

d. Pronounce initial and internal short *e* as the *e* in modern *set: welcome, ther, fressh.*

e. Pronounce long *i* and *y* as the *i* in modern *marine: I, hy.*

f. Pronounce short *i* and *y* as the *i* in modern *bit: is, his, with, driven.*

g. Pronounce *o* and *oo* as the *o* in modern *note: sone, goon.*

h. Pronounce *u* as the *u* in modern *pull: ful.*

i. Pronounce *ae, ai, ay, ei,* and *ey* as the *ay* in modern *hay: sae, mair, saynt, reid, preye.*

j. Pronounce *au* and *aw* as the *ou* in modern *how* and *house: daunce, hawkes.*

k. Pronounce *ou* and *ow* as the *oo* in modern *goose: foules, flowr.*

GEOFFREY CHAUCER (ca. 1343–1400)

from THE PARLIAMENT OF FOWLS

NOW WELCOME, SUMMER

Now welcome, somer, with thy sonné softé,
That hast this wintres wedres overshaké,
And driven away the longé nyghtés blaké!

Saynt Valentyn, that art ful hy on-lofté,
Thus syngen smalé foulés for thy saké: 5
Now welcome, somer, with thy sonné softé,
That hast this wintres wedres overshaké.

Wel han they causé for to gladen ofté,
Sith ech of hem recovered hath hys maké,
Ful blissful mowe they syngé when they waké: 10
Now welcome, somer, with thy sonné softé,
That hast this wintres wedres overshaké,
And driven away the longé nyghtés blaké!

2. *wedres:* weather; *overshake:* shaken off; 4. *on-lofte:* aloft; 5. *foules:* birds; 9. *make:* mate; 10. *mowe:* can.

from THE CANTERBURY TALES

THE SQUIRE

With him ther was his soné, a yong Squier,
A lovyere and a lusty bacheler,
With lokkés crulle as they were leyd in pressé.
Of twenty yeer of age he was, I gessé.
Of his stature he was of evene lengthé,   5
And wonderly delyvere, and of greet strengthé.
And he haddé been somtyme in chyvachié
In Flaundres, in Artoys, and Pycardié;
And born him weel, as of so litel spacé,
In hope to stondon in his lady gracé.   10
Embrouded was he, as it were a meedé
Al ful of fresshé flourés, whyte and reedé.
Syngynge he was, or floytynge, al the day;
He was as fressh as is the month of May.
Short was his gowne, with slevés longe and wydé.   15

2. *lovyere:* lover; *bacheler:* young knight; 3. *crulle:* curly; 5. *evene:* average; 6. *delyvere:* agile; 7. *chyvachie:* cavalry raid; 9. *so litel space:* shortness of time; 11. *embrouded:* embroidered; *meede:* meadow; 13. *floytynge:* playing the flute.

Wel koude he sitte on hors and fairé rydé.
He koudé songés make and wel endité,
Juste and eek daunce, and weel purtreye and writé.
So hoote he lovéde that by nyghtertalé
He sleep namoore than dooth a nyghtyngalé.   20
Curteis he was, lowely, and servysablé,
And carf biforn his fader at the tablé.

17. *endite:* compose; 18. *juste:* joust; *eek:* also; *purtreye:* draw; 19. *nyghtertale:* night-time; 21. *lowely:* modest.

EARLY BALLADS AND LYRICS

EDWARD

"Why does your brand sae drap wi' bluid,
      Edward, Edward?
Why does your brand sae drap wi' bluid,
      And why sae sad gang ye, O?"
"O I ha'e killed my hawk sae guid,   5
      Mither, mither,
O I ha'e killed my hawk sae guid,
      And I had nae mair but he, O."

"Your hawkes bluid was never sae reid,
      Edward, Edward.
Your hawkes bluid was never sae reid,
      My dear son I tell thee, O."
"O I ha'e killed my reid-roan steed,
      Mither, mither,
O I ha'e killed my reid-roan steed,   15
      That erst was sae fair and free, O."

"Your steed was auld and ye ha'e gat mair,
      Edward, Edward.
Your steed was auld and ye ha'e gat mair:
      Som other dule ye dree, O."   20
"O I ha'e killed my fader dear,
      Mither, mither,
O I ha'e killed my fader dear,
      Alas and wae is me, O!"

"And whatten penance wul ye dree for that,   25
      Edward, Edward?
And whatten penance wul ye dree for that,
      My dear son, now tell me, O?"

1. *brand:* sword; 4. *gang:* go; 16. *erst:* once; 20. *dule:* grief; *dree:* suffer.

"I'll set my feet in yonder boat,
    Mither, mither,   30
I'll set my feet in yonder boat,
    And I'll fare over the sea, O."

"And what wul ye do wi' your towers and your ha',
    Edward, Edward?
And what wul ye do wi' your towers and your ha',   35
    That were sae fair to see, O?"
"I'll let thame stand til they down fa',
    Mither, mither,
I'll let thame stand til they down fa',
    For here never mair maun I be, O."   40

"And what wul ye leave to your bairns and your wife,
    Edward, Edward,
And what wul ye leave to your bairns and your wife,
    Whan ye gang over the sea, O?"
"The warldes room: late them beg thrae life,   45
    Mither, mither,
The warldes room: late them beg thrae life,
    For thame never mair wul I see, O."

"And what wul ye leave to your ain mither dear,
    Edward, Edward?   50
And what wul ye leave to your ain mither dear,
    My dear son, now tell me, O?"
"The curse of hell frae me sal ye bear,
    Mither, mither,
The curse of hell frae me sal ye bear,   55
    Sic counseils ye gave to me, O."

40. *maun:* might; 41. *bairns:* children; 45. *warldes:* world's; *late:* let; *thrae:* through; 56. *sic:* such.

SIR PATRICK SPENS

The king sits in Dumferline town,
    Drinking the blude-reid wine:
"O whar will I get a guid sailor
    To sail this ship of mine?"

Up and spak an eldern knicht,   5
    Sat at the king's richt knee:
"Sir Patrick Spens is the best sailor
    That sails upon the sea."

The king has written a braid letter
    And signed it wi' his hand,   10

9. *braid:* broad.

And sent it to Sir Patrick Spens,
    Was walking on the sand.

The first line that Sir Patrick read,
    A loud lauch lauched he;
The next line that Sir Patrick read,   15
    The tear blinded his ee.

"O wha is this has done this deed,
    This ill deed done to me,
To send me out this time o' the year,
    To sail upon the sea?   20

"Make haste, make haste, my mirry men all,
    Our guid ship sails the morn."
"O say na sae, my master dear,
    For I fear a deadly storm.

"Late late yestre'en I saw the new moon   25
    Wi' the auld moon in her arm,
And I fear, I fear, my dear master,
    That we will come to harm."

O our Scots nobles were richt laith
    To weet their cork-heeled shoon,   30
But lang owre a' the play were played
    Their hats they swam aboon.

O lang, lang may their ladies sit,
    Wi' their fans into their hand,
Or e'er they see Sir Patrick Spens   35
    Come sailing to the land.

O lang, lang may the ladies stand,
    Wi' their gold kembs in their hair,
Waiting for their ain dear lords,
    For they'll see thame na mair.   40

Half o'er, half o'er to Aberdour
    It's fifty fadom deep,
And there lies guid Sir Patrick Spens,
    Wi' the Scots lords at his feet.

14. *lauch:* laugh; 16. *ee:* eye; 23. *na sae:* not so; 29. *richt:* right; *laith:* loath; 30. *shoon:* shoes; 31. *owre a':* before; 32. *aboon:* above; 38. *kembs:* combs.

HERE I SIT ALONE

As I walked me this endurs day
to the grene wode for to play

1. *endurs:* other; 2. *wode:* wood.

and all hevyness to put away
  my-self alone.

As I walkyd undir the grene wode bowe   5
I sawe a maide fayre i-now;
a child she happid, she song, she lough—
  that child wepid alone.

"Son," she sayd, "I have thee borne
to save mankynd that was forlorne;   10
therfor I pray thee, son, ne morne,
  but be still alone."

"Moder, me thynkith it is right ill
that men sekyth for to spill.
for them to save it is my will;   15
  therfor I cam hither alone."

"Sone," she sayd, "let it be in thi thought,
for mannys gilt is not with-sought;
for thu art he that hath all wrought,
  and I thi moder alone."   20

6. *fayre i-now:* very fair; 7. *happid:* wrapped; *lough:* laughed; 8. *wepid:* wept; 10. *forlorne:* lost; 11. *ne morne:* do not mourn; 14. *spill:* destroy; 18. *mannys:* man's; *with-sought:* searched out, pursued.

A LYKE-WAKE DIRGE

This ae nighte, this ae nighte,
  —*Every nighte and alle,*
Fire and selte and candle-lighte,
  And Christe receive thy saule.

When thou from hence away art past,   5
  —*Every nighte and alle,*
To Whinny-muir thou com'st at last;
  And Christe receive thy saule.

If ever thou gavest hosen and shoon,
  —*Every nighte and alle,*   10
Sit thee down and put them on;
  And Christe receive thy saule.

If hosen and shoon thou ne'er gav'st nane
  —*Every nighte and alle,*
The whinnes sall prick thee to the bare bane;   15
  And Christe receive thy saule.

Lyke-Wake: corpse-watch; 1. *ae:* one; 3. *selte:* salt; 7. *Whinny-muir:* or Gorsemoor, a place near Cleveland in Yorkshire, where this dirge was sung; 9. *hosen:* hose; *shoon:* shoes; 15. *whinnes:* furze, gorse.

From Whinny-muir when thou may'st pass,
   —Every nighte and alle,
To Brig o' Dread thou com'st at last;
   And Christe receive thy saule.   20

From Brig o' Dread when thou may'st pass,
   —Every nighte and alle,
To Purgatory fire thou com'st at last;
   And Christe receive thy saule.

If ever thou gavest meat or drink,   25
   —Every nighte and alle,
The fire sall never make thee shrink;
   And Christe receive thy saule.

If meat or drink thou ne'er gav'st nane,
   —Every nighte and alle,   30
The fire will burn thee to the bare bane;
   And Christe receive thy saule.

This ae nighte, this ae nighte,
   —Every nighte and alle,
Fire and selte and candle-light,   35
   And Christe receive thy saule.

19. *Brig o' Dread:* Bridge of Dread, a local place.

AS YOU CAME FROM THE HOLY LAND

As you came from the holy land
   Of Walsinghame
Met you not with my true love
   By the way as you came?

How shall I know your true love   5
   That have met many one
As I went to the holy land
   That have come, that have gone?

She is neither white nor brown
   But as the heavens fair   10
There is none hath a form so divine
   In the earth or the air.

Such an one did I meet, good Sir,
   Such an angelic face,
Who like a queen, like a nymph, did appear   15
   By her gait, by her grace.

She hath left me here all alone,
   All alone as unknown,

Who sometimes did me lead with herself,
 And me loved as her own.   20

What's the cause that she leaves you alone
 And a new way taketh;
Who loved you once as her own
 And her joy did you make?

I have loved her all my youth,   25
 But now old, as you see,
Love likes not the falling fruit
 From the withered tree.

Know that love is a careless child
 And forgets promise past,   30
He is blind, he is deaf when he list
 And in faith never fast.

His desire is a dureless content
 And a trustless joy
He is won with a world of despair   35
 And is lost with a toy.

Of women kind such indeed is the love
 Or the word Love abused
Under which many childish desires
 And conceits are excused.   40

But true Love is a durable fire
 In the mind ever burning;
Never sick, never old, never dead,
 From itself never turning.

33. *Dureless:* brief.

LULLABY

Weep you no more, sad fountains,
 What need you flow so fast?
Look how the snowy mountains
 Heaven's sun doth gently waste.
But my sun's heavenly eyes,   5
 View not your weeping,
 That now lies sleeping,
Softly, now softly lies
 Sleeping.

Sleep is a reconciling,   10
 A rest that peace begets;
Doth not the sun rise smiling
 When fair at ev'n he sets?

Rest you, then, rest sad eyes,
Melt not in weeping,   15
While she lies sleeping,
Softly, now softly lies
Sleeping.

JOHN SKELTON   (ca. 1460–1529)

TO MISTRESS MARGARET HUSSEY

Merry Margaret,
As midsummer flower,
Gentle as falcon
Or hawk of the tower;
With solace and gladness,   5
Much mirth and no madness,
All good, and no badness,
So joyously,
So maidenly,
So womanly   10
Her demeaning
In every thing,
Far, far passing
That I can endite,
Or suffice to write   15
Of merry Margaret!
As midsummer flower,
Gentle as falcon
Or hawk of the tower;
As patient and as still   20
And as full of good will
As fair Isaphill;
Colyander,
Sweet pomander,
Good Cassander;   25
Well made, well wrought;
Far may be sought
Erst that ye can find
So courteous, so kind
As merry Margaret,   30
This midsummer flower,
Gentle as falcon
Or hawk of the tower.

22. *Isaphill:* Hypsipyle, a Grecian queen; 23. *colyander:* an aromatic fruit; 24. *pomander:* a perfumed article; 25. *Cassander:* Cassandra, the Trojan prophetess.

SIR THOMAS WYATT (1503–1542)

WHO SO LIST TO HUNT

Who so list to hunt, I know where is an hind;
But as for me, *helas!* I may no more.
The vain travail hath wearied me so sore,
I am of them that farthest come behind.
Yet may I by no means my wearied mind   5
Draw from the Deer; but as she fleeth afore
Fainting I follow. I leave off, therefore,
Since in a net I seek to hold the wind.
Who list her hunt, I put him out of doubt,
As well as I may spend his time in vain.   10
And graven with diamonds in letters plain
There is written, her fair neck round about,
Noli me tangere for Caesar's I am
And wild for to hold, though I seem tame.

13. *Noli me tangere:* do not touch me.

THEY FLEE FROM ME

They flee from me, that sometime did me seek
With naked foot, stalking in my chamber.
I have seen them gentle, tame, and meek
That now are wild, and do not remember
That sometime they put themselves in danger   5
To take bread at my hand; and now they range
Busily seeking with a continual change.

Thanked be fortune it hath been otherwise
Twenty times better; but once, in special,
In thin array, after a pleasant guise,   10
When her loose gown from her shoulders did fall,
And she me caught in her arms long and small,
Therewith all sweetly did me kiss
And softly said, "Dear heart, how like you this?"

It was no dream: I lay broad waking.   15
But all is turnéd, thorough my gentleness,
Into a strange fashion of forsaking;
And I have leave to go of her goodness,
And she also to use newfangleness.
But since that I so kindly am served,   20
I would fain know what she hath deserved.

HENRY HOWARD, EARL OF SURREY   (1517–1547)

THE SOOTE SEASON

The soote season that bud and bloom forth brings
With green hath clad the hill and eke the vale,
The nightingale with feathers new she sings,
The turtle to her make hath told her tale.
Summer is come, for every spray now springs,   5
The hart hath hung his old head on the pale,
The buck in brake his winter coat he flings,
The fishes float with new repairéd scale,
The adder all her slough away she slings,
The swift swallow pursueth the fliés smale,   10
The busy bee her honey now she mings,
Winter is worn, that was the flowers' bale:
And thus I see, among these pleasant things
Each care decays—and yet my sorrow springs.

1. *soote:* sweet; 4. *turtle:* turtledove; *make:* mate; 10. *smale:* small; 11. *mings:* remembers.

GILES FLETCHER   (ca. 1549–1611)

ON THE CRUCIFIXION

It was but now their sounding clamors sung,
Blesséd is he, that comes from the most high,
And all the mountains with Hosanna rung,
And now, away with him, away they cry,
And nothing can be heard but crucify: 5
    It was but now, the crown itself they save,
    And golden name of king unto him gave,
And now, no king, but only Caesar, they will have:

It was but now they gathered blooming May,
And of his arms disrobed the branching tree,   10
To strew with boughs, and blossoms all thy way,
And now, the branchless trunk a cross for thee,
And May, dismayed, thy coronet must be:
    It was but now they were so kind, to throw
    Their own best garments, where thy feet should go,   15
And now, thyself they strip, and bleeding wounds they show.

See where the author of all life is dying:
O fearful day! he dead, what hope of living?

See where the hopes of all our lives are buying:
O cheerful day! they bought, what fear of grieving?   20
Love love for hate, and death for life is giving:
   Lo how his arms are stretched abroad to grace thee,
   And, as they open stand, call to embrace thee,
Why stay'st thou then my soul; O fly, fly; thither haste thee.

SIR WALTER RALEGH   (1552–1618)

THE WOOD, THE WEED, THE WAG

Three things there be that prosper all apace
And flourish, while they grow asunder far;
But on a day, they meet all in a place,
And when they meet they one another mar.

And they be these: the Wood, the Weed, the Wag.   5
The Wood is that that makes the gallows tree;
The Weed is that that strings the hangman's bag;
The Wag, my pretty knave, betokens thee.

Now mark, dear boy—while these assemble not,
Green springs the tree, hemp grows, the wag is wild;   10
But when they meet, it makes the timber rot,
It frets the halter, and it chokes the child.

Then bless thee, and beware, and let us pray
We part not with thee at this meeting-day.

EDMUND SPENSER   (1552–1599)

PROTHALAMION *

Calm was the day, and through the trembling air
Sweet-breathing Zephyrus did softly play
A gentle spirit, that lightly did delay
Hot Titan's beams, which then did glister fair;
When I, (whom sullen care,   5
Through discontent of my long fruitless stay
In princes' court, and expectation vain
Of idle hopes, which still do fly away
Like empty shadows, did afflict my brain,)
Walked forth to ease my pain   10
Along the shore of silver-streaming Thames;
Whose rutty bank, the which his river hems,

* The poem celebrates the double marriage of Elizabeth and Katherine Somerset, daughters of the Earl of Worcester, a soldier of Queen Elizabeth.

Was painted all with variable flowers,
And all the meads adorned with dainty gems
Fit to deck maidens' bowers,   15
And crown their paramours
Against the bridal day, which is not long:
  Sweet Thames! run softly, till I end my song.

There in a meadow by the river's side
A flock of nymphs I chancéd to espy,   20
All lovely daughters of the flood thereby,
With goodly greenish locks all loose untied
As each had been a bride;
And each one had a little wicker basket
Made of fine twigs entrailéd curiously,   25
In which they gathered flowers to fill their flasket,
And with fine fingers cropped full feateously
The tender stalks on high.
Of every sort which in that meadow grew
They gathered some; the violet, pallid blue,   30
The little daisy that at evening closes,
The virgin lily and the primrose true,
With store of vermeil roses,
To deck their bridegrooms' posies
Against the bridal day, which was not long: 35
  Sweet Thames! run softly, till I end my song.

With that I saw two swans of goodly hue
Come softly swimming down along the lee;
Two fairer birds I yet did never see;
The snow which doth the top of Pindus strew   40
Did never whiter shew
Nor Jove himself, when he a swan would be
For love of Leda, whiter did appear;
Yet Leda was, they say, as white as he,
Yet not so white as these, nor nothing near;   45
So purely white they were
That even the gentle stream, the which them bare,
Seemed foul to them, and bade his billows spare
To wet their silken feathers, lest they might
Soil their fair plumes with water not so fair,   50
And mar their beauties bright,
That shone as heaven's light,
Against their bridal day, which was not long:
  Sweet Thames! run softly, till I end my song.

Eftsoons the nymphs, which now had flowers their fill,   55
Ran all in haste to see that silver brood

27. *feateously:* dexterously.

As they came floating on the crystal flood;
Whom when they saw, they stood amazéd still
Their wondering eyes to fill;
Them seemed they never saw a sight so fair   60
Of fowls, so lovely, that they sure did deem
Them heavenly born, or to be that same pair
Which through the sky draw Venus' silver team;
For sure they did not seem
To be begot of any earthly seed,   65
But rather angels, or of angels' breed;
Yet were they bred of Somers-heat, they say.
In sweetest season, when each flower and weed
The earth did fresh array;
So fresh they seemed as day,   70
Even as their bridal day, which was not long;
   Sweet Thames, run softly, till I end my song.

Then forth they all out of their baskets drew
Great store of flowers, the honor of the field,
That to the sense did fragrant odors yield,   75
All which upon those goodly birds they threw,
And all the waves did strew,
That like old Peneus' waters they did seem,
When down along by pleasant Tempe's shore,
Scattered with flowers, through Thessaly they stream,   80
That they appear, through lilies' plenteous store,
Like a bride's chamber floor.
Two of those nymphs, meanwhile, two garlands bound
Of freshest flowers which in that mead they found,
The which presenting all in trim array,   85
Their snowy foreheads therewithal they crowned,
Whilst one did sing this lay,
Prepared against that day,
Against their bridal day, which was not long;
   Sweet Thames, run softly, till I end my song.   90

"Ye gentle birds, the world's fair ornament,
And heaven's glory, whom this happy hour
Doth lead unto your lovers' blissful bower,
Joy may you have and gentle heart's content
Of your love's complement: 95
And let fair Venus, that is Queen of Love,
With her heart-quelling sun upon you smile,
Whose smile, they say, hath virtue to remove
All love's dislike, and friendship's faulty guile
For ever to assoil.   100

67. *Somers-heat:* a play upon Somerset; 100. *assoil:* dispel.

Let endless peace your steadfast hearts accord,
And blesséd plenty wait upon your board;
And let your bed with pleasures chaste abound,
That fruitful issue may to you afford,
Which may your foes confound,   105
And make your joys redound,
Upon your bridal day, which is not long:
  Sweet Thames, run softly, till I end my song."

So ended she; and all the rest around
To her redoubled that her undersong,   110
Which said, their bridal day should not be long.
And gentle Echo from the neighbor ground
Their accents did resound.
So forth these joyous birds did pass along,
Adown the lee, that to them murmured low,   115
As he would speak, but that he lacked a tongue,
Yet did by signs his glad affection show,
Making his stream run slow.
And all the fowl which in his flood did dwell
Gan flock about these twain, that did excel   120
The rest so far as Cynthia doth shend
The lesser stars. So they, enrangéd well,
Did on those two attend,
And their best service lend,
Against their wedding day, which was not long: 125
  Sweet Thames, run softly, till I end my song.

At length they all to merry London came,
To merry London, my most kindly nurse,
That to me gave this life's first native source,
Though from another place I take my name,   130
An house of ancient fame.
There when they came whereas those bricky towers,
The which on Thames' broad agéd back do ride,
Where now the studious lawyers have their bowers,
There whilom wont the Templar knights to bide,   135
Till they decayed through pride:
Next whereunto there stands a stately place,
Where oft I gainéd gifts and goodly grace
Of that great lord which therein wont to dwell,
Whose want too well now feels my friendless case: 140
But ah! here fits not well
Old woes, but joys to tell
Against the bridal day, which is not long:
  Sweet Thames! run softly, till I end my song.

121. *shend:* shame.

Yet therein now doth lodge a noble peer,   145
Great England's glory and the world's wide wonder,
Whose dreadful name late through all Spain did thunder,
And Hercules' two pillars standing near
Did make to quake and fear:
Fair branch of honor, flower of chivalry!   150
That fillest England with thy triumphs' fame,
Joy have thou of thy noble victory,
And endless happiness of thine own name
That promiseth the same;
That through thy prowess and victorious arms   155
Thy country may be freed from foreign harms,
And great Eliza's glorious name may ring
Through all the world, filled with thy wide alarms,
Which some brave Muse may sing
To ages following,   160
Upon the bridal day, which is not long:
  Sweet Thames! run softly, till I end my song.

From those high towers this noble lord issuing,
Like radiant Hesper when his golden hair
In the ocean billows he hath bathéd fair,   165
Descended to the river's open viewing,
With a great train ensuing.
Above the rest were goodly to be seen
Two gentle knights of lovely face and feature,
Beseeming well the bower of any queen,   170
With gifts of wit and ornaments of nature
Fit for so goodly stature,
That like the twins of Jove they seemed in sight
Which deck the baldric of the heavens bright;
They two, forth pacing to the river's side,   175
Received those two fair brides, their love's delight;
Which, at the appointed tide,
Each one did make his bride
Against their bridal day, which is not long:
  Sweet Thames! run softly, till I end my song.   180

SIR PHILIP SIDNEY (1554–1586)

from ASTROPHEL AND STELLA

SONNET 5

It is most true that eyes are formed to serve
The inward light, and that the heavenly part

Ought to be King, from whose rules who do swerve,
Rebels to nature, strive for their own smart.
It is most true, what we call Cupid's dart   5
An image is, which for ourselves we carve,
And, fools, adore in temple of our heart,
Till that good god make church and churchmen starve.
True, that true beauty virtue is indeed,
Whereof this beauty can be but a shade,   10
Which elements with mortal mixture breed.
True that on earth we are but pilgrims made,
And should in soul up to our country move:
True, and yet true that I must Stella love.

SONNET 6

Some lovers speak, when they their Muses entertain,
Of hopes begot by fear, of wot not what desires,
Of force of heavenly beams infusing hellish pain,
Of living deaths, dear wounds, fair storms, and freezing fires:
Some one his song in Jove and Jove's strange tales attires,   5
Bordered with bulls and swans, powdered with golden rain:
Another, humbler wit, to shepherd's pipe retires,
Yet hiding royal blood full oft in rural vein.
To some a sweetest plaint a sweetest style affords:
While tears pour out his ink, and sighs breathe out his words,   10
His paper pale despair, and pain his pen doth move.
I can speak what I feel, and feel as much as they,
But think that all the map of my state I display
When trembling voice brings forth that I do Stella love.

("Sonnet 1," p. 17.)

WILLIAM SHAKESPEARE (1564–1616)

SONNET 19

Devouring Time, blunt thou the lion's paws,
And make the earth devour her own sweet brood;
Pluck the keen teeth from the fierce tiger's jaws
And burn the long-lived phœnix in her blood;
Make glad and sorry seasons as thou fleet'st,   5
And do whate'er thou wilt, swift-footed Time,
To the wide world and all her fading sweets,
But I forbid thee one most heinous crime:
O, carve not with thy hours my love's fair brow,
Nor draw no lines there with thine antique pen;   10
Him in thy course untainted do allow

For beauty's pattern to succeeding men.
Yet do thy worst, old Time: despite thy wrong,
My love shall in my verse ever live young.

SONNET 33

Full many a glorious morning have I seen
Flatter the mountain-tops with sovereign eye,
Kissing with golden face the meadows green,
Gilding pale streams with heavenly alchemy;
Anon permit the basest clouds to ride   5
With ugly rack on his celestial face,
And from the forlorn world his visage hide,
Stealing unseen to west with this disgrace:
Even so my sun one early morn did shine
With all-triumphant splendor on my brow;   10
But out, alack! he was but one hour mine;
The region cloud hath masked him from me now.
Yet him for this my love no whit disdaineth;
Suns of the world may stain when heaven's sun staineth.

SONNET 64

When I have seen by Time's fell hand defaced
The rich proud cost of outworn buried age,
When sometime lofty towers I see down-razed
And brass eternal slave to mortal rage;
When I have seen the hungry ocean gain   5
Advantage on the kingdom of the shore,
And the firm soil win of the wat'ry main,
Increasing store with loss and loss with store;
When I have seen such interchange of state,
Or state itself confounded, to decay,   10
Ruin hath taught me thus to ruminate,
That Time will come and take my love away.
This thought is as a death, which cannot choose
But weep to have that which it fears to lose.

SONNET 77

Thy glass will show thee how thy beauties wear,
Thy dial how thy precious minutes waste;
The vacant leaves thy mind's imprint will bear,
And of this book this learning mayst thou taste.
The wrinkles which thy glass will truly show   5
Of mouthéd graves will give thee memory;
Thou by thy dial's shady stealth mayst know

Time's thievish progress to eternity.
Look, what thy memory cannot contain
Commit to these waste blanks, and thou shalt find   10
Those children nursed, delivered from thy brain,
To take a new acquaintance of thy mind.
These offices, so oft as thou wilt look,
Shall profit thee and much enrich thy book.

SONNET 109

O, never say that I was false of heart,
Though absence seemed my flame to qualify.
As easy might I from myself depart
As from my soul, which in thy breast doth lie:
That is my home of love: if I have ranged,   5
Like him that travels, I return again;
Just to the time, not with the time exchanged,
So that myself brings water for my stain.
Never believe, though in my nature reigned
All frailties that beseige all kinds of blood,   10
That it could so preposterously be stained,
To leave for nothing all thy sum of good;
For nothing this wide universe I call,
Save thou, my rose; in it thou art my all.

SONNET 116

Let me not to the marriage of true minds
Admit impediments. Love is not love
Which alters when it alteration finds,
Or bends with the remover to remove.
O, no! it is an ever-fixéd mark   5
That looks on tempests and is never shaken;
It is the star to every wand'ring bark,
Whose worth's unknown, although his height be taken.
Love's not Time's fool, though rosy lips and cheeks
Within his bending sickle's compass come;   10
Love alters not with his brief hours and weeks,
But bears it out even to the edge of doom.
If this be error, and upon me proved,
I never writ, nor no man ever loved.

SONNET 130

My mistress' eyes are nothing like the sun;
Coral is far more red than her lips' red;
If snow be white, why then her breasts are dun;

If hairs be wires, black wires grow on her head.
I have seen roses damasked red and white,   5
But no such roses see I in her cheeks;
And in some perfumes is there more delight
Than in the breath that from my mistress reeks.
I love to hear her speak, yet well I know
That music hath a far more pleasing sound;   10
I grant I never saw a goddess go:
My mistress, when she walks, treads on the ground.
And yet, by heaven, I think my love as rare
As any she belied with false compare.

SONNET 146

Poor soul, the center of my sinful earth,
Pressed by these rebel powers that thee array,
Why dost thou pine within and suffer dearth,
Painting thy outward walls so costly gay?
Why so large cost, having so short a lease,   5
Dost thou upon thy fading mansion spend?
Shall worms, inheritors of this excess,
Eat up thy charge? Is this thy body's end?
Then, soul, live thou upon thy servant's loss,
And let that pine to aggravate thy store;   10
Buy terms divine in selling hours of dross;
Within be fed, without be rich no more:
So shalt thou feed on Death, that feeds on men,
And Death once dead, there's no more dying then.

2. *Pressed by:* a conjectural reading of a misprinted phrase in the first edition of the sonnets. Other suggestions include *fooled by, foiled by, lord of, vexed by,* and *wracked by.*

("Sonnet 15," p. 117; 18, p. 60; 65, p. 50; 71, p. 127; 73, p. 110; 87, p. 86; 100,
p. 116; 106, p. 11; 129, p. 62.)

JOHN DONNE   (1572–1631)

THE GOOD-MORROW

I wonder, by my troth, what thou and I
Did, till we loved? Were we not weaned till then?
But sucked on country pleasures, childishly?
Or snorted we in the seven sleepers' den?
'Twas so; But this, all pleasures fancies be.   5
If ever any beauty I did see,
Which I desired, and got, 'twas but a dream of thee.

4. *seven sleepers' den:* in legend, a cave to which seven youths fled to escape persecution
and in which they slept for nearly two hundred years.

And now good morrow to our waking souls,
Which watch not one another out of fear;
For love all love of other sights controls,   10
And makes one little room an everywhere.
Let sea-discoverers to new worlds have gone;
Let maps to other, worlds on worlds have shown;
Let us possess one world; each hath one, and is one.

My face in thine eye, thine in mine appears,   15
And true plain hearts do in the faces rest;
Where can we find two better hemispheres
Without sharp North, without declining West?
Whatever dies was not mixed equally;
If our two loves be one, or thou and I   20
Love so alike that none can slacken, none can die.

13. *other:* others.

SONG

Go and catch a falling star,
   Get with child a mandrake root,
Tell me where all past years are,
   Or who cleft the Devil's foot,
Teach me to hear mermaids singing,   5
Or to keep off envy's stinging,
       And find
       What wind
Serves to advance an honest mind.

If thou beest born to strange sights,   10
   Things invisible to see,
Ride ten thousand days and nights,
   Till age snow white hairs on thee,
Thou, when thou return'st, wilt tell me
All strange wonders that befell thee,   15
       And swear
       Nowhere
Lives a woman true, and fair.

If thou find'st one, let me know,
   Such a pilgrimage were sweet;   20
Yet do not, I would not go,
   Though at next door we might meet;
Though she were true when you met her,
And last till you write your letter,
       Yet she   25
       Will be
False, ere I come, to two or three.

THE SUN RISING

Busy old fool, unruly Sun,
Why dost thou thus,
Through windows, and through curtains call on us?
Must to thy motions lovers' seasons run?
Saucy pedantic wretch, go chide   5
Late school boys and sour prentices,
Go tell Court-huntsmen, that the King will ride,
Call country ants to harvest offices;
Love, all alike, no season knows nor clime,
Nor hours, days, months, which are the rags of time.   10

Thy beams, so reverend, and strong
Why shouldst thou think?
I could eclipse and cloud them with a wink,
But that I would not lose her sight so long:
If her eyes have not blinded thine,   15
Look, and tomorrow late, tell me,
Whether both th' Indias of spice and Mine
Be where thou leftst them, or lie here with me.
Ask for those Kings whom thou saw'st yesterday,
And thou shalt hear, All here in one bed lay.   20

She is all States, and all Princes, I,
Nothing else is.
Princes do but play us; compared to this,
All honor's mimic; All wealth alchemy.
Thou Sun art half as happy as we,   25
In that the world's contracted thus;
Thine age asks ease, and since thy duties be
To warm the world, that's done in warming us.
Shine here to us, and thou art everywhere;
This bed thy center is, these walls, thy sphere.   30

THE INDIFFERENT

I can love both fair and brown,
Her whom abundance melts, and her whom want betrays,
Her who loves loneness best, and her who masks and plays,
Her whom the country formed, and whom the town,
Her who believes, and her who tries,   5
Her who still weeps with spongy eyes,
And her who is dry cork and never cries;
I can love her, and her, and you, and you,
I can love any, so she be not true.

Will no other vice content you?   10
Will it not serve your turn to do as did your mothers?

Or have you all old vices spent, and now would find out others?
Or doth a fear that men are true torment you?
O we are not, be not you so;
Let me, and do you, twenty know.   15
Rob me, but bind me not, and let me go.
Must I, who came to travel thorough you,
Grow your fixed subject, because you are true?

Venus heard me sigh this song,
And by love's sweetest part, variety, she swore,   20
She heard not this till now; and that it should be so no more.
She went, examined, and returned ere long,
And said, "Alas, some two or three
Poor heretics in love there be,
Which think to 'stablish dangerous constancy.   25
But I have told them, Since you will be true,
You shall be true to them, who're false to you."

THE CANONIZATION

For God's sake hold your tongue, and let me love,
    Or chide my palsy, or my gout,
My five gray hairs, or ruined fortune flout,
      With wealth your state, your mind with arts improve,
        Take you a course, get you a place,   5
        Observe his honor, or his grace,
Or the King's real, or his stampéd face,
    Contemplate, what you will, approve,
    So you will let me love.

Alas, alas, who's injured by my love?   10
    What merchants' ships have my sighs drowned?
Who says my tears have overflowed his ground?
    When did my colds a forward spring remove?
      When did the heats which my veins fill
      Add one more to the plaguy bill?   15
Soldiers find wars, and lawyers find out still
    Litigious men, which quarrels move,
    Though she and I do love.

Call us what you will, we are made such by love;
    Call her one, me another fly,   20
We're tapers too, and at our own cost die,
    And we in us find the eagle and the dove.
      The phœnix riddle hath more wit
      By us: we two being one, are it.
So, to one neutral thing both sexes fit.   25
    We die and rise the same, and prove
    Mysterious by this love.

We can die by it, if not live by love,
　　And if unfit for tombs and hearse
Our legend be, it will be fit for verse;　　　　　　　　　　30
　　And if no piece of chronicle we prove,
　　　　We'll build in sonnets pretty rooms;
　　　　As well a well-wrought urn becomes
The greatest ashes, as half-acre tombs,
　　And by these hymns, all shall approve　　　　　　　　35
Us *Canonized* for Love:

And thus invoke us; You whom reverend love
　　Made one another's hermitage;
You, to whom love was peace, that now is rage;
　　Who did the whole world's soul contract, and drove　　40
　　Into the glasses of your eyes
　　　　(So made such mirrors, and such spies,
That they did all to you epitomize,)
　　Countries, towns, Courts: Beg from above
　　A pattern of your love!　　　　　　　　　　　　　　45

SONG

　　　　Sweetest love, I do not go,
　　　　　　For weariness of thee,
　　　　Nor in hope the world can show
　　　　　　A fitter love for me;
　　　　　　　　But since that I　　　　　　　5
　　　　At the last must part 'tis best,
　　　　Thus to use myself in jest
　　　　　　By feignéd deaths to die.

　　　　Yesternight the sun went hence,
　　　　　　And yet is here today,　　　　　　10
　　　　He hath no desire nor sense,
　　　　　　Nor half so short a way:
　　　　　　　　Then fear not me,
　　　　But believe that I shall make
　　　　Speedier journeys, since I take　　　　　15
　　　　　　More wings and spurs than he.

　　　　O how feeble is man's power,
　　　　　　That if good fortune fall,
　　　　Cannot add another hour,
　　　　　　Nor a lost hour recall!　　　　　20
　　　　　　　　But come bad chance,
　　　　And we join to it our strength,
　　　　And we teach it art and length,
　　　　　　Itself o'er us to advance.

When thou sigh'st, thou sigh'st not wind,   25
   But sigh'st my soul away,
When thou weep'st, unkindly kind,
   My life's blood doth decay.
     It cannot be
That thou lov'st me as thou say'st,   30
If in thine my life thou waste,
   That art the best of me.

Let not thy divining heart
   Forethink me any ill,
Destiny may take thy part,   35
   And may thy fears fulfil;
     But think that we
Are but turned aside to sleep;
They who one another keep
   Alive, ne'er parted be.   40

THE LEGACY

When last I died, and Dear, I die
   As often as from thee I go,
   Though it be but an hour ago,
And lovers' hours be full eternity,
I can remember yet, that I   5
   Something did say, and something did bestow;
Though I be dead, which sent me, I should be
Mine own executor and legacy.

I heard me say, Tell her anon,
   That myself, (that is you, not I,)   10
   Did kill me, and when I felt me die,
I bid me send my heart, when I was gone,
But I alas could there find none,
   When I had ripped me, and searched where hearts did lie,
It killed me again, that I who still was true   15
In life, in my last Will should cozen you.

Yet found I something like a heart,
   But colors it, and corners had,
   It was not good, it was not bad,
It was entire to none, and few had part.   20
As good as could be made by art
   It seemed; and therefore for our losses sad,
I meant to send this heart instead of mine,
But oh, no man could hold it, for 'twas thine.

A FEVER

O! do not die, for I shall hate
    All women so, when thou art gone,
That thee I shall not celebrate,
    When I remember, thou wast one.

But yet thou canst not die, I know;   5
    To leave this world behind, is death,
But when thou from this world wilt go,
    The whole world vapors with thy breath.

Or if, when thou, the world's soul, goest,
    It stay, 'tis but thy carcass then,   10
The fairest woman, but thy ghost,
    But corrupt worms, the worthiest men.

O wrangling schools, that search what fire
    Shall burn this world, had none the wit
Unto this knowledge to aspire,   15
    That this her fever might be it?

And yet she cannot waste by this,
    Nor long bear this torturing wrong,
For more corruption needful is,
    To fuel such a fever long.   20

These burning fits but meteors be,
    Whose matter in thee is soon spent.
Thy beauty, and all parts, which are thee,
    Are unchangeable firmament.

Yet 'twas of my mind, seizing thee,   25
    Though it in thee cannot perséver.
For I had rather owner be
    Of thee one hour, than all else ever.

THE ANNIVERSARY

    All Kings, and all their favorites,
    All glory of honors, beauties, wits,
The sun itself, which makes times, as they pass,
Is elder by a year, now, than it was
When thou and I first one another saw: 5
All other things, to their destruction draw,
    Only our love hath no decay;
This, no tomorrow hath, nor yesterday,

Running it never runs from us away,
But truly keeps his first, last, everlasting day.   10

Two graves must hide thine and my corse,
If one might, death were no divorce.
Alas, as well as other princes, we,
(Who prince enough in one another be,)
Must leave at last in death, these eyes, and ears,   15
Oft fed with true oaths, and with sweet salt tears;
But souls where nothing dwells but love
(All other thoughts being inmates) then shall prove
This, or a love increaséd there above,
When bodies to their graves, souls from their graves remove.   20

And then we shall be throughly blest,
But we no more, than all the rest;
Here upon earth we're Kings, and none but we
Can be such Kings, nor of such subjects be;
Who is so safe as we? where none can do   25
Treason to us, except one of us two.
True and false fears let us refrain,
Let us love nobly, and live, and add again
Years and years unto years, till we attain
To write threescore: this is the second of our reign.   30

A VALEDICTION: FORBIDDING MOURNING

As virtuous men pass mildly away,
And whisper to their souls to go,
Whilst some of their sad friends do say,
The breath goes now, and some say, No;

So let us melt, and make no noise,   5
No tear-floods, nor sigh-tempests move,
'Twere profanation of our joys
To tell the laity our love.

Moving of th' earth brings harms and fears,
Men reckon what it did and meant;   10
But trepidation of the spheres,
Though greater far, is innocent.

Dull sublunary lovers' love,
Whose soul is sense, cannot admit
Absence, because it doth remove   15
Those things which elemented it.

9. *Moving of th' earth:* earthquakes; 11. *trepidation of the spheres:* a supposed movement
of part of the universe.

But we by a love so much refined
   That ourselves know not what it is,
Inter-assuréd of the mind,
   Care less eyes, lips, and hands to miss.   20

Our two souls therefore, which are one,
   Though I must go, endure not yet
A breach, but an expansion,
   Like gold to airy thinness beat.

If they be two, they are two so   25
   As stiff twin compasses are two;
Thy soul, the fixed foot, makes no show
   To move, but doth, if th' other do.

And though it in the center sit,
   Yet when the other far doth roam,   30
It leans, and harkens after it,
   And grows erect as that comes home.

Such wilt thou be to me, who must
   Like th' other foot, obliquely run;
Thy firmness makes my circle just,   35
   And makes me end where I begun.

A JET RING SENT

   Thou art not so black, as my heart,
  Nor half so brittle, as her heart, thou art;
What would'st thou say? shall both our properties by thee be spoke,
—Nothing more endless, nothing sooner broke?

   Marriage rings are not of this stuff;   5
  Oh, why should ought less precious, or less tough
Figure our loves? Except in thy name thou have bid it say,
I am cheap, and nought but fashion; fling me away.

   Yet stay with me since thou art come,
  Circle this finger's top, which didst her thumb.   10
Be justly proud, and gladly safe, that thou dost dwell with me,
She that, Oh, broke her faith, would soon break thee.

HOLY SONNET 10

Death, be not proud, though some have calléd thee
Mighty and dreadful, for thou art not so;
For those whom thou think'st thou dost overthrow
Die not, poor Death, nor yet canst thou kill me.
From rest and sleep, which but thy pictures be,   5

Much pleasure; then from thee much more must flow,
And soonest our best men with thee do go,
Rest of their bones, and soul's delivery.
Thou art slave to fate, chance, kings, and desperate men,
And dost with poison, war, and sickness dwell,   10
And poppy or charms can make us sleep as well
And better than thy stroke; why swell'st thou then?
One short sleep past, we wake eternally
And death shall be no more; Death, thou shalt die.

("Holy Sonnet 7," p. 74; 14, p. 78.)

BEN JONSON   (1572–1637)

HIS EXCUSE FOR LOVING

Let it not your wonder move,
Less your laughter, that I love.
Though I now write fifty years,
I have had, and have, my peers;
Poets though divine are men,   5
Some have loved as old again.
And it is not always face,
Clothes, or fortune, gives the grace,
Or the feature, or the youth;
But the language and the truth,   10
With the ardor and the passion,
Gives the lover weight and fashion.
If you then will read the story,
First prepare you to be sorry
That you never knew till now   15
Either whom to love, or how;
But be glad, as soon with me,
When you know that this is she
Of whose beauty it was sung:
She shall make the old man young,   20
Keep the middle age at stay,
And let nothing high decay;
Till she be the reason why
All the world for love may die.

SLOW, SLOW, FRESH FOUNT

Slow, slow, fresh fount, keep time with my salt tears;
Yet slower, yet, oh, faintly, gentle springs;

List to the heavy part the music bears,
   Woe weeps out her division when she sings.
      Droop herbs and flowers;   5
      Fall grief in showers,
      Our beauties are not ours;
         Oh, I could still,
   Like melting snow upon some craggy hill,
      Drop, drop, drop, drop,   10
Since nature's pride is now a withered daffodil.

4. *division:* a "part" in part-singing.

ROBERT HERRICK   (1591–1674)

THE WHITE ISLAND: OR PLACE OF THE BLEST

   In this world (the *Isle of Dreams*)
   While we sit by sorrow's streams,
   Tears and terrors are our themes
           Reciting:

   But when once from hence we fly,   5
   More and more approaching nigh
   Unto young Eternity
           Uniting:

   In that whiter Island, where
   Things are evermore sincere;   10
   Candor here, and luster there
           Delighting:

   There no monstrous fancies shall
   Out of hell an horror call,
   To create (or cause at all)   15
           Affrighting.

   There in calm and cooling sleep
   We our eyes shall never steep;
   But eternal watch shall keep,
           Attending   20

   Pleasures, such as shall pursue
   Me, immortalized, and you;
   And fresh joys, as never too
           Have ending.

("Delight in Disorder," p. 8.)

HENRY KING   (1592–1669)

THE SURRENDER

My once dear love, hapless that I no more
Must call thee so, the rich affection's store
That fed our hopes lies now exhaust and spent,
Like sums of treasure unto bankrupts lent.

We that did nothing study but the way   5
To love each other, with which thoughts the day
Rose with delight to us, and with them set,
Must learn the hateful art how to forget.

We that did nothing wish that Heav'n could give
Beyond ourselves, nor did desire to live   10
Beyond that wish, all these now cancel must
As if not writ in faith, but words and dust.

Yet witness those clear vows which lovers make,
Witness the chaste desires that never break
Into unruly heats; witness that breast   15
Which in thy bosom anchored his whole rest;
'Tis no default in us, I dare acquite
Thy maiden faith, thy purpose fair and white
As thy pure self. Cross planets did envy
Us to each other, and Heav'n did untie   20
Faster than vows could bind. Oh, that the stars,
When lovers meet, should stand opposed in wars!

Since then, some higher destinies command,
Let us not strive, nor labor to withstand
What is past help. The longest date of grief   25
Can never yield a hope of our relief;
And though we waste ourselves in moist laments,
Tears may drown us, but not our discontents.

Fold back our arms, take home our fruitless loves,
That must new fortunes try, like turtledoves   30
Dislodgéd from their haunts. We must in tears
Unwind a love knit up in many years.
In this last kiss I here surrender thee
Back to thyself, so thou again art free;
Thou in another, sad as that, resend   35
The truest heart that lover e'er did lend.

Now turn from each. So fare our severed hearts
As the divorced soul from her body parts.

GEORGE HERBERT (1593–1633)

THE PEARL

I know the ways of learning; both the head
And pipes that feed the press, and make it run;
What reason hath from nature borrowéd,
Or of itself, like a good housewife, spun
In laws and policy; what the stars conspire,   5
What willing nature speaks, what forced by fire;
Both th' old discoveries and the new-found seas,
The stock and surplus, cause and history,—
All these stand open, or I have the keys:
                  Yet I love Thee.   10

I know the ways of honor, what maintains
The quick returns of courtesy and wit;
In vies of favors whether party gains;
When glory swells the heart, and moldeth it
To all expressions both of hand and eye;   15
Which on the world a true-love knot may tie,
And bear the bundle, whereso'er it goes;
How many drams of spirit there must be
To sell my life unto my friends or foes:
                  Yet I love Thee.   20

I know the ways of pleasure, the sweet strains,
The lullings and the relishes of it;
The propositions of hot blood and brains;
What mirth and music mean; what love and wit
Have done these twenty hundred years and more;   25
I know the projects of unbridled store:
My stuff is flesh, not brass; my senses live,
And grumble oft that they have more in me
Than he that curbs them, being but one to five:
                  Yet I love Thee.   30

I know all these, and have them in my hand:
Therefore not sealéd, but with open eyes
I fly to Thee, and fully understand
Both the main sale and the commodities;
And at what rate and price I have Thy love,   35
With all the circumstances that may move:
Yet through the labyrinths, not my grovelling wit,
But Thy silk-twist let down from heav'n to me,
Did both conduct and teach me how by it
                  To climb to Thee.   40

VIRTUE

Sweet day, so cool, so calm, so bright,
The bridal of the earth and sky:
The dew shall weep thy fall tonight;
      For thou must die.

Sweet rose, whose hue angry and brave   5
Bids the rash gazer wipe his eye:
Thy root is ever in its grave,
      And thou must die.

Sweet spring, full of sweet days and roses,
A box where sweets compacted lie;   10
My music shows ye have your closes,
      And all must die.

Only a sweet and virtuous soul,
Like seasoned timber, never gives;
But though the whole world turn to coal,   15
      Then chiefly lives.

11. *closes:* conclusions to musical strains.

JAMES SHIRLEY   (1596–1666)

DIRGE

The glories of our blood and state
  Are shadows, not substantial things;
There is no armor against fate;
  Death lays his icy hand on kings:
    Scepter and crown   5
    Must tumble down,
And in the dust be equal made
With the poor crooked scythe and spade.

Some men with swords may reap the field,
  And plant fresh laurels where they kill: 10
But their strong nerves at last must yield;
  They tame but one another still:
    Early or late
    They stoop to fate,
And must give up their murmuring breath   15
When they, pale captives, creep to death.

    The garlands wither on your brow;
      Then boast no more your mighty deeds;
    Upon Death's purple altar now
      See where the victor-victim bleeds: 20
      Your head must come
        To the cold tomb;
    Only the actions of the just
    Smell sweet, and blossom in their dust.

EDMUND WALLER (1606–1687)

OF THE LAST VERSES IN THE BOOK

When we for age could neither read nor write,
The subject made us able to indite;
The soul, with nobler resolutions decked,
The body stooping, does herself erect.
No mortal parts are requisite to raise   5
Her that, unbodied, can her Maker praise.
   The seas are quiet when the winds give o'er;
So calm are we when passions are no more!
For then we know how vain it was to boast
Of fleeting things, so certain to be lost.   10
Clouds of affection from our younger eyes
Conceal that emptiness which age descries.
   The soul's dark cottage, battered and decayed,
Lets in new light through chinks that time has made;
Stronger by weakness, wiser, men become   15
As they draw near to their eternal home.
Leaving the old, both worlds at once they view,
That stand upon the threshold of the new.

JOHN MILTON (1608–1674)

LYCIDAS

*In This Monody the Author Bewails a Learned Friend, Unfortunately
Drowned in His Passage, from Chester on the Irish Seas, 1637. And
by Occasion Foretells the Ruin of Our Corrupted Clergy, Then in
Their Height.*

    Yet once more, O ye laurels, and once more,
    Ye myrtles brown, with ivy never sere,

I come to pluck your berries harsh and crude,
And with forced fingers rude
Shatter your leaves before the mellowing year.   5
Bitter constraint and sad occasion dear
Compels me to disturb your season due:
For Lycidas is dead, dead ere his prime,
Young Lycidas, and hath not left his peer.
Who would not sing for Lycidas? he knew   10
Himself to sing, and build the lofty rhyme.
He must not float upon his watery bier
Unwept, and welter to the parching wind,
Without the meed of some melodious tear.
　　Begin then, Sisters of the sacred well,   15
That from beneath the seat of Jove doth spring,
Begin, and somewhat loudly sweep the string.
Hence with denial vain, and coy excuse,
So may some gentle Muse
With lucky words favor my destined urn,   20
And as he passes turn,
And bid fair peace be to my sable shroud.
For we were nursed upon the self-same hill,
Fed the same flock, by fountain, shade, and rill.
　　Together both, ere the high lawns appeared   25
Under the opening eyelids of the morn,
We drove afield, and both together heard
What time the gray-fly winds her sultry horn,
Battening our flocks with the fresh dews of night,
Oft till the star that rose, at evening, bright,   30
Toward Heaven's descent had sloped his westering wheel.
Meanwhile the rural ditties were not mute,
Tempered to th' oaten flute,
Rough Satyrs danced, and Fauns with cloven heel,
From the glad sound would not be absent long,   35
And old Damoetas loved to hear our song.
　　But O the heavy change, now thou art gone,
Now thou art gone, and never must return!
Thee shepherd, thee the woods, and desert caves,
With wild thyme and the gadding vine o'ergrown,   40
And all their echoes mourn.
The willows, and the hazel copses green,
Shall now no more be seen,
Fanning their joyous leaves to thy soft lays.
As killing as the canker to the rose,   45
Or taint-worm to the weanling herds that graze,
Or frost to flowers, that their gay wardrobe wear,

---

36. *Damoetas:* a conventional name in pastoral poetry.

When first the white-thorn blows;
Such, Lycidas, thy loss to shepherd's ear.
    Where were ye Nymphs when the remorseless deep   50
Closed o'er the head of your loved Lycidas?
For neither were ye playing on the steep,
Where your old Bards, the famous Druids, lie,
Nor on the shaggy top of Mona high,
Nor yet where Deva spreads her wizard stream: 55
Ay me, I fondly dream!
Had ye been there—for what could that have done?
What could the Muse herself that Orpheus bore,
The Muse herself for her enchanting son
Whom universal nature did lament,   60
When by the rout that made the hideous roar,
His gory visage down the stream was sent,
Down the swift Hebrus to the Lesbian shore?
    Alas! What boots it with incessant care
To tend the homely slighted shepherd's trade,   65
And strictly meditate the thankless Muse?
Were it not better done as others use,
To sport with Amaryllis in the shade,
Or with the tangles of Neæra's hair?
Fame is the spur that the clear spirit doth raise   70
(That last infirmity of noble mind)
To scorn delights, and live laborious days;
But the fair guerdon when we hope to find,
And think to burst out into sudden blaze,
Comes the blind Fury with th' abhorréd shears,   75
And slits the thin spun life. But not the praise,
Phœbus replied, and touched my trembling ears;
Fame is no plant that grows on mortal soil,
Nor in the glistering foil
Set off to th' world, nor in broad rumor lies,   80
But lives and spreads aloft by those pure eyes,
And perfect witness of all-judging Jove;
As he pronounces lastly on each deed,
Of so much fame in Heaven expect thy meed.
    O Fountain Arethuse, and thou honored flood,   85
Smooth-sliding Mincius, crowned with vocal reeds,
That strain I heard was of a higher mood.
But now my oat proceeds,

---

54. *Mona:* island to the west of England; 55. *Deva:* river in the west of England; 58. *Orpheus:* in Greek legend, the son of a goddess and master of the lyre, who was killed by a mob of women; 68. *Amaryllis:* conventional name for a shepherdess in pastoral poetry; 69. *Neæra:* another such name; 75. *Fury:* fate; 77. *Phœbus:* Phoebus Apollo, god of poetry; 85. *Arethuse:* a fountain in Sicily; 86. *Mincius:* a river in Italy; 88. *oat:* shepherd's pipe.

And listens to the herald of the sea
That came in Neptune's plea;   90
He asked the waves, and asked the felon winds,
What hard mishap hath doomed this gentle swain?
And questioned every gust of rugged wings
That blows from off each beakéd promontory:
They knew not of his story;   95
And sage Hippotades their answer brings,
That not a blast was from his dungeon strayed;
The air was calm, and on the level brine
Sleek Panope with all her sisters played.
It was that fatal and perfidious bark,   100
Built in the eclipse, and rigged with curses dark,
That sunk so low that sacred head of thine.
    Next Camus, reverend sire, went footing slow,
His mantle hairy, and his bonnet sedge,
Inwrought with figures dim, and on the edge   105
Like to that sanguine flower inscribed with woe.
"Ah! who hath reft," quoth he, "my dearest pledge?"
Last came, and last did go
The Pilot of the Galilean lake;
Two massy keys he bore of metals twain   110
(The golden opes, the iron shuts amain);
He shook his mitered locks, and stern bespake:
"How well could I have spared for thee, young swain,
Enow of such, as for their bellies' sake
Creep and intrude and climb into the fold!   115
Of other care they little reckoning make
Than how to scramble at the shearers' feast,
And shove away the worthy bidden guest;
Blind mouths! that scarce themselves know how to hold
A sheep-hook, or have learned aught else the least   120
That to the faithful herdman's art belongs!
What recks it them? What need they? They are sped;
And when they list, their lean and flashy songs
Grate on their scrannel pipes of wretched straw,
The hungry Sheep look up, and are not fed,   125
But swol'n with wind, and the rank mist they draw,
Rot inwardly, and foul contagion spread:
Besides what the grim Wolf with privy paw
Daily devours apace, and nothing said;
But that two-handed engine at the door   130
Stands ready to smite once, and smite no more."
    Return Alpheus, the dread voice is past,

96. *Hippotades:* god of the winds; 99. *Panope:* a sea nymph; 103. *Camus:* god of the river Cam at Cambridge; 109. *Pilot:* St. Peter; 132. *Alpheus:* a river associated with pastoral poetry.

That shrunk thy streams; Return Sicilian Muse,
And call the vales, and bid them hither cast
Their bells, and flowrets of a thousand hues.   135
Ye valleys low where the mild whispers use,
Of shades and wanton winds, and gushing brooks,
On whose fresh lap the swart star sparely looks,
Throw hither all your quaint enameled eyes,
That on the green turf suck the honied showers,   140
And purple all the ground with vernal flowers.
Bring the rathe primrose that forsaken dies,
The tufted crow-toe, and pale jessamine,
The white pink, and the pansy freaked with jet,
The glowing violet.   145
The musk-rose, and the well attired woodbine,
With cowslips wan that hang the pensive head,
And every flower that sad embroidery wears:
Bid Amaranthus all his beauty shed,
And daffadillies fill their cups with tears,   150
To strew the laureate hearse where Lycid lies.
For so to interpose a little ease,
Let our frail thoughts dally with false surmise.
Ay me! Whilst thee the shores, and sounding seas
Wash far away, where e'er thy bones are hurled,   155
Whether beyond the stormy Hebrides
Where thou, perhaps, under the whelming tide,
Visit'st the bottom of the monstrous world;
Or whether thou, to our moist vows denied,
Sleep'st by the fable of Bellerus old,   160
Where the great Vision of the guarded mount
Looks toward Namancos and Bayona's hold.
Look homeward, Angel, now, and melt with ruth:
And, O ye dolphins, waft the hapless youth!
    Weep no more, woeful shepherds, weep no more,   165
For Lycidas, your sorrow, is not dead,
Sunk though he be beneath the watery floor;
So sinks the day-star in the ocean bed,
And yet anon repairs his drooping head,
And tricks his beams, and with new-spangled ore   170
Flames in the forehead of the morning sky:
So Lycidas sunk low, but mounted high
Through the dear might of Him that walked the waves;

133. *Sicilian Muse:* a source of poetic inspiration, like the fountain Arethuse above; 149. *Amaranthus:* an unfading flower; 156. *Hebrides:* islands off Scotland; 160. *Bellerus:* in legend, a giant buried at the southwestern tip of England; 161. *guarded mount:* St. Michael's Mount at the southwestern tip of England; 162. *Namancos and Bayona:* places in northwestern Spain.

Where, other groves and other streams along,
With nectar pure his oozy locks he laves,   175
And hears the unexpressive nuptial song
In the blest kingdoms meek of joy and love.
There entertain him all the saints above
In solemn troops and sweet societies,
That sing, and singing in their glory move,   180
And wipe the tears for ever from his eyes.
Now, Lycidas, the shepherds weep no more;
Henceforth thou art the Genius of the shore
In thy large recompense, and shalt be good
To all that wander in that perilous flood.   185
   Thus sang the uncouth swain to the oaks and rills,
While the still morn went out with sandals gray;
He touched the tender stops of various quills,
With eager thought warbling his Doric lay:
And now the sun had stretched out all the hills,   190
And now was dropped into the western bay;
At last he rose, and twitched his mantle blue:
Tomorrow to fresh woods, and pastures new.

("On the Late Massacre in Piedmont," p. 78.)

RICHARD CRASHAW (ca. 1613–1649)

ON OUR CRUCIFIED LORD, NAKED AND BLOODY

Th' have left Thee naked, Lord, O that they had;
This garment too I would they had denied.
Thee with Thyself they have too richly clad,
Opening the purple wardrobe of Thy side.
   O never could be found garments too good   5
   For Thee to wear, but these, of Thine own blood.

HENRY VAUGHAN (1621–1695)

PEACE

My soul, there is a country
  Far beyond the stars,
Where stands a wingéd sentry
  All skillful in the wars,

There above noise, and danger   5
  Sweet Peace sits crowned with smiles,
And One born in a manger
  Commands the beauteous files,
He is thy gracious friend,
  And (O my soul awake!)   10
Did in pure love descend
  To die here for thy sake.
If thou canst get but thither,
  There grows the flower of peace,
The rose that cannot wither,   15
  Thy fortress, and thy ease.
Leave then thy foolish ranges;
  For none can thee secure,
But One, who never changes,
  Thy God, thy life, thy cure.   20

ANDREW MARVELL (1621–1678)

THE UNFORTUNATE LOVER

Alas, how pleasant are their days
With whom the infant Love yet plays!
Sorted by pairs, they still are seen
By fountains cool, and shadows green.
But soon these flames do lose their light,   5
Like meteors of a summer's night:
Nor can they to that region climb,
To make impression upon time.

'Twas in a shipwreck, when the seas
Ruled, and the winds did what they please,   10
That my poor lover floating lay,
And, ere brought forth, was cast away:
Till at the last the master-wave
Upon the rock his mother drave;
And there she split against the stone,   15
In a Caesarean sectiön.

The sea him lent these bitter tears
Which at his eyes he always bears:
And from the winds the sighs he bore,
Which through his surging breast do roar.   20
No day he saw but that which breaks,
Through frightéd clouds in forkéd streaks:

While round the rattling thunder hurled,
As at the fun'ral of the world.

While Nature to his birth presents   25
This masque of quarreling elements,
A num'rous fleet of corm'rants black,
That sailed insulting o'er the wrack,
Received into their cruel care
Th' unfortunate and abject heir: 30
Guardians most fit to entertain
'The orphan of the hurricane.

They fed him up with hopes and air,
Which soon digested to despair:
And as one corm'rant fed him, still   35
Another on his heart did bill.
Thus while they famish him, and feast,
He both consuméd, and increased:
And languishéd with doubtful breath,
Th' amphibium of life and death.   40

And now, when angry heaven would
Behold a spectacle of blood,
Fortune and he are called to play
At sharp before it all the day:
And tyrant Love his breast does ply   45
With all his winged artillery:
Whilst he, betwixt the flames and waves,
Like Ajax, the mad tempest braves.

See how he nak'd and fierce does stand,
Cuffing the thunder with one hand;   50
While with the other he does lock,
And grapple, with the stubborn rock:
From which he with each wave rebounds,
Torn into flames, and ragg'd with wounds.
And all he says, a lover dressed   55
In his own blood does relish best.

This is the only banneret
That ever Love created yet:
Who though by the malignant stars,
Forced to live in storms and wars;   60
Yet dying leaves a perfume here,
And music within every ear:
And he in story only rules,
In a field sable a lover gules.

28. *insulting:* assaulting.

JOHN BUNYAN (1628–1688)

WHO WOULD TRUE VALOR SEE

Who would true valor see,
Let him come hither;
One here will constant be,
Come wind, come weather.
There's no discouragement,   5
Shall make him once relent,
His first avowed intent,
To be a pilgrim.

Whoso beset him round,
With dismal stories,   10
Do but themselves confound;
His strength the more is.
No lion can him fright,
He'll with a giant fight,
But he will have a right,   15
To be a pilgrim.

Hobgoblin, nor foul fiend,
Can daunt his spirit:
He knows, he at the end,
Shall life inherit.   20
Then fancies fly away,
He'll fear not what men say,
He'll labor night and day,
To be a pilgrim.

("He that is down," p. 38.)

JOHN DRYDEN (1631–1700)

SONG

I feed a flame within which so torments me
That it both pains my heart, and yet contents me:
'Tis such a pleasing smart, and I so love it,
That I had rather die, than once remove it.

Yet he for whom I grieve shall never know it,   5
My tongue does not betray, nor my eyes show it:

Not a sigh nor a tear my pain discloses,
But they fall silently like dew on roses.

Thus to prevent my love from being cruel,
My heart's the sacrifice as 'tis the fuel: 10
And while I suffer this to give him quiet,
My faith rewards my love, though he deny it.

On his eyes will I gaze, and there delight me;
While I conceal my love, no frown can fright me:
To be more happy I dare not aspire;   15
Nor can I fall more low, mounting no higher.

SONG

Ah how sweet it is to love,
Ah how gay is young desire!
And what pleasing pains we prove
When we first approach love's fire!
　　Pains of love be sweeter far   5
　　Than all other pleasures are.

Sighs which are from lovers blown,
Do but gently heave the heart:
Ev'n the tears they shed alone
Cure, like trickling balm their smart.   10
　　Lovers when they lose their breath,
　　Bleed away in easy death.

Love and time with reverence use,
Treat 'em like a parting friend:
Nor the golden gifts refuse   15
Which in youth sincere they send:
　　For each year their price is more,
　　And they less simple than before.

Love, like spring-tides full and high,
Swells in every youthful vein: 20
But each tide does less supply,
Till they quite shrink in again:
　　If a flow in age appear,
　　'Tis but rain, and runs not clear.

SONG

Can life be a blessing,
Or worth the possessing,
Can life be a blessing if love were away?
Ah no! though our love all night keep us waking,

And though he torment us with cares all the day,   5
Yet he sweetens, he sweetens our pains in the taking,
There's an hour at the last, there's an hour to repay.

In every possessing,
The ravishing blessing,
In every possessing the fruit of our pain,   10
Poor lovers forget long ages of anguish,
Whate'er they have suffered and done to obtain;
'Tis a pleasure, a pleasure to sigh and to languish,
When we hope, when we hope to be happy again.

TO THE MEMORY OF MR. OLDHAM *

Farewell, too little, and too lately known,
Whom I began to think and call my own:
For sure our souls were near allied, and thine
Cast in the same poetic mold with mine.
One common note on either lyre did strike,   5
And knaves and fools we both abhorred alike.
To the same goal did both our studies drive;
The last set out the soonest did arrive.
Thus Nisus fell upon the slippery place,
While his young friend performed and won the race.   10
O early ripe! to thy abundant store
What could advancing age have added more?
It might (what nature never gives the young)
Have taught the numbers of thy native tongue.
But satire needs not those, and wit will shine   15
Through the harsh cadence of a rugged line:
A noble error, and but seldom made,
When poets are by too much force betrayed.
Thy generous fruits, though gathered ere their prime,
Still showed a quickness; and maturing time   20
But mellows what we write to the dull sweets of rhyme.
Once more, hail and farewell; farewell, thou young,
But ah too short, Marcellus of our tongue;
Thy brows with ivy, and with laurels bound;
But fate and gloomy night encompass thee around.   25

SONG

Fair Iris I love, and hourly I die,
But not for a lip, nor a languishing eye:
She's fickle and false, and there we agree;
For I am as false, and as fickle as she:

* *John Oldham:* a satiric poet, died in 1683 at the age of twenty.

We neither believe what either can say;   5
And, neither believing, we neither betray.

'Tis civil to swear, and say things of course;
We mean not the taking for better for worse.
When present, we love; when absent, agree:
I think not of Iris, nor Iris of me: 10
The legend of love no couple can find
So easy to part, or so equally joined.

APHRA BEHN   (1640–1689)

SONG

Love in fantastic triumph sat,
Whilst bleeding hearts around him flowed,
For whom fresh pains he did create,
And strange tyrannic power he showed;

From thy bright eyes he took his fire,   5
Which round about, in sport he hurled;
But 'twas from mine he took desire,
Enough to undo the amorous world.

From me he took his sighs and tears,
From thee his pride and cruelty;   10
From me his languishments and fears.
And every killing dart from thee;

Thus thou and I the God have armed,
And set him up a deity;
But my poor heart alone is harmed,   15
Whilst thine the victor is, and free.

ALEXANDER POPE   (1688–1744)

AN ESSAY ON MAN

To Henry St. John, Lord Bolingbroke

Epistle I. Of the Nature and State of Man, With Respect
to the Universe

Awake, my St. John! leave all meaner things
To low ambition, and the pride of kings.
Let us (since life can little more supply
Than just to look about us and to die)

Expatiate free o'er all this scene of man;   5
A mighty maze! but not without a plan;
A wild, where weeds and flowers promiscuous shoot,
Or garden, tempting with forbidden fruit.
Together let us beat this ample field,
Try what the open, what the covert yield;   10
The latent tracts, the giddy heights, explore
Of all who blindly creep, or sightless soar;
Eye Nature's walks, shoot folly as it flies,
And catch the manners living as they rise;
Laugh where we must, be candid where we can;   15
But vindicate the ways of God to man.

   1. Say first, of God above, or man below,
What can we reason, but from what we know?
Of man, what see we but his station here,
From which to reason, or to which refer?   20
Through worlds unnumbered though the God be known,
'Tis ours to trace him only in our own.
He, who through vast immensity can pierce,
See worlds on worlds compose one universe,
Observe how system into system runs,   25
What other planets circle other suns,
What varied Being peoples every star,
May tell why Heaven has made us as we are.
But of this frame the bearings, and the ties,
The strong connections, nice dependencies,   30
Gradations just, has thy pervading soul
Looked through? or can a part contain the whole?
   Is the great chain, that draws all to agree,
And drawn supports, upheld by God, or thee?

   2. Presumptuous man! the reason wouldst thou find,   35
Why formed so weak, so little, and so blind?
First if thou canst, the harder reason guess,
Why formed no weaker, blinder and no less!
Ask of thy mother earth, why oaks are made
Taller or stronger than the weeds they shade?   40
Or ask of yonder argent fields above,
Why Jove's satellites are less than Jove?
   Of systems possible, if 'tis confessed
That Wisdom Infinite must form the best,
Where all must full or not coherent be,   45
And all that rises, rise in due degree;
Then, in the scale of reasoning life, 'tis plain,
There must be, somewhere, such a rank as man:
And all the question (wrangle e'er so long)
Is only this, if God has placed him wrong?   50

Respecting man, whatever wrong we call,
May, must be right, as relative to all.
In human works, though labored on with pain,
A thousand movements scarce one purpose gain;
In God's, one single can its end produce;   55
Yet serves to second too some other use.
So man, who here seems principal alone,
Perhaps acts second to some sphere unknown,
Touches some wheel, or verges to some goal;
'Tis but a part we see, and not the whole.   60
  When the proud steed shall know why man restrains
His fiery course, or drives him o'er the plains;
When the dull ox, why now he breaks the clod,
Is now a victim, and now Egypt's god:
Then shall man's pride and dullness comprehend   65
His actions', passions', beings' use and end;
Why doing, suffering, checked, impelled; and why
This hour a slave, the next a deity.
  Then say not man's imperfect, Heaven in fault;
Say rather, man's as perfect as he ought: 70
His knowledge measured to his state and place,
His time a moment, and a point his space.
If to be perfect in a certain sphere,
What matter, soon or late, or here or there?
The blest today is as completely so,   75
As who began a thousand years ago.

  3. Heaven from all creatures hides the book of Fate,
All but the page prescribed, their present state:
From brutes what men, from men what spirits know:
Or who could suffer Being here below?   80
The lamb thy riot dooms to bleed today,
Had he thy reason, would he skip and play?
Pleased to the last, he crops the flowery food,
And licks the hand just raised to shed his blood.
O blindness to the future! kindly given,   85
That each may fill the circle marked by Heaven:
Who sees with equal eye, as God of all,
A hero perish, or a sparrow fall,
Atoms or systems into ruin hurled,
And now a bubble burst, and now a world.   90
  Hope humbly then; with trembling pinions soar;
Wait the great teacher Death, and God adore!
What future bliss, he gives thee not to know,
But gives that hope to be thy blessing now.
Hope springs eternal in the human breast: 95
Man never is, but always to be blest:

The soul, uneasy and confined from home,
Rests and expatiates in a life to come.
    Lo! the poor Indian, whose untutored mind
Sees God in clouds, or hears him in the wind;   100
His soul proud Science never taught to stray
Far as the solar walk, or milky way;
Yet simple Nature to his hope has given,
Behind the cloud-topped hill, an humbler heaven;
Some safer world in depth of woods embraced,   105
Some happier island in the watery waste,
Where slaves once more their native land behold,
No fiends torment, no Christians thirst for gold!
To be, contents his natural desire,
He asks no angel's wing, no seraph's fire;   110
But thinks, admitted to that equal sky,
His fathful dog shall bear him company.

    4. Go, wiser thou! and, in thy scale of sense,
Weigh thy opinion against Providence;
Call imperfection what thou fancy'st such,   115
Say, here he gives too little, there too much;
Destroy all creatures for thy sport or gust.
Yet cry, if man's unhappy, God's unjust;
If man alone engross not Heaven's high care,
Alone made perfect here, immortal there: 120
Snatch from his hand the balance and the rod,
Rejudge his justice, be the God of God!
In pride, in reasoning pride, our error lies;
All quit their sphere, and rush into the skies.
Pride still is aiming at the blest abodes,   125
Men would be angels, angels would be gods.
Aspiring to be gods, if angels fell,
Aspiring to be angels, men rebel:
And who but wishes to invert the laws
Of order, sins against the Eternal Cause.   130

    5. Ask for what end the heavenly bodies shine,
Earth for whose use? Pride answers, " 'Tis for mine:
For me kind Nature wakes her genial power,
Suckles each herb, and spreads out every flower;
Annual for me, the grape, the rose renew   135
The juice nectareous, and the balmy dew;
For me, the mine a thousand treasures brings;
For me, health gushes from a thousand springs;
Seas roll to waft me, suns to light me rise;
My footstool earth, my canopy the skies."   140
    But errs not Nature from this gracious end,
From burning suns when livid deaths descend,

When earthquakes swallow, or when tempests sweep
Towns to one grave, whole nations to the deep?
"No," 'tis replied, "the first Almighty Cause   145
Acts not by partial, but by general laws;
The exceptions few; some change since all began,
And what created perfect?"—Why then man?
If the great end be human happiness,
Then Nature deviates; and can man do less?   150
As much that end a constant course requires
Of showers and sunshine, as of man's desires;
As much eternal springs and cloudless skies,
As men forever temperate, calm, and wise.
If plagues or earthquakes break not Heaven's design,   155
Why then a Borgia, or a Cataline?
Who knows but he whose hand the lightning forms,
Who heaves old ocean, and who wings the storms,
Pours fierce ambition in a Caesar's mind,
Or turns young Ammon loose to scourge mankind?   160
From pride, from pride, our very reasoning springs;
Account for moral, as for natural things:
Why charge we Heaven in those, in these acquit?
In both, to reason right is to submit.
    Better for us, perhaps, it might appear,   165
Were there all harmony, all virtue here;
That never air or ocean felt the wind;
That never passion discomposed the mind:
But ALL subsists by elemental strife;
And passions are the elements of life.   170
The general ORDER, since the whole began,
Is kept in Nature, and is kept in man.

    6. What would this man? Now upward will he soar,
And little less than angel, would be more;
Now looking downwards, just as grieved appears   175
To want the strength of bulls, the fur of bears.
Made for his use all creatures if he call,
Say what their use, had he the powers of all?
Nature to these, without profusion, kind,
The proper organs, proper powers assigned;   180
Each seeming want compénsated of course,
Here with degrees of swiftness, there of force;
All in exact proportion to the state;
Nothing to add, and nothing to abate.
Each beast, each insect, happy in its own;   185
Is Heaven unkind to man, and man alone?
Shall he alone, whom rational we call,
Be pleased with nothing, if not blessed with all?

The bliss of man (could pride that blessing find)
Is not to act or think beyond mankind;   190
No powers or body or of soul to share,
But what his nature and his state can bear.
Why has not man a microscopic eye?
For this plain reason, man is not a fly.
Say what the use, were finer optics given,   195
To inspect a mite, not comprehend the heaven?
Or touch, if tremblingly alive all o'er,
To smart and agonize at every pore?
Or quick effluvia darting through the brain,
Die of a rose in aromatic pain?   200
If nature thundered in his opening ears,
And stunned him with the music of the spheres,
How would he wish that Heaven had left him still
The whispering zephyr, and the purling rill?
Who finds not Providence all good and wise,   205
Alike in what it gives, and what denies?

7. Far as creation's ample range extends,
The scale of sensual, mental powers ascends:
Mark how it mounts, to man's imperial race,
From the green myriads in the peopled grass: 210
What modes of sight betwixt each wide extreme,
The mole's dim curtain, and the lynx's beam:
Of smell, the headlong lioness between,
And hound sagacious on the tainted green:
Of hearing, from the life that fills the flood,   215
To that which warbles through the vernal wood:
The spider's touch, how exquisitely fine!
Feels at each thread, and lives along the line:
In the nice bee, what sense so subtly true
From poisonous herbs extracts the healing dew: 220
How instinct varies in the groveling swine,
Compared, half-reasoning elephant, with thine!
'Twixt that, and reason, what a nice barrier;
Forever separate, yet forever near!
Remembrance and reflection how allied;   225
What thin partitions sense from thought divide:
And middle natures, how they long to join,
Yet never pass the insuperable line!
Without this just gradation, could they be
Subjected, these to those, or all to thee?   230
The powers of all subdued by thee alone,
Is not thy reason all these powers in one?

8. See, through this air, this ocean, and this earth,
All matter quick, and bursting into birth.

Above, how high progressive life may go!   235
Around, how wide! how deep extend below!
Vast Chain of Being! which from God began,
Natures ethereal, human, angel, man,
Beast, bird, fish, insect, what no eye can see,
No glass can reach! from Infinite to thee,   240
From thee to nothing.—On superior powers
Were we to press, inferior might on ours:
Or in the full creation leave a void,
Where, one step broken, the great scale's destroyed:
From Nature's chain whatever link you strike,   245
Tenth or ten thousandth, breaks the chain alike.
   And, if each system in gradation roll
Alike essential to the amazing Whole,
The least confusion but in one, not all
That system only, but the Whole must fall.   250
Let earth unbalanced from her orbit fly,
Planets and suns run lawless through the sky,
Let ruling angels from their spheres be hurled,
Being on being wrecked, and world on world,
Heaven's whole foundations to their center nod,   255
And Nature tremble to the throne of God:
All this dread ORDER break—for whom? for thee?
Vile worm!—oh, madness, pride, impiety!

   9. What if the foot, ordained the dust to tread,
Or hand, to toil, aspired to be the head?   260
What if the head, the eye, or ear repined
To serve mere engines to the ruling Mind?
Just as absurd for any part to claim
To be another, in this general frame:
Just as absurd, to mourn the tasks or pains,   265
The great directing MIND of ALL ordains.
   All are but parts of one stupendous whole,
Whose body Nature is, and God the soul;
That, changed through all, and yet in all the same,
Great in the earth, as in the ethereal frame,   270
Warms in the sun, refreshes in the breeze,
Glows in the stars, and blossoms in the trees,
Lives through all life, extends through all extent,
Spreads undivided, operates unspent,
Breathes in our soul, informs our mortal part,   275
As full, as perfect, in a hair as heart;
As full, as perfect, in vile man that mourns,
As the rapt seraph that adores and burns;
To him no high, no low, no great, no small;
He fills, he bounds, connects, and equals all.   280

10. Cease then, nor ORDER imperfection name:
Our proper bliss depends on what we blame.
Know thy own point: this kind, this due degree
Of blindness, weakness, Heaven bestows on thee.
Submit—In this, or any other sphere   285
Secure to be as blest as thou canst bear:
Safe in the hand of one disposing Power,
Or in the natal, or the mortal hour.
All Nature is but art, unknown to thee;
All chance, direction, which thou canst not see;   290
All discord, harmony not understood;
All partial evil, universal good:
And, spite of pride, in erring reason's spite,
One truth is clear: Whatever IS, is RIGHT.

WILLIAM COWPER   (1731–1800)

THE SHRUBBERY

Oh, happy shades—to me unblessed!
    Friendly to peace, but not to me!
How ill the scene that offers rest,
    And heart that cannot rest, agree!

This glassy stream, that spreading pine,   5
    Those alders quivering in the breeze,
Might soothe a soul less hurt than mine,
    And please, if anything could please.

But fixed unalterable care
    Foregoes not what she feels within,   10
Shows the same sadness everywhere,
    And slights the season and the scene.

For all that pleased in wood or lawn,
    While peace possessed these silent bowers,
Her animating smile withdrawn,   15
    Has lost its beauties and its powers.

The saint or moralist should tread
    This moss-grown alley, musing slow;
They seek, like me, the secret shade,
    But not, like me, to nourish woe!   20

Me fruitful scenes and prospects waste
    Alike admonish not to roam;
These tell me of enjoyments past,
    And those of sorrows yet to come.

WILLIAM BLAKE (1757–1827)

INTRODUCTION TO SONGS OF INNOCENCE

Piping down the valleys wild,
Piping songs of pleasant glee,
On a cloud I saw a child,
And he laughing said to me:

"Pipe a song about a lamb!"   5
So I piped with merry cheer.
"Piper, pipe that song again";
So I piped: he wept to hear.

"Drop thy pipe, thy happy pipe;
Sing thy songs of happy cheer":   10
So I sung the same again,
While he wept with joy to hear.

"Piper, sit thee down and write
In a book, that all may read."
So he vanished from my sight,   15
And I plucked a hollow reed,

And I made a rural pen,
And I stained the water clear,
And I wrote my happy songs
Every child may joy to hear.   20

THE ECHOING GREEN

The sun does arise,
And make happy the skies;
The merry bells ring
To welcome the spring;
The skylark and thrush,   5
The birds of the bush,
Sing louder around
To the bells' cheerful sound,
While our sports shall be seen
On the echoing green.   10

Old John, with white hair,
Does laugh away care,
Sitting under the oak,
Among the old folk.

They laugh at our play,   15
And soon they all say:
"Such, such were the joys
When we all, girls and boys,
In our youth-time were seen
On the echoing green."   20

Till the little ones, weary,
No more can be merry;
The sun does descend,
And our sports have an end.
Round the laps of their mothers   25
Many sisters and brothers,
Like birds in their nest,
Are ready for rest,
And sport no more seen
On the darkening green.   30

THE LAMB

Little Lamb, who made thee?
Dost thou know who made thee?
Gave thee life, and bid thee feed
By the stream and o'er the mead;
Gave thee clothing of delight,   5
Softest clothing, woolly, bright;
Gave thee such a tender voice,
Making all the vales rejoice?
   Little Lamb, who made thee?
   Dost thou know who made thee?   10

   Little Lamb, I'll tell thee,
   Little Lamb, I'll tell thee:
He is calléd by thy name,
For he calls himself a Lamb.
He is meek, and he is mild;   15
He became a little child.
I a child, and thou a lamb,
We are calléd by his name.
   Little Lamb, God bless thee!
   Little Lamb, God bless thee!   20

INFANT JOY

"I have no name:
I am but two days old."
What shall I call thee?

"I happy am,
Joy is my name."   5
Sweet joy befall thee!

Pretty joy!
Sweet joy, but two days old.
Sweet joy I call thee:
Thou dost smile,   10
I sing the while,
Sweet joy befall thee!

AH! SUN-FLOWER

Ah, Sun-flower! weary of time,
Who countest the steps of the Sun;
Seeking after that sweet golden clime,
Where the traveller's journey is done:

Where the Youth pined away with desire,   5
And the pale Virgin shrouded in snow,
Arise from their graves, and aspire
Where my Sun-flower wishes to go.

THE GARDEN OF LOVE

I went to the Garden of Love,
And saw what I never had seen:
A chapel was built in the midst,
Where I used to play on the green.

And the gates of this chapel were shut,   5
And "Thou shalt not" writ over the door;
So I turned to the Garden of Love,
That so many sweet flowers bore;

And I saw it was filléd with graves,
And tombstones where flowers should be: 10
And priests in black gowns were walking their rounds,
And binding with briars my joys and desires.

THE HUMAN ABSTRACT

Pity would be no more
If we did not make somebody Poor;
And Mercy no more could be
If all were as happy as we.

And mutual fear brings peace,   5
Till the selfish loves increase;

Then Cruelty knits a snare,
And spreads his baits with care.

He sits down with holy fears,
And waters the ground with tears;   10
Then Humility takes its root
Underneath his foot.

Soon spreads the dismal shade
Of Mystery over his head;
And the Caterpillar and Fly   15
Feed on the Mystery.

And it bears the fruit of Deceit,
Ruddy and sweet to eat;
And the Raven his nest has made
In its thickest shade.   20

The Gods of the earth and sea
Sought through Nature to find this Tree;
But their search was all in vain:
There grows one in the Human Brain.

INFANT SORROW

My mother groaned, my father wept.
Into the dangerous world I leapt;
Helpless, naked, piping loud,
Like a fiend hid in a cloud.

Struggling in my father's hands,   5
Striving against my swaddling bands,
Bound and weary I thought best
To sulk upon my mother's breast.

A POISON TREE

I was angry with my friend:
I told my wrath, my wrath did end.
I was angry with my foe:
I told it not, my wrath did grow.

And I watered it in fears,   5
Night and morning with my tears;
And I sunnéd it with smiles,
And with soft deceitful wiles.

And it grew both day and night,
Till it bore an apple bright;   10

And my foe beheld it shine,
And he knew that it was mine,

And into my garden stole
When the night had veiled the pole:
In the morning glad I see   15
My foe outstretched beneath the tree.

AND DID THOSE FEET

And did those feet in ancient time
Walk upon England's mountain green?
And was the holy Lamb of God
On England's pleasant pastures seen?

And did the Countenance Divine   5
Shine forth upon our clouded hills?
And was Jerusalem builded here
Among these dark Satanic Mills?

Bring me my Bow of burning gold!
Bring me my Arrows of desire!   10
Bring me my Spear! O clouds unfold!
Bring me my Chariot of fire!

I will not cease from Mental Fight,
Nor shall my Sword sleep in my hand,
Till we have built Jerusalem   15
In England's green and pleasant Land.

("The Sick Rose," p. 139; "The Tiger," p. 141; "London," p. 95; Epigrams,
p. 142.)

ROBERT BURNS   (1759–1796)

THE HENPECKED HUSBAND

Cursed be the man, the poorest wretch in life,
The crouching vassal to the tyrant wife!
Who has no will but by her high permission;
Who has not sixpence but in her possession;
Who must to her his dear friend's secret tell;   5
Who dreads a curtain lecture worse than hell.
Were such the wife had fallen to my part,
I'd break her spirit, or I'd break her heart:
I'd charm her with the magic of a switch,
I'd kiss her maids, and kick the perverse bitch.   10

ON SEEING THE BEAUTIFUL SEAT OF LORD GALLOWAY

What dost thou in that mansion fair?
  Flit, Galloway, and find
Some narrow, dirty, dungeon cave,
  The picture of thy mind!

EPITAPH ON JAMES GRIEVE, LAIRD OF BOGHEAD

Here lies Boghead amang the dead
  In hopes to get salvation;
But if such as he in Heaven may be,
  Then welcome—hail! damnation.

O, WERT THOU IN THE CAULD BLAST

O, wert thou in the cauld blast,
  On yonder lea, on yonder lea,
My plaidie to the angry airt,
  I'd shelter thee, I'd shelter thee.
Or did misfortune's bitter storms   5
  Around thee blaw, around thee blaw,
Thy bield should be my bosom,
  To share it a', to share it a'.

Or were I in the wildest waste,
  Sae black and bare, sae black and bare,   10
The desert were a paradise,
  If thou wert there, if thou wert there.
Or were I monarch o' the globe,
  Wi' thee to reign, wi' thee to reign,
The brightest jewel in my crown   15
  Wad be my queen, wad be my queen.

3. *plaidie:* plaid; *airt:* quarter of the sky; 7. *bield:* shelter.

THE JOYFUL WIDOWER

I married with a scolding wife
  The fourteenth of November;
She made me weary of my life,
  By one unruly member.
Long did I bear the heavy yoke,   5
  And many griefs attended;
But, to my comfort be it spoke,
  Now, now her life is ended.

We lived full one-and-twenty years
  A man and wife together; 10
At length from me her course she steered,
  And gone I know not whither:
Would I could guess! I do profess,
  I speak, and do not flatter,
Of all the women in the world, 15
  I never would come at her.

Her body is bestowéd well,
  A handsome grave does hide her;
But sure her soul is not in hell,
  The deil would ne'er abide her. 20
I rather think she is aloft,
  And imitating thunder;
For why,—methinks I hear her voice
  Tearing the clouds asunder.

20. *deil:* devil.

WILLIAM WORDSWORTH (1770–1850)

LINES

Composed a Few Miles Above Tintern Abbey, on Revisiting the Banks of the Wye During a Tour, July 13, 1798

Five years have passed; five summers, with the length
Of five long winters! and again I hear
These waters, rolling from their mountain-springs
With a soft inland murmur.—Once again
Do I behold these steep and lofty cliffs, 5
That on a wild secluded scene impress
Thoughts of more deep seclusion; and connect
The landscape with the quiet of the sky.
The day is come when I again repose
Here, under this dark sycamore, and view 10
These plots of cottage-ground, these orchard-tufts,
Which at this season, with their unripe fruits,
Are clad in one green hue, and lose themselves
'Mid groves and copses. Once again I see
These hedge-rows, hardly hedge-rows, little lines 15
Of sportive wood run wild: these pastoral farms,
Green to the very door; and wreaths of smoke
Sent up, in silence, from among the trees!
With some uncertain notice, as might seem

Of vagrant dwellers in the houseless woods,   20
Or of some hermit's cave, where by his fire
The hermit sits alone.

              These beauteous forms,
Through a long absence, have not been to me
As is a landscape to a blind man's eye:
But oft, in lonely rooms, and 'mid the din   25
Of towns and cities, I have owed to them,
In hours of weariness, sensations sweet,
Felt in the blood, and felt along the heart;
And passing even into my purer mind,
With tranquil restoration:—feelings too   30
Of unremembered pleasure: such, perhaps,
As have no slight or trivial influence
On that best portion of a good man's life,
His little, nameless, unremembered, acts
Of kindness and of love. Nor less, I trust,   35
To them I may have owed another gift,
Of aspect more sublime; that blessed mood,
In which the burthen of the mystery,
In which the heavy and the weary weight
Of all this unintelligible world,   40
Is lightened:—that serene and blessed mood,
In which the affections gently lead us on,—
Until, the breath of this corporeal frame
And even the motion of our human blood
Almost suspended, we are laid asleep   45
In body, and become a living soul:
While with an eye made quiet by the power
Of harmony, and the deep power of joy,
We see into the life of things.

                 If this
Be but a vain belief, yet, oh! how oft—   50
In darkness and amid the many shapes
Of joyless daylight; when the fretful stir
Unprofitable, and the fever of the world,
Have hung upon the beatings of my heart—
How oft, in spirit, have I turned to thee,   55
O sylvan Wye! thou wanderer through the woods,
How often has my spirit turned to thee!

   And now, with gleams of half-extinguished thought,
With many recognitions dim and faint,
And somewhat of a sad perplexity,   60
The picture of the mind revives again:
While here I stand, not only with the sense

Of present pleasure, but with pleasing thoughts
That in this moment there is life and food
For future years. And so I dare to hope,   65
Though changed, no doubt, from what I was when first
I came among these hills; when like a roe
I bounded o'er the mountains, by the sides
Of the deep rivers, and the lonely streams,
Wherever nature led: more like a man   70
Flying from something that he dreads than one
Who sought the thing he loved. For nature then
(The coarser pleasures of my boyish days,
And their glad animal movements all gone by)
To me was all in all.—I cannot paint   75
What then I was. The sounding cataract
Haunted me like a passion: the tall rock,
The mountain, and the deep and gloomy wood,
Their colors and their forms, were then to me
An appetite; a feeling and a love,   80
That had no need for a remoter charm,
By thought supplied, nor any interest
Unborrowed from the eye.—That time is past,
And all its aching joys are now no more,
And all its dizzy raptures. Not for this   85
Faint I, nor mourn nor murmur; other gifts
Have followed; for such loss, I would believe,
Abundant recompense. For I have learned
To look on nature, not as in the hour
Of thoughtless youth; but hearing oftentimes   90
The still, sad music of humanity,
Nor harsh nor grating, though of ample power
To chasten and subdue. And I have felt
A presence that disturbs me with the joy
Of elevated thoughts; a sense sublime   95
Of something far more deeply interfused,
Whose dwelling is the light of setting suns,
And the round ocean and the living air,
And the blue sky, and in the mind of man:
A motion and a spirit, that impels   100
All thinking things, all objects of all thought,
And rolls through all things. Therefore am I still
A lover of the meadows and the woods,
And mountains; and of all that we behold
From this green earth; of all the mighty world   105
Of eye, and ear,—both what they half create,
And what perceive; well pleased to recognize
In nature and the language of the sense
The anchor of my purest thoughts, the nurse,

The guide, the guardian of my heart, and soul   110
Of all my moral being.

                Nor perchance,
If I were not thus taught, should I the more
Suffer my genial spirits to decay:
For thou art with me here upon the banks
Of this fair river; thou my dearest Friend,   115
My dear, dear Friend; and in thy voice I catch
The language of my former heart, and read
My former pleasures in the shooting lights
Of thy wild eyes. Oh! yet a little while
May I behold in thee what I was once,   120
My dear, dear Sister! and this prayer I make,
Knowing that Nature never did betray
The heart that loved her; 'tis her privilege,
Through all the years of this our life, to lead
From joy to joy: for she can so inform   125
The mind that is within us, so impress
With quietness and beauty, and so feed
With lofty thoughts, that neither evil tongues,
Rash judgments, nor the sneers of selfish men,
Nor greetings where no kindness is, nor all   130
The dreary intercourse of daily life,
Shall e'er prevail against us, or disturb
Our cheerful faith, that all which we behold
Is full of blessings. Therefore let the moon
Shine on thee in thy solitary walk;   135
And let the misty mountain-winds be free
To blow against thee: and, in after years,
When these wild ecstasies shall be matured
Into a sober pleasure; when thy mind
Shall be a mansion for all lovely forms,   140
Thy memory be as a dwelling-place
For all sweet sounds and harmonies; oh! then,
If solitude, or fear, or pain, or grief,
Should be thy portion, with what healing thoughts
Of tender joy wilt thou remember me,   145
And these my exhortations! Nor, perchance—
If I should be where I no more can hear
Thy voice, nor catch from thy wild eyes these gleams
Of past existence—wilt thou then forget
That on the banks of this delightful stream   150
We stood together; and that I, so long
A worshipper of Nature, hither came
Unwearied in that service: rather say
With warmer love—oh! with far deeper zeal

Of holier love. Nor wilt thou then forget 155
That after many wanderings, many years
Of absence, these steep woods and lofty cliffs,
And this green pastoral landscape, were to me
More dear, both for themselves and for thy sake!

SURPRISED BY JOY

Surprised by joy—impatient as the Wind
I turned to share the transport—Oh! with whom
But thee, deep buried in the silent tomb,
That spot which no vicissitude can find?
Love, faithful love, recalled thee to my mind— 5
But how could I forget thee? Through what power,
Even for the least division of an hour,
Have I been so beguiled as to be blind
To my most grievous loss!—That thought's return
Was the worst pang that sorrow ever bore, 10
Save one, one only, when I stood forlorn,
Knowing my heart's best treasure was no more;
That neither present time, nor years unborn
Could to my sight that heavenly face restore.

("A Slumber Did My Spirit Seal," p. 86; "There Was a Boy," p. 112; "Yew
Trees," p. 117.)

SIR WALTER SCOTT (1771–1832)

TO A LADY
WITH FLOWERS FROM THE ROMAN WALL

Take these flowers which, purple waving,
   On the ruined rampart grew,
Where, the sons of freedom braving,
   Rome's imperial banner flew.

Warriors from the breach of danger 5
   Pluck no longer laurels there;
They but yield the passing stranger
   Wild-flower wreaths for Beauty's hair.

PROUD MAISIE

Proud Maisie is in the wood
   Walking so early;
Sweet Robin sits on the bush,
   Singing so rarely.

"Tell me, thou bonny bird,
  When shall I marry me?"— 5
"When six braw gentlemen
  Kirkward shall carry ye."

"Who makes the bridal bed,
  Birdie, say truly?"— 10
"The gray-headed sexton
  That delves the grave duly.

"The glowworm o'er grave and stone
  Shall light thee steady,
The owl from the steeple sing, 15
  'Welcome, proud lady.' "

SAMUEL TAYLOR COLERIDGE (1772–1834)

THE NIGHTINGALE

No cloud, no relique of the sunken day
Distinguishes the West, no long thin slip
Of sullen light, no obscure trembling hues.
Come, we will rest on this old mossy bridge!
You see the glimmer of the stream beneath, 5
But hear no murmuring: it flows silently,
O'er its soft bed of verdure. All is still,
A balmy night! and though the stars be dim,
Yet let us think upon the vernal showers
That gladden the green earth, and we shall find 10
A pleasure in the dimness of the stars.
And hark! the Nightingale begins its song,
"Most musical, most melancholy" bird!
A melancholy bird? Oh! idle thought!
In Nature there is nothing melancholy. 15
But some night-wandering man whose heart was pierced
With the remembrance of a grievous wrong,
Or slow distemper, or neglected love,
(And so, poor wretch! filled all things with himself,
And made all gentle sounds tell back the tale 20
Of his own sorrow) he, and such as he,
First named these notes a melancholy strain.
And many a poet echoes the conceit;
Poet who hath been building up the rhyme
When he had better far have stretched his limbs 25
Beside a brook in mossy forest-dell,
By sun or moon-light, to the influxes
Of shapes and sounds and shifting elements

Surrendering his whole spirit, of his song
And of his fame forgetful! so his fame   30
Should share in Nature's immortality,
A venerable thing! and so his song
Should make all Nature lovelier, and itself
Be loved like Nature! But 'twill not be so;
And youths and maidens most poetical,   35
Who lose the deepening twilights of the spring
In ball-rooms and hot theatres, they still
Full of meek sympathy must heave their sighs
O'er Philomela's pity-pleading strains.

My Friend, and thou, our Sister! we have learnt   40
A different lore: we may not thus profane
Nature's sweet voices, always full of love
And joyance! 'Tis the merry Nightingale
That crowds, and hurries, and precipitates
With fast thick warble his delicious notes,   45
As he were fearful that an April night
Would be too short for him to utter forth
His love-chant, and disburthen his full soul
Of all its music!

        And I know a grove
Of large extent, hard by a castle huge,   50
Which the great lord inhabits not; and so
This grove is wild with tangling underwood,
And the trim walks are broken up, and grass,
Thin grass and king-cups grow within the paths.
But never elsewhere in one place I knew   55
So many nightingales; and far and near,
In wood and thicket, over the wide grove,
They answer and provoke each other's song,
With skirmish and capricious passagings,
And murmurs musical and swift jug jug,   60
And one low piping sound more sweet than all—
Stirring the air with such a harmony,
That should you close your eyes, you might almost
Forget it was not day! On moon-light bushes,
Whose dewy leaflets are but half-disclosed,   65
You may perchance behold them on the twigs,
Their bright, bright eyes, their eyes both bright and full,
Glistening, while many a glow-worm in the shade
Lights up her love-torch.

        A most gentle Maid,
Who dwelleth in her hospitable home   70
Hard by the castle, and at latest eve

(Even like a Lady vowed and dedicate
To something more than Nature in the grove)
Glides through the pathways; she knows all their notes,
That gentle Maid! and oft, a moment's space,   75
What time the moon was lost behind a cloud,
Hath heard a pause of silence; till the moon
Emerging, hath awakened earth and sky
With one sensation, and those wakeful birds
Have all burst forth in choral minstrelsy,   80
As if some sudden gale had swept at once
A hundred airy harps! And she hath watched
Many a nightingale perch giddily
On blossomy twig still swinging from the breeze,
And to that motion tune his wanton song   85
Like tipsy Joy that reels with tossing head.

Farewell, O Warbler! till tomorrow eve,
And you, my friends! farewell, a short farewell!
We have been loitering long and pleasantly,
And now for our dear homes.—That strain again!   90
Full fain it would delay me! My dear babe,
Who, capable of no articulate sound,
Mars all things with his imitative lisp,
How he would place his hand beside his ear,
His little hand, the small forefinger up,   95
And bid us listen! And I deem it wise
To make him Nature's play-mate. He knows well
The evening-star; and once, when he awoke
In most distressful mood (some inward pain
Had made up that strange thing, an infant's dream—)   100
I hurried with him to our orchard-plot,
And he beheld the moon, and, hushed at once,
Suspends his sobs, and laughs most silently,
While his fair eyes, that swam with undropped tears,
Did glitter in the yellow moon-beams! Well!—   105
It is a father's tale: But if that Heaven
Should give me life, his childhood shall grow up
Familiar with these songs, that with the night
He may associate joy.—Once more, farewell,
Sweet Nightingale! once more, my friends! farewell.   110

KUBLA KHAN

In Xanadu did Kubla Khan
A stately pleasure-dome decree:
Where Alph, the sacred river, ran

Through caverns measureless to man
   Down to a sunless sea.   5
So twice five miles of fertile ground
With walls and towers were girdled round:
And there were gardens bright with sinuous rills,
Where blossomed many an incense-bearing tree;
And here were forests ancient as the hills,   10
Enfolding sunny spots of greenery.

But oh, that deep romantic chasm which slanted
Down the green hill athwart a cedarn cover!
A savage place! as holy and enchanted
As e'er beneath a waning moon was haunted   15
By woman wailing for her demon-lover!
And from this chasm, with ceaseless turmoil seething,
As if this earth in fast thick pants were breathing,
A mighty fountain momently was forced:
Amid whose swift half-intermitted burst   20
Huge fragments vaulted like rebounding hail,
Or chaffy grain beneath the thresher's flail:
And 'mid these dancing rocks at once and ever
It flung up momently the sacred river.
Five miles meandering with a mazy motion   25
Through wood and dale the sacred river ran,
Then reached the caverns measureless to man,
And sank in tumult to a lifeless ocean:
And 'mid this tumult Kubla heard from far
Ancestral voices prophesying war!   30
   The shadow of the dome of pleasure
   Floated midway on the waves;
   Where was heard the mingled measure
   From the fountain and the caves.
It was a miracle of rare device,   35
A sunny pleasure-dome with caves of ice!

   A damsel with a dulcimer
   In a vision once I saw:
   It was an Abyssinian maid,
   And on her dulcimer she played,   40
   Singing of Mount Abora.
Could I revive within me
Her symphony and song,
To such a deep delight 'twould win me,
That with music loud and long,   45
I would build that dome in air,
That sunny dome! those caves of ice!
And all who heard should see them there,
And all should cry, Beware! Beware!

His flashing eyes, his floating hair!   50
Weave a circle round him thrice.
And close your eyes with holy dread,
For he on honey-dew hath fed,
And drunk the milk of Paradise.

GEORGE GORDON, LORD BYRON   (1788–1824)

THE DREAM

I

Our life is twofold: Sleep hath its own world,
A boundary between the things misnamed
Death and existence: Sleep hath its own world,
And a wide realm of wild reality,
And dreams in their development have breath,   5
And tears, and tortures, and the touch of joy;
They leave a weight upon our waking thoughts,
They take a weight from off our waking toils,
They do divide our being; they become
A portion of ourselves as of our time,   10
And look like heralds of eternity;
They pass like spirits of the past,—they speak
Like sibyls of the future; they have power—
The tyranny of pleasure and of pain;
They make us what we were not—what they will,   15
And shake us with the vision that's gone by,
The dread of vanished shadows—Are they so?
Is not the past all shadow? What are they?
Creations of the mind?—The mind can make
Substance, and people planets of its own   20
With beings brighter than have been, and give
A breath to forms which can outlive all flesh.
I would recall a vision which I dreamed
Perchance in sleep—for in itself a thought,
A slumbering thought, is capable of years,   25
And curdles a long life into one hour.

II

I saw two beings in the hues of youth
Standing upon a hill, a gentle hill,
Green and of mild declivity, the last
As 'twere the cape of a long ridge of such,   30
Save that there was no sea to lave its base,
But a most living landscape, and the wave
Of woods and cornfields, and the abodes of men

Scattered at intervals, and wreathing smoke
Arising from such rustic roofs;—the hill   35
Was crowned with a peculiar diadem
Of trees, in circular array, so fixed,
Not by the sport of nature, but of man:
These two, a maiden and a youth, were there
Gazing—the one on all that was beneath   40
Fair as herself—but the boy gazed on her;
And both were young, and one was beautiful:
And both were young—yet not alike in youth.
As the sweet moon on the horizon's verge,
The maid was on the eve of womanhood;   45
The boy had fewer summers, but his heart
Had far outgrown his years, and to his eye
There was but one belovéd face on earth,
And that was shining on him; he had looked
Upon it till it could not pass away;   50
He had no breath, no being, but in hers:
She was his voice; he did not speak to her,
But trembled on her words: she was his sight,
For his eyes followed hers, and saw with hers,
Which colored all his objects:—he had ceased   55
To live within himself; she was his life,
The ocean to the river of his thoughts,
Which terminated all: upon a tone,
A touch of hers, his blood would ebb and flow,
And his cheek change tempestuously—his heart   60
Unknowing of its cause of agony.
But she in these fond feelings had no share:
Her sighs were not for him; to her he was
Even as a brother—but no more; t'was much,
For brotherless she was, save in the name   65
Her infant friendship had bestowed on him;
Herself the solitary scion left
Of a time-honored race.—It was a name
Which pleased him, and yet pleased him not—and why?
Time taught him a deep answer—when she loved   70
Another; even *now* she loved another,
And on the summit of that hill she stood
Looking afar if yet her lover's steed
Kept pace with her expectancy, and flew.

III
A change came o'er the spirit of my dream.   75
There was an ancient mansion, and before
Its walls there was a steed caparisoned:
Within an antique Oratory stood

The Boy of whom I spake;—he was alone,
And pale, and pacing to and fro: anon   80
He sat him down, and seized a pen, and traced
Words which I could not guess of; then he leaned
His bowed head on his hands, and shook as 'twere
With a convulsion—then arose again,
And with his teeth and quivering hands did tear   85
What he had written, but he shed no tears.
And he did calm himself, and fix his brow
Into a kind of quiet: as he paused,
The Lady of his love re-entered there;
She was serene and smiling then, and yet   90
She knew she was by him beloved,—she knew,
For quickly comes such knowledge, that his heart
Was darkened with her shadow, and she saw
That he was wretched, but she saw not all.
He rose, and with a cold and gentle grasp   95
He took her hand; a moment o'er his face
A tablet of unutterable thoughts
Was traced, and then it faded, as it came;
He dropped the hand he held, and with slow steps
Retired, but not as bidding her adieu,   100
For they did part with mutual smiles; he passed
From out the massy gate of that old Hall,
And mounting on his steed he went his way;
And ne'er repassed that hoary threshold more.

IV

A change came o'er the spirit of my dream.   105
The Boy was sprung to manhood: in the wilds
Of fiery climes he made himself a home,
And his Soul drank their sunbeams: he was girt
With strange and dusky aspects; he was not
Himself like what he had been; on the sea   110
And on the shore he was a wanderer;
There was a mass of many images
Crowded like waves upon me, but he was
A part of all; and in the last he lay
Reposing from the noontide sultriness,   115
Couched among fallen columns, in the shade
Of ruined walls that had survived the names
Of those who reared them; by his sleeping side
Stood camels grazing, and some goodly steeds
Were fastened near a fountain; and a man   120
Clad in a flowing garb did watch the while,
While many of his tribe slumbered around:
And they were canopied by the blue sky,

So cloudless, clear, and purely beautiful,
That God alone was to be seen in Heaven.   125

V

A change came o'er the spirit of my dream.
The Lady of his love was wed with One
Who did not love her better:—in her home,
A thousand leagues from his,—her native home,
She dwelt, begirt with growing Infancy,   130
Daughters and sons of Beauty,—but behold!
Upon her face there was the tint of grief,
The settled shadow of an inward strife,
And an unquiet drooping of the eye,
As if its lid were charged with unshed tears.   135
What could her grief be?—she had all she loved,
And he who had so loved her was not there
To trouble with bad hopes, or evil wish,
Or ill-repressed affliction, her pure thoughts.
What could her grief be?—she had loved him not,   140
Nor given him cause to deem himself beloved,
Nor could he be a part of that which preyed
Upon her mind—a specter of the past.

VI

A change came o'er the spirit of my dream.
The Wanderer was returned.—I saw him stand   145
Before an Altar—with a gentle bride;
Her face was fair, but was not that which made
The Starlight of his Boyhood;—as he stood
Even at the altar, o'er his brow there came
The selfsame aspect, and the quivering shock   150
That in the antique Oratory shook
His bosom in its solitude; and then—
As in that hour—a moment o'er his face
The tablet of unutterable thoughts
Was traced—and then it faded as it came,   155
And he stood calm and quiet, and he spoke
The fitting vows, but heard not his own words,
And all things reeled around him; he could see
Not that which was, nor that which should have been—
But the old mansion, and the accustomed hall,   160
And the remembered chambers, and the place,
The day, the hour, the sunshine, and the shade,
All things pertaining to that place and hour,
And her who was his destiny, came back
And thrust themselves between him and the light: 165
What business had they there at such a time?

VII

A change came o'er the spirit of my dream.
The Lady of his love;—Oh! she was changed,
As by the sickness of the soul; her mind
Had wandered from its dwelling, and her eyes,   170
They had not their own luster, but the look
Which is not of the earth; she was become
The queen of a fantastic realm; her thoughts
Were combinations of disjointed things;
And forms impalpable and unperceived   175
Of others' sight familiar were to hers.
And this the world calls frenzy; but the wise
Have a far deeper madness, and the glance
Of melancholy is a fearful gift;
What is it but a telescope of truth?   180
Which strips the distance of its fantasies,
And brings life near in utter nakedness,
Making the cold reality too real!

VIII

A change came o'er the spirit of my dream
The Wanderer was alone as heretofore,   185
The beings which surrounded him were gone,
Or were at war with him; he was a mark
For blight and desolation, compassed round
With Hatred and Contention; Pain was mixed
In all which was served up to him, until,   190
Like to the Pontic monarch of old days,
He fed on poisons, and they had no power,
But were a kind of nutriment; he lived
Through that which had been death to many men,
And made him friends of mountains: with the stars   195
And the quick Spirit of the Universe
He held his dialogues! and they did teach
To him the magic of their mysteries;
To him the book of Night was opened wide,
And voices from the deep abyss revealed   200
A marvel and a secret—Be it so.

IX

My dream was past; it had no further change.
It was of a strange order, that the doom
Of these two creatures should be thus traced out
Almost like a reality—the one   205
To end in madness—both in misery.

191. *Pontic monarch:* Mithridates, who survived the poison fed to him by his enemies.

EPIGRAMS

Oh, Castlereagh! thou art a patriot now;
Cato died for his country, so didst thou:
He perished rather than see Rome enslaved,
Thou cut'st thy throat that Britain may be saved!

So Castlereagh has cut his throat!—The worst
Of this is,—that his own was not the first.

So *He* has cut his throat at last!—He! Who?
The man who cut his country's long ago.

LINES TO MR. HODGSON
WRITTEN ON BOARD THE LISBON PACKET

Huzza! Hodgson, we are going,
   Our embargo's off at last;
Favorable breezes blowing
   Bend the canvas o'er the mast.
From aloft the signal's streaming,   5
   Hark! the farewell gun is fired;
Women screeching, tars blaspheming,
   Tell us that our time's expired.
      Here's a rascal
      Come to task all,   10
Prying from the custom-house;
      Trunks unpacking
      Cases cracking,
Not a corner for a mouse
'Scapes unsearched amid the racket,   15
Ere we sail on board the Packet.

Now our boatmen quit the mooring,
   And all hands must ply the oar;
Baggage from the quay is lowering,
   We're impatient, push from shore.   20
"Have a care! that case holds liquor—
   Stop the boat—I'm sick—oh Lord!"
"Sick, Ma'am, damme, you'll be sicker,
   Ere you've been an hour on board."
      Thus are screaming   25
      Men and women,
Gemmen, ladies, servants, Jacks;
      Here entangling,
      All are wrangling,

Stuck together close as wax.—   30
Such the general noise and racket,
Ere we reach the Lisbon Packet.

Now we've reached her, lo! the Captain,
    Gallant Kidd, commands the crew;
Passengers their berths are clapped in,   35
    Some to grumble, some to spew.
"Hey day! call you that a cabin?
Why 'tis hardly three feet square:
Not enough to stow Queen Mab in—
    Who the deuce can harbor there?"   40
        "Who, sir? plenty—
        Nobles twenty
Did at once my vessel fill."—
        "Did they? Jesus,
        How you squeeze us!
    Would to God they did so still: 45
Then I'd 'scape the heat and racket
Of the good ship, Lisbon Packet."

Fletcher! Murray! Bob! where are you?
    Stretched along the deck like logs—   50
Bear a hand, you jolly tar, you!
    Here's a rope's end for the dogs.
Hobhouse muttering fearful curses,
    As the hatchway down he rolls,
Now his breakfast, now his verses,   55
    Vomits forth—and damns our souls.
        "Here's a stanza
        On Braganza—
Help!"—"A couplet?"—"No, a cup
        Of warm water—"   60
        "What's the matter?"
    "Zounds! my liver's coming up;
I shall not survive the racket
Of this brutal Lisbon Packet."

Now at length we're off for Turkey,   65
    Lord knows when we shall come back!
Breezes foul and tempests murky
    May unship us in a crack.
But, since Life at most a jest is,
    As philosophers allow,   70
Still to laugh by far the best is,
    Then laugh on—as I do now.
        Laugh at all things,

49. *Fletcher, Murray, and Bob:* Byron's servants; 53. *Hobhouse:* John Hobhouse, a friend.

Great and small things,
Sick or well, at sea or shore;   75
While we're quaffing,
Let's have laughing—
Who the devil cares for more?—
Some good wine! and who would lack it,
Ev'n on board the Lisbon Packet?

PERCY BYSSHE SHELLEY (1792–1822)

ODE TO THE WEST WIND

I
O wild West Wind, thou breath of Autumn's being,
Thou, from whose unseen presence the leaves dead
Are driven, like ghosts from an enchanter fleeing,

Yellow, and black, and pale, and hectic red,
Pestilence-stricken multitudes: O thou,   5
Who chariotest to their dark wintry bed

The wingéd seeds, where they lie cold and low,
Each like a corpse within its grave, until
Thine azure sister of the Spring shall blow

Her clarion o'er the dreaming earth, and fill   10
(Driving sweet buds like flocks to feed in air)
With living hues and odors plain and hill:

Wild Spirit, which art moving everywhere;
Destroyer and preserver; hear, oh, hear!

II
Thou on whose stream, mid the steep sky's commotion,   15
Loose clouds like earth's decaying leaves are shed,
Shook from the tangled boughs of Heaven and Ocean,

Angels of rain and lightning: there are spread
On the blue surface of thine aëry surge,
Like the bright hair uplifted from the head   20

Of some fierce Maenad, even from the dim verge
Of the horizon to the zenith's height,
The locks of the approaching storm. Thou dirge

Of the dying year, to which this closing night
Will be the dome of a vast sepulcher,   25
Vaulted with all thy congregated might

Of vapors, from whose solid atmosphere
Black rain, and fire, and hail will burst: oh, hear!

III

Thou who didst waken from his summer dreams
The blue Mediterranean, where he lay,   30
Lulled by the coil of his crystálline streams,

Beside a pumice isle in Baiæ's bay,
And saw in sleep old palaces and towers
Quivering within the wave's intenser day,

All overgrown with azure moss and flowers   35
So sweet, the sense faints picturing them! Thou
For whose path the Atlantic's level powers

Cleave themselves into chasms, while far below
The sea-blooms and the oozy woods which wear
The sapless foliage of the ocean, know   40

Thy voice, and suddenly grow gray with fear,
And tremble and despoil themselves: oh, hear!

IV

If I were a dead leaf thou mightest bear;
If I were a swift cloud to fly with thee;
A wave to pant beneath thy power, and share   45

The impulse of thy strength, only less free
Than thou, O uncontrollable! If even
I were as in my boyhood, and could be

The comrade of thy wanderings over Heaven,
As then, when to outstrip thy skiey speed   50
Scarce seemed a vision; I would ne'er have striven

As thus with thee in prayer in my sore need.
Oh, lift me as a wave, a leaf, a cloud!
I fall upon the thorns of life! I bleed!

A heavy weight of hours has chained and bowed   55
One too like thee: tameless, and swift, and proud.

V

Make me thy lyre, even as the forest is:
What if my leaves are falling like its own!
The tumult of thy mighty harmonies

Will take from both a deep, autumnal tone,   60
Sweet though in sadness. Be thou, Spirit fierce,
My spirit! Be thou me, impetuous one!

32. *Baiæ's bay:* a bay near Naples.

Drive my dead thoughts over the universe
Like withered leaves to quicken a new birth!
And, by the incantation of this verse,   65

Scatter, as from an unextinguished hearth
Ashes and sparks, my words among mankind!
Be through my lips to unawakened Earth

The trumpet of a prophecy! O Wind,
If Winter comes, can Spring be far behind?   70

("Music, When Soft Voices Die," p. 94.)

JOHN CLARE   (1793–1864)

SONG LAST DAY

There is a day a dreadful day
Still following the past
When sun and moon are past away
And mingle with the blast
There is a vision in my eye   5
A vacuum o'er my mind
Sometimes as on the sea I lie
Mid roaring waves and wind

When valleys rise to mountain waves
And mountains sink to seas   10
When towns and cities temples graves
All vanish like a breeze
The skies that were are past and o'er
That almanac of days
Year chronicles are kept no more   15
Oblivions ruin pays

Pays in destruction shades and hell
Sin goes in darkness down
And there in sulphurs shadows dwell
Worth wins and wears the crown   20
The very shore if shore I see
All shrivelled to a scroll
The Heaven's rend away from me
And thunders sulphurs roll

Black as the deadly thunder cloud   25
The stars shall turn to dun
And heaven by that darkness bowed
Shall make days light be done

When stars and skies shall all decay
And earth no more shall be   30
When heaven itself shall pass away
Then thou'lt remember me

MARCH VIOLET

Where last year leaves and weeds decay
March violets are in blow
I'd rake the rubbish all away
And give them room to grow

Near neighbor to the Arum proud   5
Where dew drops fall and sleep
As purple as a fallen cloud
March violets bloom and creep

Scenting the gales of early morn
They smell before they're seen   10
Peeping beneath the old white thorn
That shows its tender green

The lamb will nibble by their bloom
And eat them day by day
Till briars forbid his steps to come   15
And then he skips away

Mid nettle stalks that wither there
And on the greensward lie
All bleaching in the thin March air
The scattered violets lie   20

I know the place it is a place
In spring where nettles come
There milk white violets show their face
And blue ones earlier bloom

JOHN KEATS   (1795–1821)

ON THE SONNET

If by dull rhymes our English must be chained,
     And, like Andromeda, the Sonnet sweet
Fettered, in spite of painéd loveliness;
Let us find out, if we must be constrained,
     Sandals more interwoven and complete   5
To fit the naked foot of poesy;

Let us inspect the lyre, and weigh the stress
Of every chord, and see what may be gained
 By ear industrious, and attention meet;
Misers of sound and syllable, no less   10
Than Midas of his coinage, let us be
 Jealous of dead leaves in the bay-wreath crown;
So, if we may not let the Muse be free,
 She will be bound with garlands of her own.

ODE TO PSYCHE

O Goddess! hear these tuneless numbers, wrung
 By sweet enforcement and remembrance dear,
And pardon that thy secrets should be sung
 Even into thine own soft-conchéd ear:
Surely I dreamt today, or did I see   5
 The wingéd Psyche with awakened eyes?
I wandered in a forest thoughtlessly,
 And, on the sudden, fainting with surprise,
Saw two fair creatures, couchéd side by side
 In deepest grass, beneath the whisp'ring roof 10
Of leaves and trembled blossoms, where there ran
 A brooklet, scarce espied:

'Mid hushed, cool-rooted flowers, fragrant-eyed,
 Blue, silver-white, and budded Tyrian,
They lay calm-breathing on the bedded grass; 15
 Their arms embracéd, and their pinions too;
 Their lips touched not, but had not bade adieu,
As if disjoinéd by soft-handed slumber,
And ready still past kisses to outnumber
 At tender eye-dawn of aurorean love: 20
  The wingéd boy I knew;
 But who wast thou, O happy, happy dove?
  His Psyche true!

O latest born and loveliest vision far
 Of all Olympus' faded hierarchy!   25
Fairer than Phoebe's sapphire-regioned star,
 Or Vesper, amorous glowworm of the sky;
Fairer than these, though temple thou hast none,
 Nor altar heaped with flowers;
Nor virgin choir to make delicious moan   30
 Upon the midnight hours;
No voice, no lute, no pipe, no incense sweet
 From chain-swung censer teeming;
No shrine, no grove, no oracle, no heat
 Of pale-mouthed prophet dreaming.   35

O brightest! though too late for antique vows,
    Too, too late for the fond believing lyre,
When holy were the haunted forest boughs,
    Holy the air, the water, and the fire;
Yet even in these days so far retired   40
    From happy pieties, thy lucent fans,
    Fluttering among the faint Olympians,
I see, and sing, by my own eyes inspired.
So let me be thy choir, and make a moan
        Upon the midnight hours;   45
Thy voice, thy lute, thy pipe, thy incense sweet
    From swingéd censer teeming;
Thy shrine, thy grove, thy oracle, thy heat
    Of pale-mouthed prophet dreaming.

Yes, I will be thy priest, and build a fane   50
    In some untrodden region of my mind,
Where branchéd thoughts, new grown with pleasant pain,
    Instead of pines shall murmur in the wind:
Far, far around shall those dark-clustered trees
    Fledge the wild-ridged mountains steep by steep,   55
And there by zephyrs, streams, and birds, and bees,
    The moss-lain Dryads shall be lulled to sleep;
And in the midst of this wide quietness
A rosy sanctuary will I dress
With the wreathed trellis of a working brain,   60
    With buds, and bells, and stars without a name,
With all the gardener Fancy e'er could feign,
    Who breeding flowers, will never breed the same:
And there shall be for thee all soft delight
    That shadowy thought can win,   65
A bright torch, and a casement ope at night,
    To let the warm Love in!

ODE ON A GRECIAN URN

I

Thou still unravished bride of quietness,
    Thou foster-child of silence and slow time,
Sylvan historian, who canst thus express
    A flowery tale more sweetly than our rhyme:
What leaf-fringed legend haunts about thy shape   5
    Of deities or mortals, or of both,
        In Tempe or the dales of Arcady?
What men or gods are these? What maidens loth?
    What mad pursuit? What struggle to escape?
        What pipes and timbrels? What wild ecstacy?   10

II

Heard melodies are sweet, but those unheard
  Are sweeter; therefore, ye soft pipes, play on;
Not to the sensual ear, but, more endeared,
  Pipe to the spirit ditties of no tone:
Fair youth, beneath the trees, thou canst not leave   15
  Thy song, nor ever can those trees be bare;
    Bold Lover, never, never canst thou kiss,
Though winning near the goal—yet, do not grieve;
  She cannot fade, though thou hast not thy bliss,
    For ever wilt thou love, and she be fair!   20

III

Ah, happy, happy boughs! that cannot shed
  Your leaves, nor ever bid the Spring adieu;
And, happy melodist, unweariéd,
  For ever piping songs for ever new;
More happy love! more happy, happy love!   25
  For ever warm and still to be enjoyed,
    For ever panting, and for ever young;
All breathing human passion far above,
  That leaves a heart high-sorrowful and cloyed,
    A burning forehead, and a parching tongue.   30

IV

Who are these coming to the sacrifice?
  To what green altar, O mysterious priest,
Lead'st thou that heifer lowing at the skies,
  And all her silken flanks with garlands dressed?
What little town by river or sea shore,   35
  Or mountain-built with peaceful citadel,
    Is emptied of this folk, this pious morn?
And, little town, thy streets for evermore
  Will silent be; and not a soul to tell
    Why thou art desolate, can e'er return.   40

V

O Attic shape! Fair attitude! with brede
  Of marble men and maidens overwrought,
With forest branches and the trodden weed;
  Thou, silent form, dost tease us out of thought
As doth eternity: Cold Pastoral!   45
  When old age shall this generation waste,
    Thou shalt remain, in midst of other woe
Than ours, a friend to man, to whom thou say'st,
  Beauty is truth, truth beauty,—that is all
    Ye know on earth, and all ye need to know.   50

ODE ON MELANCHOLY

I

No, no, go not to Lethe, neither twist
   Wolf's bane, tight-rooted, for its poisonous wine,
Nor suffer thy pale forehead to be kissed
   By nightshade, ruby grape of Proserpine;
Make not your rosary of yew-berries,   5
    Nor let the beetle, nor the death-moth be
      Your mournful Psyche, nor the downy owl
A partner in your sorrow's mysteries;
    For shade to shade will come too drowsily,
      And drown the wakeful anguish of the soul.   10

II

But when the melancholy fit shall fall
   Sudden from heaven like a weeping cloud,
That fosters the droop-headed flowers all,
   And hides the green hill in an April shroud;
Then glut thy sorrow on a morning rose,   15
    Or on the rainbow of the salt sand-wave,
      Or on the wealth of globèd-peonies;
Or if thy mistress some rich anger shows,
    Emprison her soft hand, and let her rave,
      And feed deep, deep upon her peerless eyes.   20

III

She dwells with Beauty—Beauty that must die;
   And Joy, whose hand is ever at his lips
Bidding adieu; and aching Pleasure nigh,
   Turning to Poison while the bee-mouth sips:
Ay, in the very temple of Delight   25
    Veiled Melancholy has her sov'reign shrine,
      Though seen of none save him whose strenuous tongue
Can burst Joy's grape against his palate fine;
   His soul shall taste the sadness of her might,
    And be among her cloudy trophies hung.   30

TO AUTUMN

I

Season of mists and mellow fruitfulness,
   Close bosom-friend of the maturing sun;
Conspiring with him how to load and bless
   With fruit the vines that round the thatch-eves run;
To bend with apples the mossed cottage-trees,   5

And fill all fruit with ripeness to the core;
  To swell the gourd, and plump the hazel shells
With a sweet kernel; to set budding more,
  And still more, later flowers for the bees,
  Until they think warm days will never cease,   10
  For Summer has o'er-brimmed their clammy cells.

II
Who hath not seen thee oft amid thy store?
  Sometimes whoever seeks abroad may find
Thee sitting careless on a granary floor,
  Thy hair soft-lifted by the winnowing wind;   15
Or on a half-reaped furrow sound asleep,
  Drowsed with the fume of poppies, while thy hook
  Spares the next swath and all its twinéd flowers:
And sometimes like a gleaner thou dost keep
  Steady thy laden head across a brook;   20
  Or by a cider-press, with patient look,
  Thou watchest the last oozings hours by hours.

III
Where are the songs of Spring? Ay, where are they?
  Think not of them, thou hast thy music too,—
While barréd clouds bloom the soft-dying day,   25
  And touch the stubble-plains with rosy hue;
Then in a wailful choir the small gnats mourn
  Among the river sallows, borne aloft
  Or sinking as the light wind lives or dies;
And full-grown lambs loud bleat from hilly bourn;   30
  Hedge-crickets sing; and now with treble soft
  The red-breast whistles from a garden-croft;
  And gathering swallows twitter in the skies.

("When I Have Fears," p. 15; "Bright Star," p. 93; "La Belle Dame Sans Merci,"
p. 150.)

ALFRED, LORD TENNYSON   (1809–1892)
ULYSSES

It little profits that an idle king,
By this still hearth, among these barren crags,
Matched with an agéd wife, I mete and dole
Unequal laws unto a savage race,
That hoard, and sleep, and feed, and know not me.   5
I cannot rest from travel; I will drink
Life to the lees. All times I have enjoyed
Greatly, have suffered greatly, both with those

That loved me, and alone; on shore, and when
Through scudding drifts the rainy Hyades   10
Vexed the dim sea. I am become a name;
For always roaming with a hungry heart
Much have I seen and known,—cities of men
And manners, climates, councils, governments,
Myself not least, but honored of them all,—   15
And drunk delight of battle with my peers,
Far on the ringing plains of windy Troy.
I am a part of all that I have met;
Yet all experience is an arch wherethrough
Gleams that untravelled world whose margin fades   20
For ever and for ever when I move.
How dull it is to pause, to make an end,
To rust unburnished, not to shine in use!
As though to breathe were life! Life piled on life
Were all too little, and of one to me   25
Little remains; but every hour is saved
From that eternal silence, something more,
A bringer of new things; and vile it were
For some three suns to store and hoard myself,
And this gray spirit yearning in desire   30
To follow knowledge like a sinking star,
Beyond the utmost bound of human thought.
    This is my son, mine own Telemachus,
To whom I leave the scepter and the isle,—
Well-loved of me, discerning to fulfil   35
This labor, by slow prudence to make mild
A rugged people, and through soft degrees
Subdue them to the useful and the good.
Most blameless is he, centered in the sphere
Of common duties, decent not to fail   40
In offices of tenderness, and pay
Meet adoration to my household gods,
When I am gone. He works his work, I mine.
    There lies the port; the vessel puffs her sail;
There gloom the dark, broad seas. My mariners,   45
Souls that have toiled, and wrought, and thought with me,—
That ever with a frolic welcome took
The thunder and the sunshine, and opposed
Free hearts, free foreheads,—you and I are old;
Old age hath yet his honor and his toil.   50
Death closes all; but something ere the end,
Some work of noble note, may yet be done,
Not unbecoming men that strove with Gods.
The lights begin to twinkle from the rocks:

The long day wanes: the slow moon climbs: the deep   55
Moans round with many voices. Come, my friends,
'Tis not too late to seek a newer world.
Push off, and sitting well in order smite
The sounding furrows; for my purpose holds
To sail beyond the sunset, and the baths   60
Of all the western stars, until I die.
It may be that the gulfs will wash us down:
It may be we shall touch the Happy Isles,
And see the great Achilles, whom we knew.
Though much is taken, much abides; and though   65
We are not now that strength which in old days
Moved earth and heaven; that which we are, we are;
One equal temper of heroic hearts,
Made weak by time and fate, but strong in will
To strive, to seek, to find, and not to yield.   70

TITHONUS

The woods decay, the woods decay and fall,
The vapors weep their burthen to the ground,
Man comes and tills the field and lies beneath,
And after many a summer dies the swan.
Me only cruel immortality   5
Consumes: I wither slowly in thine arms,
Here at the quiet limit of the world,
A white-haired shadow roaming like a dream
The ever-silent spaces of the East,
Far-folded mists, and gleaming halls of morn.   10
   Alas! for this gray shadow, once a man—
So glorious in his beauty and thy choice,
Who madest him thy chosen, that he seemed
To his great heart none other than a God!
I asked thee, "Give me immortality."   15
Then didst thou grant mine asking with a smile,
Like wealthy men who care not how they give.
But thy strong Hours indignant worked their wills,
And beat me down and marred and wasted me,
And though they could not end me, left me maimed   20
To dwell in presence of immortal youth,
Immortal age beside immortal youth,
And all I was, in ashes. Can thy love,
Thy beauty, make amends, though even now
Close over us, the silver star, thy guide,   25
Shines in those tremulous eyes that fill with tears
To hear me? Let me go: take back thy gift:

Why should a man desire in any way
To vary from the kindly race of men,
Or pass beyond the goal of ordinance   30
Where all should pause, as is most meet for all?
   A soft air fans the cloud apart: there comes
A glimpse of that dark world where I was born.
Once more the old mysterious glimmer steals
From thy pure brows, and from thy shoulders pure,   35
And bosom beating with a heart renewed.
Thy cheek begins to redden through the gloom,
Thy sweet eyes brighten slowly close to mine,
Ere yet they blind the stars, and the wild team
Which love thee, yearning for thy yoke, arise,   40
And shake the darkness from their loosened manes,
And beat the twilight into flakes of fire.
   Lo! ever thus thou growest beautiful
In silence, then before thine answer given
Departest, and thy tears are on my cheek.   45
   Why wilt thou ever scare me with thy tears,
And make me tremble lest a saying learnt,
In days far-off, on that dark earth, be true?
"The Gods themselves cannot recall their gifts."
   Ay me! ay me! with what another heart   50
In days far-off, and with what other eyes
I used to watch—if I be he that watched—
The lucid outline forming round thee; saw
The dim curls kindle into sunny rings;
Changed with thy mystic change, and felt my blood   55
Glow with the glow that slowly crimsoned all
Thy presence and thy portals, while I lay,
Mouth, forehead, eyelids, growing dewy-warm
With kisses balmier than half-opening buds
Of April, and could hear the lips that kissed   60
Whispering I knew not what of wild and sweet,
Like that strange song I heard Apollo sing,
While Ilion like a mist rose into towers.
   Yet hold me not for ever in thine East;
How can my nature longer mix with thine?   65
Coldly thy rosy shadows bathe me, cold
Are all thy lights, and cold my wrinkled feet
Upon thy glimmering thresholds, when the steam
Floats up from those fields about the homes
Of happy men that have the power to die,   70
And grassy barrows of the happier dead.
Release me, and restore me to the ground.
Thou seest all things, thou wilt see my grave;
Thou wilt renew thy beauty morn by morn,

I earth in earth forget these empty courts,   75
   And thee returning on thy silver wheels.

("Sonnet," p. 91; "Break, Break, Break," p. 75; "Crossing the Bar," p. 10.)

ROBERT BROWNING   (1812–1889)

CHILDE ROLAND TO THE DARK TOWER CAME

(See Edgar's Song in *Lear*)

1

My first thought was, he lied in every word,
   That hoary cripple, with malicious eye
   Askance to watch the working of his lie
On mine, and mouth scarce able to afford
Suppression of the glee, that pursed and scored   5
   Its edge, at one more victim gained thereby.

2

What else should he be set for, with his staff?
   What, save to waylay with his lies, ensnare
   All travelers who might find him posted there,
And ask the road? I guessed what skull-like laugh   10
Would break, what crutch 'gin write my epitaph
   For pastime in the dusty thoroughfare,

3

If at his counsel I should turn aside
   Into that ominous tract which, all agree,
   Hides the Dark Tower. Yet acquiescingly   15
I did turn as he pointed: neither pride
Nor hope rekindling at the end descried,
   So much as gladness that some end might be.

4

For, what with my whole world-wide wandering,
   What with my search drawn out through years, my hope   20
   Dwindled into a ghost not fit to cope
With that obstreperous joy success would bring,
I hardly tried now to rebuke the spring
   My heart made, finding failure in its scope.

5

As when a sick man very near to death   25
   Seems dead indeed, and feels begin and end
   The tears and takes the farewell of each friend,

And hears one bid the other go, draw breath
Freelier outside ("since all is o'er," he saith,
    "And the blow fallen no grieving can amend").   30

6

While some discuss if near the other graves
    Be room enough for this, and when a day
    Suits best for carrying the corpse away,
With care about the banners, scarves and staves:
And still the man hears all, and only craves   35
    He may not shame such tender love and stay.

7

Thus, I had so long suffered in this quest,
    Heard failure prophesied so oft, been writ
    So many times among "The Band"—to wit,
The knights who to the Dark Tower's search addressed   40
Their steps—that just to fail as they, seemed best,
    And all the doubt was now—should I be fit?

8

So, quiet as despair, I turned from him,
    That hateful cripple, out of his highway
    Into the path he pointed. All the day   45
Had been a dreary one at best, and dim
Was settling to its close, yet shot one grim
    Red leer to see the plain catch its estray.

9

For mark! no sooner was I fairly found
    Pledged to the plain, after a pace or two,   50
    Than, pausing to throw backward a last view
O'er the safe road, 'twas gone; gray plain all round:
Nothing but plain to the horizon's bound.
    I might go on; naught else remained to do.

10

So, on I went. I think I never saw   55
    Such starved ignoble nature; nothing throve:
    For flowers—as well expect a cedar grove!
But cockle, spurge, according to their law
Might propagate their kind, with none to awe,
    You'd think; a burr had been a treasure trove.   60

11

No! penury, inertness and grimace,
    In some strange sort, were the land's portion. "See
    Or shut your eyes," said Nature peevishly,
"It nothing skills: I cannot help my case;

'Tis the Last Judgment's fire must cure this place, 65
    Calcine its clods and set my prisoners free."

12

If there pushed any ragged thistle stalk
    Above its mates, the head was chopped; the bents
    Were jealous else. What made those holes and rents
In the dock's harsh swarth leaves, bruised as to balk 70
All hope of greenness? 'tis a brute must walk
    Pashing their life out, with a brute's intents.

13

As for the grass, it grew as scant as hair
    In leprosy; thin dry blades pricked the mud
    Which underneath looked kneaded up with blood. 75
One stiff blind horse, his every bone a-stare,
Stood stupefied, however he came there:
    Thrust out past service from the devil's stud!

14

Alive? he might be dead for aught I know,
    With that red gaunt and colloped neck a-strain, 80
    And shut eyes underneath the rusty mane;
Seldom went such grotesqueness with such woe;
I never saw a brute I hated so;
    He must be wicked to deserve such pain.

15

I shut my eyes and turned them on my heart. 85
    As a man calls for wine before he fights,
    I asked one draught of earlier, happier sights,
Ere fitly I could hope to play my part.
Think first, fight afterwards—the soldier's art:
    One taste of the old times sets all to rights. 90

16

Not it! I fancied Cuthbert's reddened face
    Beneath its garniture of curly gold,
    Dear fellow, till I almost felt him fold
An arm in mine to fix me to the place,
That way he used. Alas, one night's disgrace! 95
    Out went my heart's new fire and left it cold.

17

Giles then, the soul of honor—there he stands
    Frank as ten years ago when knighted first.
    What honest man should dare (he said) he durst.
Good—but the scene shifts—faugh! what hangman hands 100
Pin to his breast a parchment? His own bands
    Read it. Poor traitor, spit upon and cursed!

18

Better this present than a past like that;
　　Back therefore to my darkening path again!
　　No sound, no sight as far as eye could strain.　　105
Will the night send a howlet or a bat?
I asked: when something on the dismal flat
　　Came to arrest my thoughts and change their train.

19

A sudden little river crossed my path
　　As unexpected as a serpent comes.　　110
　　No sluggish tide congenial to the glooms;
This, as it frothed by, might have been a bath
For the fiend's glowing hoof—to see the wrath
　　Of its black eddy bespate with flakes and spumes.

20

So petty yet so spiteful! All along,　　115
　　Low scrubby alders kneeled down over it;
　　Drenched willows flung them headlong in a fit
Of mute despair, a suicidal throng:
The river which had done them all the wrong,
　　Whate'er that was, rolled by, deterred no whit.　　120

21

Which, while I forded—good saints, how I feared
　　To set my foot upon a dead man's cheek,
　　Each step, or feel the spear I thrust to seek
For hollows, tangled in his hair or beard!
—It may have been a water rat I speared,　　125
　　But, ugh! it sounded like a baby's shriek.

22

Glad was I when I reached the other bank.
　　Now for a better country. Vain presage!
　　Who were the strugglers, what war did they wage,
Whose savage trample thus could pad the dank　　130
Soil to a plash? Toads in a poisoned tank,
　　Or wild cats in a red-hot iron cage—

23

The fight must so have seemed in that fell cirque.
　　What penned them there, with all the plain to choose?
　　No footprint leading to that horrid mews,　　135
None out of it. Mad brewage set to work
Their brains, no doubt, like galley slaves the Turk
　　Pits for his pastime, Christians against Jews.

24

And more than that—a furlough on—why, there!
    What bad use was that engine for, that wheel,   140
    Or brake, not wheel—that harrow fit to reel
Men's bodies out like silk? with all the air
Of Tophet's tool, on earth left unaware,
    Or brought to sharpen its rusty teeth of steel.

25

Then came a bit of stubbed ground, once a wood,   145
    Next a marsh, it would seem, and now mere earth
    Desperate and done with; (so a fool finds mirth,
Makes a thing and then mars it, till his mood
Changes and off he goes!) within a rood—
    Bog, clay and rubble, sand and stark black dearth.   150

26

Now blotches rankling, colored gay and grim,
    Now patches where some leanness of the soil's
    Broke into moss, or substance like boils;
Then came some palsied oak, a cleft in him
Like a distorted mouth that splits its rim   155
    Gaping at death, and dies while it recoils.

27

And just as far as ever from the end!
    Naught in the distance but the evening, naught
    To point my footstep further! At the thought,
A great black bird, Apollyon's bosom friend,   160
Sailed past, nor beat his wide wing dragon-penned
    That brushed my cap—perchance the guide I sought.

28

For, looking up, aware I somehow grew,
    'Spite of the dusk, the plain had given place
    All round to mountains—with such name to grace   165
Mere ugly heights and heaps now stolen in view.
How thus they had surprised me—solve it, you!
    How to get from them was no clearer case.

29

Yet half I seemed to recognize some trick
    Of mischief happened to me, God knows when—   170
    In a bad dream perhaps. Here ended, then,
Progress this way. When, in the very nick
Of giving up, one time more, came a click
    As when a trap shuts—you're inside the den!

30

Burningly it came on me all at once.   175
    This was the place! those two hills on the right,
    Crouched like two bulls locked horn in horn in fight;
While to the left, a tall scalped mountain . . . Dunce,
Dotard, a-dozing at the very nonce,
    After a life spent training for the sight!   180

31

What in the midst lay but the Tower itself?
    The round squat turret, blind as the fool's heart,
    Built of brown stone, without a counterpart
In the whole world. The tempest's mocking elf
Points to the shipman thus the unseen shelf   185
    He strikes on, only when the timbers start.

32

Not see? because of night perhaps?—why, day
    Came back again for that! before it left,
    The dying sunset kindled through a cleft:
The hills, like giants at a hunting, lay,   190
Chin upon hand, to see the game at bay—
    "Now stab and end the creature—to the heft!"

33

Not hear? when noise was everywhere! it tolled
    Increasing like a bell. Names in my ears
    Of all the lost adventurers my peers—   195
How such a one was strong, and such was bold,
And such was fortunate, yet each of old
    Lost, lost! one moment knelled the woe of years

34

There they stood, ranged along the hillsides, met
    To view the last of me, a living frame   200
    For one more picture! in a sheet of flame
I saw them and I knew them all. And yet
Dauntless the slug-horn to my lips I set,
    And blew. *"Childe Roland to the Dark Tower came."*

PROSPICE

Fear death?—to feel the fog in my throat,
    The mist in my face,
When the snows begin, and the blasts denote
    I am nearing the place,
The power of the night, the press of the storm,   5
    The post of the foe;

Where he stands, the Arch Fear in a visible form,
   Yet the strong man must go:
For the journey is done and the summit attained,
   And the barriers fall,   10
Though a battle's to fight ere the guerdon be gained,
   The reward of it all.
I was ever a fighter, so—one fight more,
   The best and the last!
I would hate that death bandaged my eyes and forbore,   15
   And bade me creep past.
No! let me taste the whole of it, fare like my peers
   The heroes of old,
Bear the brunt, in a minute pay glad life's arrears
   Of pain, darkness and cold.   20
For sudden the worst turns the best to the brave,
   The black minute's at end,
And the elements' rage, the fiend-voices that rave,
   Shall dwindle, shall blend,
Shall change, shall become first a peace, out of pain,   25
   Then a light, then thy breast,
O thou soul of my soul! I shall clasp thee again
   And with God be the rest!

("My Last Duchess," p. 136.)

WALT WHITMAN   (1819–1892)

WHEN LILACS LAST IN THE DOORYARD BLOOMED *

1

When lilacs last in the dooryard bloomed,
And the great star early drooped in the western sky in the night,
I mourned, and yet shall mourn with ever-returning spring.

Ever-returning spring, trinity sure to me you bring,
Lilac blooming perennial and drooping star in the west,   5
And thought of him I love.

2

O powerful western fallen star!
O shades of night—O moody, tearful night!
O great star disappeared—O the black murk that hides the star!
O cruel hands that hold me powerless—O helpless soul of me!   10
O harsh surrounding cloud that will not free my soul.

* The occasion of the poem was the death of Abraham Lincoln.

3

In the dooryard fronting an old farm-house near the white-washed
    palings,
Stands the lilac-bush tall-growing with heart-shaped leaves of rich
    green,
With many a pointed blossom rising delicate, with the perfume
    strong I love,
With every leaf a miracle—and from this bush in the dooryard,   15
With delicate-colored blossoms and heart-shaped leaves of rich green,
A sprig with its flower I break.

4

In the swamp in secluded recesses,
A shy and hidden bird is warbling a song.

Solitary the thrush,   20
The hermit withdrawn to himself, avoiding the settlements,
Sings by himself a song.

Song of the bleeding throat,
Death's outlet song of life, (for well dear brother I know,
If thou wast not granted to sing thou would'st surely die.)   25

5

Over the breast of the spring, the land, amid cities,
Amid lanes and through old woods, where lately the violets peeped
    from the ground, spotting the gray debris,
Amid the grass in the fields each side of the lanes, passing the end-
    less grass,
Passing the yellow-speared wheat, every grain from its shroud in
    the dark-brown fields uprisen,
Passing the apple-tree blows of white and pink in the orchards,   30
Carrying a corpse to where it shall rest in the grave,
Night and day journeys a coffin.

6

Coffin that passes through lanes and streets,
Through day and night with the great cloud darkening the land,
With the pomp of the inlooped flags with the cities draped in black,   35
With the show of the States themselves as of crepe-veiled women
    standing,
With processions long and winding and the flambeaus of the night,
With the countless torches lit, with the silent sea of faces and the
    unbared heads,
With the waiting depot, the arriving coffin, and the sombre faces,
With dirges through the night, with the thousand voices rising
    strong and solemn,   40
With all the mournful voices of the dirges poured around the coffin,

The dim-lit churches and the shuddering organs—where amid these
  you journey,
With the tolling tolling bells' perpetual clang,
Here, coffin that slowly passes,
I give you my sprig of lilac.   45

7

(Nor for you, for one alone,
Blossoms and branches green to coffins all I bring,
For fresh as the morning, thus would I chant a song for you O sane
  and sacred death.

All over bouquets of roses,
O death, I cover you over with roses and early lilies,   50
But mostly and now the lilac that blooms the first,
Copious I break, I break the sprigs from the bushes,
With loaded arms I come, pouring for you,
For you and the coffins all of you O death.)

8

O western orb sailing the heaven,   55
Now I know what you must have meant as a month since I walked,
As I walked in silence the transparent shadowy night,
As I saw you had something to tell as you bent to me night after
  night,
As you drooped from the sky low down as if to my side, (while the
  other stars all looked on,)
As we wandered together the solemn night, (for something I know
  not what kept me from sleep,)   60
As the night advanced, and I saw on the rim of the west how full
  you were of woe,
As I stood on the rising ground in the breeze in the cool transparent
  night,
As I watched where you passed and was lost in the netherward
  black of the night,
As my soul in its trouble dissatisfied sank, as where you sad orb,
Concluded, dropped in the night, and was gone.   65

9

Sing on there in the swamp,
O singer bashful and tender, I hear your notes, I hear your call,
I hear, I come presently, I understand you,
But a moment I linger, for the lustrous star has detained me,
The star my departing comrade holds and detains me.   70

10

O how shall I warble myself for the dead one there I loved?
And how shall I deck my song for the large sweet soul that has
  gone?
And what shall my perfume be for the grave of him I love?

Sea-winds blown from east and west,
Blown from the Eastern sea and blown from the Western sea, till
    there on the prairies meeting,   75
These and with these and the breath of my chant,
I'll perfume the grave of him I love.

11

O what shall I hang on the chamber walls?
And what shall the pictures be that I hang on the walls,
To adorn the burial-house of him I love?   80

Pictures of growing spring and farms and homes,
With the Fourth-month eve at sundown, and the gray smoke lucid
    and bright,
With floods of the yellow gold of the gorgeous, indolent, sinking
    sun, burning, expanding the air,
With the fresh sweet herbage under foot, and the pale green leaves
    of the trees prolific,
In the distance the flowing glaze, the breast of the river, with a
    wind-dapple here and there,   85
With ranging hills on the banks, with many a line against the sky,
    and shadows,
And the city at hand with dwellings so dense, and stacks of chim-
    neys,
And all the scenes of life and the workshops, and the workmen
    homeward returning.

12

Lo, body and soul—this land,
My own Manhattan with spires, and the sparkling and hurrying
    tides, and the ships,   90
The varied and ample land, the South and the North in the light,
    Ohio's shores and flashing Missouri,
And ever the far-spreading prairies covered with grass and corn.

Lo, the most excellent sun so calm and haughty,
The violet and purple morn with just-felt breezes,
The gentle soft-born measureless light,   95
The miracle spreading bathing all, the fulfilled noon,
The coming eve delicious, the welcome night and the stars,
Over my cities shining all, enveloping man and land.

13

Sing on, sing on you gray-brown bird,
Sing from the swamps, the recesses, pour your chant from the
    bushes,   100
Limitless out of the dusk, out of the cedars and pines.
Sing on dearest brother, warble your reedy song,
Loud human song, with voice of uttermost woe.
O liquid and free and tender!

O wild and loose to my soul!—O wondrous singer! 105
You only I hear—yet the star holds me, (but will soon depart,)
Yet the lilac with mastering odor holds me.

14

Now while I sat in the day and looked forth,
In the close of the day with its light and the fields of spring, and
    the farmers preparing their crops,
In the large unconscious scenery of my land with its lakes and
    forests, 110
In the heavenly aerial beauty, (after the perturbed winds and the
    storms,)
Under the arching heavens of the afternoon swift passing, and the
    voices of children and women,
The many-moving sea-tides, and I saw the ships how they sailed,
And the summer approaching with richness and the fields all busy
    with labor,
And the infinite separate houses, how they all went on, each with
    its meals and minutia of daily usages, 115
And the streets how their throbbings throbbed, and the cities pent
    —lo, then and there,
Falling upon them all and among them all, enveloping me with
    the rest,
Appeared the cloud, appeared the long black trail,
And I knew death, its thought, and the sacred knowledge of death.

Then with the knowledge of death as walking one side of me, 120
And the thought of death close-walking the other side of me,
And I in the middle as with companions, and as holding the hands
    of companions,
I fled forth to the hiding receiving night that talks not,
Down to the shores of the water, the path by the swamp in the
    dimness,
To the solemn shadowy cedars and ghostly pines so still. 125

And the singer so shy to the rest received me,
The gray-brown bird I know received us comrades three,
And he sang the carol of death, and a verse for him I love.

From deep secluded recesses,
From the fragrant cedars and the ghostly pines so still, 130
Came the carol of the bird.

And the charm of the carol rapt me
As I held as if by their hands my comrades in the night,
And the voice of my spirit tallied the song of the bird.

Come lovely and soothing death, 135
Undulate round the world, serenely arriving, arriving,

In the day, in the night, to all, to each,
Sooner or later delicate death.

Praised be the fathomless universe,
For life and joy, and for objects and knowledge curious,   140
And for love, sweet love—but praise! praise! praise!
For the sure-enwinding arms of cool-enfolding death.

Dark mother always gliding near with soft feet,
Have none chanted for thee a chant of fullest welcome?
Then I chant it for thee, I glorify thee above all,   145
I bring thee a song that when thou must indeed come, come un-
*   falteringly.*

Approach strong deliveress,
When it is so, when thou hast taken them I joyously sing the dead,
Lost in the loving floating ocean of thee,
Laved in the flood of thy bliss O death.   150

From me to thee glad serenades,
Dances for thee I propose saluting thee, adornments and feastings
*   for thee,*
And the sights of the open landscape and the high-spread sky are
*   fitting,*
And life and the fields, and the huge and thoughtful night.

The night in silence under many a star,   155
The ocean shore and the husky whispering wave whose voice I
*   know,*
And the soul turning to thee O vast and well-veiled death,
And the body gratefully nestling close to thee.

Over the tree-tops I float thee a song,
Over the rising and sinking waves, over the myriad fields and the
*   prairies wide,*   160
Over the dense-packed cities all and the teeming wharves and ways,
I float this carol with joy, with joy to thee O death.

15

To the tally of my soul,
Loud and strong kept up the gray-brown bird,
With pure deliberate notes spreading filling the night.   165

Loud in the pines and cedars dim,
Clear in the freshness moist and the swamp-perfume,
And I with my comrades there in the night.

While my sight that was bound in my eyes unclosed,
As to long panoramas of visions.   170

And I saw askant the armies,
I saw as in noiseless dreams hundreds of battle-flags,

Borne through the smoke of the battles and pierced with missiles I
    saw them,
And carried hither and yon through the smoke, and torn and
    bloody,
And at last but a few shreds left on the staffs, (and all in silence,)   175
And the staffs all splintered and broken.

I saw battle-corpses, myriads of them,
And the white skeletons of young men, I saw them,
I saw the debris and debris of all the slain soldiers of the war,
But I saw they were not as was thought,   180
They themselves were fully at rest, they suffered not,
The living remained and suffered, the mother suffered,
And the wife and the child and the musing comrade suffered,
And the armies that remained suffered.

16

Passing the visions, passing the night,   185
Passing, unloosing the hold of my comrades' hands,
Passing the song of the hermit bird and the tallying song of my
    soul,
Victorious song, death's outlet song, yet varying ever-altering song,
As low and wailing, yet clear the notes, rising and falling, flooding
    the night,
Sadly sinking and fainting, as warning and warning, and yet again
    bursting with joy,   190
Covering the earth and filling the spread of the heaven,
As that powerful psalm in the night I heard from recesses,
Passing, I leave thee lilac with heart-shaped leaves,
I leave thee there in the door-yard, blooming, returning with
    spring.

I cease from my song for thee,   195
From my gaze on thee in the west, fronting the west, communing
    with thee,
O comrade lustrous with silver face in the night.

Yet each to keep and all, retrievements out of the night,
The song, the wondrous chant of the gray-brown bird,
And the tallying chant, the echo aroused in my soul,   200
With the lustrous and drooping star with the countenance full of
    woe,
With the holders holding my hand nearing the call of the bird,
Comrades mine and I in the midst, and their memory ever to keep,
    for the dead I loved so well,
For the sweetest, wisest soul of all my days and lands—and this for
    his dear sake,
Lilac and star and bird twined with the chant of my soul,   205
There in the fragrant pines and the cedars dusk and dim.

MATTHEW ARNOLD (1822–1888)

PHILOMELA

Hark! ah, the nightingale—
The tawny-throated!
Hark, from that moonlit cedar what a burst!
What triumph! hark!—what pain!

O wanderer from a Grecian shore,   5
Still, after many years, in distant lands,
Still nourishing in thy bewildered brain
That wild, unquenched, deep-sunken, old world pain—
Say, will it never heal?
And can this fragrant lawn   10
With its cool trees, and night,
And the sweet, tranquil Thames,
And moonshine, and the dew,
To thy racked heart and brain
Afford no balm?   15

Dost thou tonight behold,
Here, through the moonlight on this English grass,
The unfriendly palace in the Thracian wild?
Dost thou again peruse
With hot cheeks and seared eyes   20
The too clear web, and thy dumb sister's shame?
Dost thou once more assay
Thy flight, and feel come over thee,
Poor fugitive, the feathery change
Once more, and once more seem to make resound   25
With love and hate, triumph and agony,
Lone Daulis, and the high Cephissian vale?
Listen, Eugenia—
How thick the bursts come crowding through the leaves!
Again—thou hearest?   30
Eternal passion!
Eternal pain!

GROWING OLD

What is it to grow old?
Is it to lose the glory of the form,
The luster of the eye?

Is it for beauty to forego her wreath?
Yes, but not this alone.   5

Is it to feel our strength—
Not our bloom only, but our strength—decay?
Is it to feel each limb
Grow stiffer, every function less exact,
Each nerve more weakly strung?   10

Yes, this, and more! but not,
Ah, 'tis not what in youth we dreamed 'twould be!
'Tis not to have our life
Mellowed and softened as with sunset glow,
A golden day's decline!   15

'Tis not to see the world
As from a height, with rapt prophetic eyes,
And heart profoundly stirred;
And weep, and feel the fullness of the past,
The years that are no more!   20

It is to spend long days
And not once feel that we were ever young.
It is to add, immured
In the hot prison of the present, month
To month with weary pain.   25

It is to suffer this,
And feel but half, and feebly, what we feel.
Deep in our hidden heart
Festers the dull remembrance of a change,
But no emotion,—none.   30

It is—last stage of all—
When we are frozen up within, and quite
The phantom of ourselves,
To hear the world applaud the hollow ghost
Which blamed the living man.   35

GEORGE MEREDITH   (1828–1909)

from MODERN LOVE

1

By this he knew she wept with waking eyes:
That, at his hand's light quiver by her head,
The strange low sobs that shook their common bed,
Were called into her with a sharp surprise,

And strangled mute, like little gaping snakes,   5
Dreadfully venomous to him. She lay
Stone-still, and the long darkness flowed away
With muffled pulses. Then, as midnight makes
Her giant heart of Memory and Tears
Drink the pale drug of silence, and so beat   10
Sleep's heavy measure, they from head to feet
Were moveless, looking through their dead black years,
By vain regret scrawled over the blank wall.
Like sculptured effigies they might be seen
Upon their marriage tomb, the sword between;   15
Each wishing for the sword that severs all.

16

In our old shipwrecked days there was an hour,
When in the firelight steadily aglow,
Joined slackly, we beheld the red chasm grow
Among the clicking coals. Our library-bower
That eve was left to us: and hushed we sat   5
As lovers to whom Time is whispering.
From sudden-opened doors we heard them sing:
The nodding elders mixed good wine with chat.
Well knew we that Life's greatest treasure lay
With us, and of it was our talk. "Ah, yes!   10
Love dies!" I said: I never thought it less.
She yearned to me that sentence to unsay.
Then when the fire domed blackening, I found
Her cheek was salt against my kiss, and swift
Up the sharp scale of sobs her breast did lift:—   15
Now am I haunted by that taste! that sound!

29

Am I failing? For no longer can I cast
A glory round about this head of gold.
Glory she wears, but springing from the mold
Not like the consecration of the Past!
Is my soul beggared? Something more than earth   5
I cry for still: I cannot be at peace
In having Love upon a mortal lease.
I cannot take the woman at her worth!
Where is the ancient wealth wherewith I clothed
Our human nakedness, and could endow   10
With spiritual splendor a white brow
That else had grinned at me the fact I loathed?
A kiss is but a kiss now! and no wave
Of a great flood that whirls me to the sea.
But, as you will! we'll sit contentedly,   15
And eat our pot of honey on the grave.

EMILY DICKINSON (1830–1886)

THE SOUL SELECTS HER OWN SOCIETY

The Soul selects her own Society—
Then—shuts the Door—
To her divine Majority—
Present no more—

Unmoved—she notes the Chariots—pausing—   5
At her low Gate—
Unmoved—an Emperor be kneeling
Upon her Mat—

I've known her—from an ample nation—
Choose One—   10
Then—close the Valves of her attention—
Like Stone—

AFTER GREAT PAIN, A FORMAL FEELING COMES

After great pain, a formal feeling comes—
The Nerves sit ceremonious, like Tombs—
The stiff Heart questions was it He, that bore,
And Yesterday, or Centuries before?

The Feet, mechanical, go round—   5
Of Ground, or Air, or Ought—
A Wooden way
Regardless grown,
A Quartz contentment, like a stone—

This is the Hour of Lead—   10
Remembered, if outlived,
As Freezing persons, recollect the Snow—
First—Chill—then Stupor—then the letting go—

I DIED FOR BEAUTY

I died for Beauty—but was scarce
Adjusted in the Tomb
When One who died for Truth, was lain
In an adjoining Room—

He questioned softly "Why I failed?"   5
"For Beauty" I replied—
"And I—for Truth—Themself are One—
We Brethren are," He said—

And so, as Kinsmen, met a Night—
We talked between the Rooms— 10
Until the Moss had reached our lips—
And covered up—our names—

BECAUSE I COULD NOT STOP FOR DEATH

Because I could not stop for Death—
He kindly stopped for me—
The Carriage held but just Ourselves—
And Immortality.

We slowly drove—He knew no haste, 5
And I had put away
My labor, and my leisure too,
For his Civility—

We passed the School, where Children strove
At Recess—in the Ring— 10
We passed the Fields of Gazing Grain—
We passed the Setting Sun—

Or rather—He passed Us—
The Dews drew quivering and chill—
For only Gossamer, my Gown— 15
My Tippet—only Tulle—

We paused before a House that seemed
A Swelling of the Ground—
The Roof was scarcely visible—
The Cornice—in the Ground— 20

Since then—'tis Centuries—and yet
Feels shorter than the Day
I first surmised the Horses' Heads
Were toward Eternity—

MY LIFE CLOSED TWICE BEFORE ITS CLOSE

My life closed twice before its close—
It yet remains to see
If Immortality unveil
A third event to me

So huge, so hopeless to conceive
As these that twice befell. 5
Parting is all we know of heaven.
And all we need of hell.

("Success is counted sweetest," p. 56.)

ALGERNON CHARLES SWINBURNE   (1837–1909)

A FORSAKEN GARDEN

In a coign of the cliff between lowland and highland,
    At the sea-down's edge between windward and lee,
Walled round with rocks as an inland island,
    The ghost of a garden fronts the sea.
A girdle of brushwood and thorn encloses   5
    The steep square slope of the blossomless bed
Where the weeds that grew green from the graves of its roses
    Now lie dead.

The fields fall southward, abrupt and broken,
    To the low last edge of the long lone land.   10
If a step should sound or a word be spoken,
    Would a ghost not rise at the strange guest's hand?
So long have the grey bare walks lain guestless,
    Through branches and briars if a man makes way,
He shall find no life but the sea-wind's, restless   15
    Night and day.

The dense hard passage is blind and stifled
    That crawls by a track none turn to climb
To the strait waste place that the years have rifled
    Of all but the thorns that are touched not of time.   20
The thorns he spares when the rose is taken;
    The rocks are left when he wastes the plain.
The wind that wanders, the weeds wind-shaken,
    These remain.

Not a flower to be pressed of the foot that falls not;   25
    As the heart of a dead man the seed-plots are dry;
From the thicket of thorns whence the nightingale calls not,
    Could she call, there were never a rose to reply.
Over the meadows that blossom and wither
    Rings but the note of a sea-bird's song;   30
Only the sun and the rain come hither
    All year long.

The sun burns sere and the rain dishevels
    One gaunt bleak blossom of scentless breath.
Only the wind here hovers and revels   35
    In a round where life seems barren as death.

Here there was laughing of old, there was weeping,
    Haply, of lovers none ever will know,
Whose eyes went seaward a hundred sleeping
      Years ago. 40

Heart handfast in heart as they stood, "Look thither,"
    Did he whisper? "look forth from the flowers to the sea;
For the foam-flowers endure when the rose-blossoms wither,
    And men that love lightly may die—but we?"
And the same wind sang and the same waves whitened, 45
    And or ever the garden's last petals were shed,
In the lips that had whispered, the eyes that had lightened,
      Love was dead.

Or they loved their life through, and then went whither?
    And were one to the end—but what end who knows? 50
Love deep as the sea as a rose must wither,
    As the rose-red seaweed that mocks the rose.
Shall the dead take thought for the dead to love them?
    What love was ever as deep as a grave?
They are loveless now as the grass above them 55
      Or the wave.

All are at one now, roses and lovers,
    Not known of the cliffs and the fields and the sea.
Not a breath of the time that has been hovers
    In the air now soft with a summer to be. 60
Not a breath there shall sweeten the seasons hereafter
    Of the flowers or the lovers that laugh now or weep,
When as they that are free now of weeping and laughter
      We shall sleep.

Here death may deal not again for ever; 65
    Here change may come not till all change end.
From the graves they have made they shall rise up never,
    Who have left nought living to ravage and rend.
Earth, stones, and thorns of the wild ground growing,
    While the sun and the rain live, these shall be; 70
Till a last wind's breath upon all these blowing
      Roll the sea.

Till the slow sea rise and the sheer cliff crumble,
    Till terrace and meadow the deep gulfs drink,
Till the strength of the waves of the high tides humble 75
    The fields that lessen, the rocks that shrink,
Here now in his triumph where all things falter,
    Stretched out on the spoils that his own hand spread,
As a god self-slain on his own strange altar,
      Death lies dead. 80

THOMAS HARDY   (1840–1928)

ON AN INVITATION TO THE UNITED STATES

I

My ardors for emprize nigh lost
Since Life has bared its bones to me,
I shrink to see a modern coast
Whose riper times have yet to be;
Where the new regions claim them free   5
From that long drip of human tears
Which peoples old in tragedy
Have left upon the centuried years.

II

For, wonning in these ancient lands,
Enchased and lettered as a tomb,   10
And scored with prints of perished hands,
And chronicled with dates of doom,
Though my own Being bear no bloom
I trace the lives such scenes enshrine,
Give past exemplars present room,   15
And their experience count as mine.

THE DARKLING THRUSH

(*December 31, 1900*)

I leant upon a coppice gate
    When Frost was specter-gray,
And Winter's dregs made desolate
    The weakening eye of day.
The tangled bine-stems scored the sky   5
    Like strings of broken lyres,
And all mankind that haunted nigh
    Had sought their household fires.

The land's sharp features seemed to be
    The Century's corpse outleant,   10
His crypt the cloudy canopy,
    The wind his death-lament.
The ancient pulse of germ and birth
    Was shrunken hard and dry,
And every spirit upon earth   15
    Seemed fervorless as I.

At once a voice arose among
    The bleak twigs overhead
In a full-hearted evensong
    Of joy illimited;   20
An aged thrush, frail, gaunt, and small,
    In blast-beruffled plume,
Had chosen thus to fling his soul
    Upon the growing gloom.

So little cause for carolings   25
    Of such ecstatic sound
Was written on terrestrial things
    Afar or nigh around,
That I could think there trembled through
    His happy good-night air   30
Some blessed Hope, whereof he knew
    And I was unaware.

20. *illimited:* without limit.

IN TENEBRIS

    Wintertime nighs;
But my bereavement-pain
It cannot bring again:
    Twice no one dies.

    Flower-petals flee;   5
But, since it once hath been,
No more that severing scene
    Can harrow me.

    Birds faint in dread:
I shall not lose old strength   10
In the lone frost's black length:
    Strength long since fled!

    Leaves freeze to dun;
But friends can not turn cold
This season as of old   15
    For him with none.

    Tempests may scath;
But love can not make smart
Again this year his heart
    Who no heart hath.   20

    Black is night's cope;
But death will not appal
One who, past doubtings all,
    Waits in unhope.

THE CONVERGENCE OF THE TWAIN

(*Lines on the loss of the "Titanic"*)

In a solitude of the sea
Deep from human vanity,
And the Pride of Life that planned her, stilly couches she.

Steel chambers, late the pyres
Of her salamandrine fires,   5
Cold currents thrid, and turn to rhythmic tidal lyres.

Over the mirrors meant
To glass the opulent
The sea-worm crawls—grotesque, slimed, dumb, indifferent.

Jewels in joy designed   10
To ravish the sensuous mind
Lie lightless, all their sparkles bleared and black and blind.

Dim moon-eyed fishes near
Gaze at the gilded gear
And query: "What does this vaingloriousness down here?" . . .   15

Well: while was fashioning
This creature of cleaving wing,
The Immanent Will that stirs and urges everything

Prepared a sinister mate
For her—so gaily great—   20
A Shape of Ice, for the time far and dissociate.

And as the smart ship grew
In stature, grace, and hue,
In shadowy silent distance grew the Iceberg too.

Alien they seemed to be: 25
No mortal eye could see
The intimate welding of their later history.

Or sign that they were bent
By paths coincident
On being anon twin halves of one august event.   30

Till the Spinner of the Years
Said "Now!" And each one hears,
And consummation comes, and jars two hemispheres.

6. *thrid:* thread.

THE GOING

Why did you give no hint that night
That quickly after the morrow's dawn,
And calmly, as if indifferent quite,
You would close your term here, up and be gone
      Where I could not follow   5
      With wing of swallow
To gain one glimpse of you ever anon!

      Never to bid goodbye,
      Or lip me the softest call,
Or utter a wish for a word, while I   10
Saw morning harden upon the wall,
      Unmoved, unknowing
      That your great going
Had place that moment, and altered all.

Why do you make me leave the house   15
And think for a breath it is you I see
At the end of the alley of bending boughs
Where so often at dusk you used to be;
      Till in darkening dankness
      The yawning blankness   20
Of the perspective sickens me!

      You were she who abode
      By those red-veined rocks far West,
You were the swan-necked one who rode
Along the beetling Beeny Crest,   25
      And, reining nigh me,
      Would muse and eye me,
While Life unrolled us its very best.

Why, then, latterly did we not speak,
Did we not think of those days long dead,   30
And ere your vanishing strive to seek
That time's renewal? We might have said,
      "In this bright spring weather
      We'll visit together
Those places that once we visited."   35

      Well, well! All's past amend,
      Unchangeable. It must go.
I seem but a dead man held on end
To sink down soon. . . . O you could not know
      That such swift fleeing   40
      No soul foreseeing—
Not even I—would undo me so!

"REGRET NOT ME"

Regret not me;
Beneath the sunny tree
I lie uncaring, slumbering peacefully.

Swift as the light
I flew my faery flight;   5
Ecstatically I moved, and feared no night.

I did not know
That heydays fade and go,
But deemed that what was would be always so.

I skipped at morn   10
Between the yellowing corn,
Thinking it good and glorious to be born.

I ran at eves
Among the piled-up sheaves,
Dreaming, "I grieve not, therefore nothing grieves."   15

Now soon will come
The apple, pear, and plum,
And hinds will sing, and autumn insects hum.

Again you will fare
To cider-makings rare,   20
And junketings; but I shall not be there.

Yet gaily sing
Until the pewter ring
Those songs we sang when we went gipsying.

And lightly dance   25
Some triple-timed romance
In coupled figures, and forget mischance;

And mourn not me
Beneath the yellowing tree;
For I shall mind not, slumbering peacefully.   30

HIS HEART

A Woman's Dream

At midnight, in the room where he lay dead
Whom in his life I had never clearly read,
I thought if I could peer into that citadel
His heart, I should at last know full and well

What hereto had been known to him alone,   5
Despite our long sit-out of years foreflown,
"And if," I said, "I do this for his memory's sake,
    It would not wound him, even if he could wake."

So I bent over him. He seemed to smile
With a calm confidence the whole long while   10
That I, withdrawing his heart, held it and, bit by bit,
    Perused the unguessed things found written on it.

It was inscribed like a terrestrial sphere
With quaint vermiculations close and clear—
His graving. Had I known, would I have risked the stroke   15
    Its reading brought, and my own heart nigh broke!

Yes, there at last, eyes opened, did I see
His whole sincere symmetric history;
There were his truth, his simple singlemindedness,
    Strained, maybe, by time's storms, but there no less.   20

There were the daily deeds from sun to sun
In blindness, but good faith, that he had done;
There were regrets, at instances wherein he swerved
    (As he conceived) from cherishings I had deserved.

There were old hours all figured down as bliss—   25
Those spent with me—(how little had I thought this!)
There those when, at my absence, whether he slept or waked,
    (Though I knew not 'twas so!) his spirit ached.

There that when we were severed, how day dulled
Till time joined us anew, was chronicled: 30
And arguments and battlings in defence of me
    That heart recorded clearly and ruddily.

I put it back, and left him as he lay
While pierced the morning pink and then the gray
Into each dreary room and corridor around,   35
    Where I shall wait, but his step will not sound.

TRANSFORMATIONS

Portion of this yew
Is a man my grandsire knew,
Bosomed here at its foot:
This branch may be his wife,
A ruddy human life   5
Now turned to a green shoot.

These grasses must be made
Of her who often prayed,

Last century, for repose;
And the fair girl long ago   10
Whom I often tried to know
May be entering this rose.

So, they are not underground,
But as nerves and veins abound
In the growths of upper air,   15
And they feel the sun and rain,
And the energy again
That made them what they were!

EPITAPH ON A PESSIMIST

I'm Smith of Stoke, aged sixty-odd,
  I've lived without a dame
From youth-time on; and would to God
  My dad had done the same.

IN TIME OF "THE BREAKING OF NATIONS"

I
Only a man harrowing clods
  In a slow silent walk
With an old horse that stumbles and nods
  Half asleep as they stalk.

II
Only thin smoke without flame   5
  From the heaps of couch-grass;
Yet this will go onward the same
  Though Dynasties pass.

III
Yonder a maid and her wight
  Come whispering by: 10
War's annals will cloud into night
  Ere their story die.

("The Ruined Maid," p. 35; "When I Set Out for Lyonnesse," p. 10; "The Wound," p. 44; "At the Piano," p. 14.)

GERARD MANLEY HOPKINS   (1844–1889)

THE HABIT OF PERFECTION

Elected Silence, sing to me
And beat upon my whorlèd ear,
Pipe me to pastures still and be
The music that I care to hear.

Shape nothing, lips; be lovely-dumb: 5
It is the shut, the curfew sent
From there where all surrenders come
Which only makes you eloquent.

Be shelléd, eyes, with double dark
And find the uncreated light: 10
This ruck and reel which you remark
Coils, keeps, and teases simple sight.

Palate, the hutch of tasty lust,
Desire not to be rinsed with wine:
The can must be so sweet, the crust   15
So fresh that come in fasts divine!

Nostrils, your careless breath that spend
Upon the stir and keep of pride,
What relish shall the censers send
Along the sanctuary side!   20

O feel-of-primrose hands, O feet
That want the yield of plushy sward,
But you shall walk the golden street
And you unhouse and house the Lord.

And, Poverty, be thou the bride   25
And now the marriage feast begun,
And lily-colored clothes provide
Your spouse not labored-at nor spun.

THE LANTERN OUT OF DOORS

Sometimes a lantern moves along the night,
   That interests our eyes. And who goes there?
   I think; where from and bound, I wonder, where,
With, all down darkness wide, his wading light?

Men go by me whom either beauty bright   5
   In mold or mind or what not else makes rare:
   They rain against our much-thick and marsh air
Rich beams, till death or distance buys them quite.

Death or distance soon consumes them: wind
   What most I may eye after, be in at the end   10
I cannot, and out of sight is out of mind.

Christ minds; Christ's interest, what to avow or amend
   There, éyes them, heart wánts, care háunts, foot fóllows kind,
Their ránsom, théir rescue, ánd first, fást, last friénd.

THE WINDHOVER

To Christ Our Lord

I caught this morning morning's minion, king-
 dom of daylight's dauphin, dapple-dawn-drawn Falcon, in
  his riding
Of the rolling level underneath him steady air, and striding
High there, how he rung upon the rein of a wimpling wing
In his ecstasy! then off, off forth on swing,   5
 As a skate's heel sweeps smooth on a bow-bend: the hurl and
  gliding
 Rebuffed the big wind. My heart in hiding
Stirred for a bird,—the achieve of, the mastery of the thing!

Brute beauty and valor and act, oh, air, pride, plume here
 Buckle! AND the fire that breaks from thee then, a billion   10
Times told lovelier, more dangerous, O my chevalier!

 No wonder of it: shéer plód makes plough down sillion
Shine, and blue-bleak embers, ah my dear,
 Fall, gall themselves, and gash gold-vermilion.

12. *sillion:* ridges of a plowed field.

SPRING AND FALL

To a Young Child

 Márgarét, are you grieving
 Over Goldengrove unleaving?
 Leáves, líke the things of man, you
 With your fresh thoughts care for, can you?
 Áh! ás the heart grows older   5
 It will come to such sights colder
 By and by, nor spare a sigh
 Though worlds of wanwood leafmeal lie;
 And yet you wíll weep and know why.
 Now no matter, child, the name: 10
 Sórrow's springs áre the same.
 Nor mouth had, no nor mind, expressed
 Whát heart heard of, ghost guessed:
 It ís the blight man was born for,
 It is Margaret you mourn for.   15

("God's Grandeur," p. 48.)

A. E. HOUSMAN (1859–1936)

1887

From Clee to heaven the beacon burns,
   The shires have seen it plain,
From north and south the sign returns
   And beacons burn again.

Look left, look right, the hills are bright,   5
   The dales are light between,
Because 'tis fifty years tonight
   That God has saved the Queen.

Now, when the flame they watch not towers
   Above the soil they trod,   10
Lads, we'll remember friends of ours
   Who shared the work with God.

To skies that knit their heartstrings right,
   To fields that bred them brave,
The saviors come not home tonight: 15
   Themselves they could not save.

It dawns in Asia, tombstones show
   And Shropshire names are read;
And the Nile spills his overflow
   Beside the Severn's dead.   20

We pledge in peace by farm and town
   The Queen they served in war,
And fire the beacons up and down
   The land they perished for.

"God save the Queen" we living sing,   25
   From height to height 'tis heard;
And with the rest your voices ring,
   Lads of the Fifty-third.

Oh, God will save her, fear you not:
   Be you the men you've been,
Get you the sons your fathers got,   30
   And God will save the Queen.

"IS MY TEAM PLOUGHING?"

"Is my team ploughing,
   That I was used to drive

And hear the harness jingle
  When I was man alive?"

Ay, the horses trample,   5
  The harness jingles now;
No change though you lie under
  The land you used to plough.

"Is football playing
  Along the river shore,   10
With lads to chase the leather,
  Now I stand up no more?"

Ay, the ball is flying,
  The lads play heart and soul;
The goal stands up, the keeper   15
  Stands up to keep the goal.

"Is my girl happy,
  That I thought hard to leave,
And has she tired of weeping
  As she lies down at eve?"   20

Ay, she lies down lightly,
  She lies not down to weep:
Your girl is well contented.
  Be still, my lad, and sleep.

"Is my friend hearty,   25
  Now I am thin and pine,
And he has found to sleep in
  A better bed than mine?"

Yes, lad, I lie easy,
  I lie as lads would choose;   30
I cheer a dead man's sweetheart,
  Never ask me whose.

THE CHESTNUT CASTS HIS FLAMBEAUX, AND THE FLOWERS

The chestnut casts his flambeaux, and the flowers
  Stream from the hawthorn on the wind away,
The doors clap to, the pane is blind with showers.
  Pass me the can, lad; there's an end of May.

There's one spoilt spring to scant our mortal lot,   5
  One season ruined of our little store.
May will be fine next year as like as not:
  Oh ay, but then we shall be twenty-four.

We for a certainty are not the first
    Have sat in taverns while the tempest hurled   10
Their hopeful plans to emptiness, and cursed
    Whatever brute and blackguard made the world.

It is in truth iniquity on high
    To cheat our sentenced souls of aught they crave,
And mar the merriment as you and I   15
    Fare on our long fool's-errand to the grave.

Iniquity it is; but pass the can.
    My lad, no pair of kings our mothers bore;
Our only portion is the estate of man:
    We want the moon, but we shall get no more.   20

If here today the cloud of thunder lours
    Tomorrow it will hie on far behests;
The flesh will grieve on other bones than ours
    Soon, and the soul will mourn in other breasts.

The troubles of our proud and angry dust   25
    Are from eternity, and shall not fail.
Bear them we can, and if we can we must.
    Shoulder the sky, my lad, and drink your ale.

("Be still, my soul, be still," p. 27; "In the morning, in the morning," p. 1; "Epitaph on an Army of Mercenaries," p. 127; "They say my verse is sad," p. 85; "I did not lose my heart in summer's even," p. 22.)

RUDYARD KIPLING (1865–1936)

DANNY DEEVER

"What are the bugles blowin' for?" said Files-on-Parade.
"To turn you out, to turn you out," the Color-Sergeant said.
"What makes you look so white, so white?" said Files-on-Parade.
"I'm dreadin' what I've got to watch," the Color-Sergeant said.
    For they're hangin' Danny Deever, you can hear the Dead
      March play,   5
    The Regiment's in 'ollow square—they're hangin' him today;
    They've taken of his buttons off an' cut his stripes away,
    An' they're hangin' Danny Deever in the mornin'.

"What makes the rear rank breathe so 'ard?" said Files-on-Parade.
"It's bitter cold, it's bitter cold," the Color-Sergeant said.   10
"What makes that front-rank man fall down?" said Files-on-Parade.
"A touch o' sun, a touch o' sun," the Color-Sergeant said.
    They are hangin' Danny Deever, they are marchin' of 'im round,

They 'ave 'alted Danny Deever by 'is coffin on the ground;
An' 'e'll swing in 'arf a minute for a sneakin' shootin' hound—   15
O they're hangin' Danny Deever in the mornin'!

" 'Is cot was right-'and cot to mine," said Files-on-Parade.
" 'E's sleepin' out an' far tonight," the Color-Sergeant said.
"I've drunk 'is beer a score o' times," said Files-on-Parade.
" 'E's drinkin' bitter beer alone," the Color-Sergeant said.   20
They are hangin' Danny Deever, you must mark 'im to 'is place,
For 'e shot a comrade sleepin'—you must look 'im in the face;
Nine 'undred of 'is country an' the Regiment's disgrace,
While they're hangin' Danny Deever in the mornin'.

"What's that so black agin the sun?" said Files-on-Parade.   25
"It's Danny fightin' 'ard for life," the Color-Sergeant said.
"What's that that whimpers over'ead?" said Files-on-Parade.
"It's Danny's soul that's passin' now," the Color-Sergeant said.
For they're done with Danny Deever, you can 'ear the quickstep play,
The Regiment's in column, an' they're marchin' us away;   30
Ho! the young recruits are shakin', an' they'll want their beer today,
After hangin' Danny Deever in the mornin'.

WILLIAM BUTLER YEATS   (1865–1939)

WHEN YOU ARE OLD

When you are old and gray and full of sleep,
And nodding by the fire, take down this book,
And slowly read, and dream of the soft look
Your eyes had once, and of their shadows deep;

How many loved your moments of glad grace,   5
And loved your beauty with love false or true,
But one man loved the pilgrim soul in you,
And loved the sorrows of your changing face;

And bending down beside the glowing bars,
Murmur, a little sadly, how Love fled   10
And paced upon the mountains overhead
And hid his face amid a crowd of stars.

NO SECOND TROY

Why should I blame her that she filled my days
With misery, or that she would of late

Have taught to ignorant men most violent ways,
Or hurled the little streets upon the great,
Had they but courage equal to desire?   5
What could have made her peaceful with a mind
That nobleness made simple as a fire,
With beauty like a tightened bow, a kind
That is not natural in an age like this,
Being high and solitary and most stern?   10
Why, what could she have done, being what she is?
Was there another Troy for her to burn?

THE WILD SWANS AT COOLE

The trees are in their autumn beauty,
The woodland paths are dry,
Under the October twilight the water
Mirrors a still sky;
Upon the brimming water among the stones   5
Are nine-and-fifty swans.

The nineteenth autumn has come upon me
Since I first made my count;
I saw, before I had well finished,
All suddenly mount   10
And scatter wheeling in great broken rings
Upon their clamorous wings.

I have looked upon those brilliant creatures,
And now my heart is sore.
All's changed since I, hearing at twilight,   15
The first time on this shore,
The bell-beat of their wings above my head,
Trod with a lighter tread.

Unwearied still, lover by lover,
They paddle in the cold   20
Companionable streams or climb the air;
Their hearts have not grown old;
Passion or conquest, wander where they will,
Attend upon them still.

But now they drift on the still water,   25
Mysterious, beautiful;
Among what rushes will they build,
By what lake's edge or pool
Delight men's eyes when I awake some day
To find they have flown away?   30

THE SECOND COMING

Turning and turning in the widening gyre
The falcon cannot hear the falconer;
Things fall apart; the center cannot hold;
Mere anarchy is loosed upon the world,
The blood-dimmed tide is loosed, and everywhere   5
The ceremony of innocence is drowned;
The best lack all conviction, while the worst
Are full of passionate intensity.

Surely some revelation is at hand;
Surely the Second Coming is at hand.   10
The Second Coming! Hardly are those words out
When a vast image out of *Spiritus Mundi*
Troubles my sight: somewhere in sands of the desert
A shape with lion body and the head of a man,
A gaze blank and pitiless as the sun,   15
Is moving its slow thighs, while all about it
Reel shadows of the indignant desert birds.
The darkness drops again; but now I know
That twenty centuries of stony sleep
Were vexed to nightmare by a rocking cradle,   20
And what rough beast, its hour come round at last,
Slouches towards Bethlehem to be born?

12. *Spiritus Mundi:* spirit of the world.

SAILING TO BYZANTIUM

I

That is no country for old men. The young
In one another's arms, birds in the trees
—Those dying generations—at their song,
The salmon-falls, the mackerel-crowded seas,
Fish, flesh, or fowl, commend all summer long   5
Whatever is begotten, born, and dies.
Caught in that sensual music all neglect
Monuments of unaging intellect.

II

An aged man is but a paltry thing,
A tattered coat upon a stick, unless   10
Soul clap its hands and sing, and louder sing
For every tatter in its mortal dress,
Nor is there singing school but studying
Monuments of its own magnificence;

And therefore I have sailed the seas and come   15
To the holy city of Byzantium.

III

O sages standing in God's holy fire
As in the gold mosaic of a wall,
Come from the holy fire, perne in a gyre,
And be the singing-masters of my soul.   20
Consume my heart away; sick with desire
And fastened to a dying animal
It knows not what it is; and gather me
Into the artifice of eternity.

IV

Once out of nature I shall never take   25
My bodily form from any natural thing,
But such a form as Grecian goldsmiths make
Of hammered gold and gold enamelling
To keep a drowsy Emperor awake;
Or set upon a golden bough to sing   30
To lords and ladies of Byzantium
Of what is past, or passing, or to come.

19. *perne:* turning.

AMONG SCHOOL CHILDREN

I

I walk through the long schoolroom questioning;
A kind old nun in a white hood replies;
The children learn to cipher and to sing,
To study reading-books and histories,
To cut and sew, be neat in everything   5
In the best modern way—the children's eyes
In momentary wonder stare upon
A sixty-year-old smiling public man.

II

I dream of a Ledaean body, bent
Above a sinking fire, a tale that she   10
Told of a harsh reproof, or trivial event
That changed some childish day to tragedy—
Told, and it seemed that our two natures blent
Into a sphere from youthful sympathy,
Or else, to alter Plato's parable,   15
Into the yolk and white of the one shell.

III

And thinking of that fit of grief or rage
I look upon one child or t'other there

9. *Ledaean:* like Leda, the beautiful queen desired by Zeus.

And wonder if she stood so at that age—
For even daughters of the swan can share   20
Something of every paddler's heritage—
And had that color upon cheek or hair,
And thereupon my heart is driven wild:
She stands before me as a living child.

IV

Her present image floats into the mind—   25
Did Quattrocento finger fashion it
Hollow of cheek as though it drank the wind
And took a mess of shadows for its meat?
And I though never of Ledaean kind
Had pretty plumage once—enough of that,   30
Better to smile on all that smile, and show
There is a comfortable kind of old scarecrow.

V

What youthful mother, a shape upon her lap
Honey of generation had betrayed,
And that must sleep, shriek, struggle to escape   35
As recollection or the drug decide,
Would think her son, did she but see that shape
With sixty or more winters on its head,
A compensation for the pang of his birth,
Or the uncertainty of his setting forth?   40

VI

Plato thought nature but a spume that plays
Upon a ghostly paradigm of things;
Solider Aristotle played the taws
Upon the bottom of a king of kings;
World-famous golden-thighed Pythagoras   45
Fingered upon a fiddle-stick or strings
What a star sang and careless Muses heard:
Old clothes upon old sticks to scare a bird.

VII

Both nuns and mothers worship images,
But those the candles light are not as those   50
That animate a mother's reveries,
But keep a marble or a bronze repose.
And yet they too break hearts—O Presences
That passion, piety or affection knows,

---

44. *king of kings:* Alexander the Great, who as a youth was a pupil of Aristotle's; the stanza as a whole alludes to the varying views of human life of Plato, Aristotle, and Pythagoras.

And that all heavenly glory symbolize—   55
O self-born mockers of man's enterprise;

VIII

Labor is blossoming or dancing where
The body is not bruised to pleasure soul,
Nor beauty born out of its own despair,
Nor blear-eyed wisdom out of midnight oil.   60
O chestnut-tree, great-rooted blossomer,
Are you the leaf, the blossom or the bole?
O body swayed to music, O brightening glance,
How can we know the dancer from the dance?

AFTER LONG SILENCE

Speech after long silence; it is right,
All other lovers being estranged or dead,
Unfriendly lamplight hid under its shade,
The curtains drawn upon unfriendly night,
That we descant and yet again descant   5
Upon the supreme theme of Art and Song:
Bodily decrepitude is wisdom; young
We loved each other and were ignorant.

LAPIS LAZULI

I have heard that hysterical women say
They are sick of the palette and fiddle-bow,
Of poets that are always gay,
For everybody knows or else should know
That if nothing drastic is done   5
Aeroplane and Zeppelin will come out,
Pitch like King Billy bomb-balls in
Until the town lie beaten flat.

All perform their tragic play,
There struts Hamlet, there is Lear,   10
That's Ophelia, that Cordelia;
Yet they, should the last scene be there,
The great stage curtain about to drop,
If worthy their prominent part in the play,
Do not break up their lines to weep.   15
They know that Hamlet and Lear are gay;
Gaiety transfiguring all that dread.
All men have aimed at, found and lost;
Black out; Heaven blazing into the head:
Tragedy wrought to its uttermost.   20

Though Hamlet rambles and Lear rages,
And all the drop-scenes drop at once
Upon a hundred thousand stages,
It cannot grow by an inch or an ounce.

On their own feet they came, or on shipboard,   25
Camel-back, horse-back, ass-back, mule-back,
Old civilizations put to the sword.
Then they and their wisdom went to rack:
No handiwork of Callimachus,
Who handled marble as if it were bronze,   30
Made draperies that seemed to rise
When sea-wind swept the corner, stands;
His long lamp-chimney shaped like the stem
Of a slender palm, stood but a day;
All things fall and are built again,   35
And those that build them again are gay.

Two Chinamen, behind them a third,
Are carved in lapis lazuli,
Over them flies a long-legged bird,
A symbol of longevity;   40
The third, doubtless a serving-man,
Carries a musical instrument.

Every discoloration of the stone,
Every accidental crack or dent,
Seems a water-course or an avalanche,   45
Or lofty slope where it still snows
Though doubtless plum or cherry-branch
Sweetens the little half-way house
Those Chinamen climb towards, and I
Delight to imagine them seated there;   50
There, on the mountain and the sky,
On all the tragic scene they stare.
One asks for mournful melodies;
Accomplished fingers begin to play.
Their eyes mid many wrinkles, their eyes,   55
Their ancient, glittering eyes, are gay.

THE CIRCUS ANIMALS' DESERTION

I

I sought a theme and sought for it in vain,
I sought it daily for six weeks or so.
Maybe at last, being but a broken man,
I must be satisfied with my heart, although
Winter and summer till old age began   5

My circus animals were all on show,
Those stilted boys, that burnished chariot,
Lion and woman and the Lord knows what.

II

What can I but enumerate old themes?
First that sea-rider Oisin led by the nose   10
Through three enchanted islands, allegorical dreams,
Vain gaiety, vain battle, vain repose,
Themes of the embittered heart, or so it seems,
That might adorn old songs or courtly shows;
But what cared I that set him on to ride,   15
I, starved for the bosom of his faery bride?

And then a counter-truth filled out its play,
The Countess Cathleen was the name I gave it;
She, pity-crazed, had given her soul away,
But masterful Heaven had intervened to save it.   20
I thought my dear must her own soul destroy,
So did fanaticism and hate enslave it,
And this brought forth a dream and soon enough
This dream itself had all my thought and love.

And when the Fool and Blind Man stole the bread   25
Cuchulain fought the ungovernable sea;
Heart-mysteries there, and yet when all is said
It was the dream itself enchanted me:
Character isolated by a deed
To engross the present and dominate memory.   30
Players and painted stage took all my love,
And not those things that they were emblems of.

III

Those masterful images because complete
Grew in pure mind, but out of what began?
A mound of refuse or the sweepings of a street,   35
Old kettles, old bottles, and a broken can,
Old iron, old bones, old rags, that raving slut
Who keeps the till. Now that my ladder's gone,
I must lie down where all the ladders start,
In the foul rag-and-bone shop of the heart.   40

10. *Oisin:* a figure from Irish legend whom Yeats wrote a poem about; Cathleen and Cuchulain in lines below are similar figures.

("The Coming of Wisdom with Time," p. 83; "On Hearing That the Students . . . ," p. 123; "Leda and the Swan," p. 130; "Crazy Jane Talks with the Bishop," p. 132; "The Spur," p. 134.)

EDWIN ARLINGTON ROBINSON (1869–1935)

LUKE HAVERGAL

Go to the western gate, Luke Havergal,
There where the vines cling crimson on the wall,
And in the twilight wait for what will come.
The leaves will whisper there of her, and some,
Like flying words, will strike you as they fall;   5
But go, and if you listen she will call.
Go to the western gate, Luke Havergal—
Luke Havergal.

No, there is not a dawn in eastern skies
To rift the fiery night that's in your eyes;   10
But there, where western glooms are gathering,
The dark will end the dark, if anything:
God slays himself with every leaf that flies,
And hell is more than half of paradise.
No, there is not a dawn in eastern skies—   15
In eastern skies.

Out of a grave I come to tell you this,
Out of a grave I come to quench the kiss
That flames upon your forehead with a glow
That blinds you to the way that you must go.   20
Yes, there is yet one way to where she is,
Bitter, but one that faith may never miss.
Out of a grave I come to tell you this—
To tell you this.

There is the western gate, Luke Havergal,   25
There are the crimson leaves upon the wall.
Go, for the winds are tearing them away,—
Nor think to riddle the dead words they say,
Nor any more to feel them as they fall;
But go, and if you trust her she will call.   30
There is the western gate, Luke Havergal—
Luke Havergal.

EROS TURANNOS

She fears him, and will always ask
    What fated her to choose him;
She meets in his engaging mask
    All reasons to refuse him;

But what she meets and what she fears   5
Are less than are the downward years,
Drawn slowly to the foamless weirs
    Of age, were she to lose him.

Between a blurred sagacity
    That once had power to sound him,   10
And Love, that will not let him be
    The Judas that she found him,
Her pride assuages her almost,
As if it were alone the cost.
He sees that he will not be lost,   15
    And waits and looks around him.

A sense of ocean and old trees
    Envelops and allures him;
Tradition, touching all he sees,
    Beguiles and reassures him;   20
And all her doubts of what he says
Are dimmed with what she knows of days—
Till even prejudice delays
    And fades, and she secures him.

The falling leaf inaugurates   25
    The reign of her confusion;
The pounding wave reverberates
    The dirge of her illusion;
And home, where passion lived and died,
Becomes a place where she can hide,   30
While all the town and harbor-side
    Vibrate with her seclusion.

We tell you, tapping on our brows,
    The story as it should be,
As if the story of a house   35
    Were told, or ever could be;
We'll have no kindly veil between
Her visions and those we have seen,—
As if we guessed what hers have been,
    Or what they are or would be.   40

Meanwhile we do no harm; for they
    That with a god have striven,
Not hearing much of what we say,
    Take what the god has given;
Though like waves breaking it may be,   45
Or like a changed familiar tree,
Or like a stairway to the sea
    Where down the blind are driven.

FOR A DEAD LADY

No more with overflowing light
Shall fill the eyes that now are faded,
Nor shall another's fringe with night
Their woman-hidden world as they did.
No more shall quiver down the days   5
The flowing wonder of her ways,
Whereof no language may requite
The shifting and the many-shaded.

The grace, divine, definitive,
Clings only as a faint forestalling;   10
The laugh that love could not forgive
Is hushed, and answers to no calling;
The forehead and the little ears
Have gone where Saturn keeps the years;
The breast where roses could not live   15
Has done with rising and with falling.

The beauty, shattered by the laws
That have creation in their keeping,
No longer trembles at applause,
Or over children that are sleeping;   20
And we who delve in beauty's lore
Know all that we have known before
Of what inexorable cause
Makes Time so vicious in his reaping.

("Richard Cory," p. 104; "The House on the Hill," p. 154.)

ROBERT FROST (1874–1963)

"OUT, OUT—"

The buzz-saw snarled and rattled in the yard
And made dust and dropped stove-length sticks of wood,
Sweet-scented stuff when the breeze drew across it.
And from there those that lifted eyes could count
Five mountain ranges one behind the other   5
Under the sunset far into Vermont.
And the saw snarled and rattled, snarled and rattled,
As it ran light, or had to bear a load.
And nothing happened: day was all but done.
Call it a day, I wish they might have said   10

To please the boy by giving him the half hour
That a boy counts so much when saved from work.
His sister stood beside them in her apron
To tell them "Supper." At the word, the saw,
As if to prove saws knew what supper meant,   15
Leaped out at the boy's hand, or seemed to leap—
He must have given the hand. However it was,
Neither refused the meeting. But the hand!
The boy's first outcry was a rueful laugh,
As he swung toward them holding up the hand   20
Half in appeal, but half as if to keep
The life from spilling. Then the boy saw all—
Since he was old enough to know, big boy
Doing a man's work, though a child at heart—
He saw all spoiled. "Don't let him cut my hand off—   25
The doctor, when he comes. Don't let him, sister!"
So. But the hand was gone already.
The doctor put him in the dark of ether.
He lay and puffed his lips out with his breath.
And then—the watcher at his pulse took fright.   30
No one believed. They listened at his heart.
Little—less—nothing!—and that ended it.
No more to build on there. And they, since they
Were not the one dead, turned to their affairs.

FIRE AND ICE

Some say the world will end in fire,
Some say in ice.
From what I've tasted of desire
I hold with those who favor fire.
But if it had to perish twice,   5
I think I know enough of hate
To say that for destruction ice
Is also great
And would suffice.

ONCE BY THE PACIFIC

The shattered water made a misty din.
Great waves looked over others coming in,
And thought of doing something to the shore
That water never did to land before.
The clouds were low and hairy in the skies,   5
Like locks blown forward in the gleam of eyes.
You could not tell, and yet it looked as if
The shore was lucky in being backed by cliff,

The cliff in being backed by continent;
It looked as if a night of dark intent   10
Was coming, and not only a night, an age.
Someone had better be prepared for rage.
There would be more than ocean-water broken
Before God's last *Put out the Light* was spoken.

ACQUAINTED WITH THE NIGHT

I have been one acquainted with the night.
I have walked out in rain—and back in rain.
I have outwalked the furthest city light.

I have looked down the saddest city lane.
I have passed by the watchman on his beat   5
And dropped my eyes, unwilling to explain.

I have stood still and stopped the sound of feet
When far away an interrupted cry
Came over houses from another street,

But not to call me back or say good-by;   10
And further still at an unearthly height,
One luminary clock against the sky

Proclaimed the time was neither wrong nor right.
I have been one acquainted with the night.

PROVIDE, PROVIDE

The witch that came (the withered hag)
To wash the steps with pail and rag,
Was once the beauty Abishag,

The picture pride of Hollywood.
Too many fall from great and good   5
For you to doubt the likelihood.

Die early and avoid the fate.
Or if predestined to die late,
Make up your mind to die in state.

Make the whole stock exchange your own!   10
If need be occupy a throne,
Where nobody can call *you* crone.

Some have relied on what they knew;
Others on being simply true.
What worked for them might work for you.   15

No memory of having starred
Atones for later disregard,
Or keeps the end from being hard.

Better to go down dignified
With boughten friendship at your side   20
Than none at all. Provide, provide!

THE SUBVERTED FLOWER

She drew back; he was calm:
"It is this that had the power."
And he lashed his open palm
With the tender-headed flower.
He smiled for her to smile,   5
But she was either blind
Or willfully unkind.
He eyed her for a while
For a woman and a puzzle.
He flicked and flung the flower,   10
And another sort of smile
Caught up like finger tips
The corners of his lips
And cracked his ragged muzzle.
She was standing to the waist   15
In goldenrod and brake,
Her shining hair displaced.
He stretched her either arm
As if she made it ache
To clasp her—not to harm;   20
As if he could not spare
To touch her neck and hair.
"If this has come to us
And not to me alone—"
So she thought she heard him say;   25
Though with every word he spoke
His lips were sucked and blown
And the effort made him choke
Like a tiger at a bone.
She had to lean away.   30
She dared not stir a foot,
Lest movement should provoke
The demon of pursuit
That slumbers in a brute.
It was then her mother's call   35
From inside the garden wall
Made her steal a look of fear

To see if he could hear
And would pounce to end it all
Before her mother came.   40
She looked and saw the shame:
A hand hung like a paw,
An arm worked like a saw
As if to be persuasive,
An ingratiating laugh   45
That cut the snout in half,
An eye become evasive.
A girl could only see
That a flower had marred a man,
But what she could not see   50
Was that the flower might be
Other than base and fetid:
That the flower had done but part,
And what the flower began
Her own too meager heart   55
Had terribly completed.
She looked and saw the worst.
And the dog or what it was,
Obeying bestial laws,
A coward save at night,   60
Turned from the place and ran.
She heard him stumble first
And use his hands in flight.
She heard him bark outright.
And oh, for one so young   65
The bitter words she spit
Like some tenacious bit
That will not leave the tongue.
She plucked her lips for it,
And still the horror clung.   70
Her mother wiped the foam
From her chin, picked up her comb
And drew her backward home.

IT BIDS PRETTY FAIR

The play seems out for an almost infinite run.
Don't mind a little thing like the actors fighting.
The only thing I worry about is the sun.
We'll be all right if nothing goes wrong with the lighting.

WALLACE STEVENS   (1879–1955)

DOMINATION OF BLACK

At night, by the fire,
The colors of the bushes
And of the fallen leaves,
Repeating themselves,
Turned in the room,   5
Like the leaves themselves
Turning in the wind.
Yes: but the color of the heavy hemlocks
Came striding.
And I remembered the cry of the peacocks.   10

The colors of their tails
Were like the leaves themselves
Turning in the wind,
In the twilight wind.
They swept over the room,   15
Just as they flew from the boughs of the hemlocks
Down to the ground.
I heard them cry—the peacocks.
Was it a cry against the twilight
Or against the leaves themselves   20
Turning in the wind,
Turning as the flames
Turned in the fire,
Turning as the tails of the peacocks
Turned in the loud fire,   25
Loud as the hemlocks
Full of the cry of the peacocks?
Or was it a cry against the hemlocks?

Out of the window,
I saw how the planets gathered   30
Like the leaves themselves
Turning in the wind.
I saw how the night came,
Came striding like the color of the heavy hemlocks
I felt afraid.   35
And I remembered the cry of the peacocks.

THIRTEEN WAYS OF LOOKING AT A BLACKBIRD

I

Among twenty snowy mountains,
The only moving thing
Was the eye of the blackbird.

II

I was of three minds,
Like a tree   5
In which there are three blackbirds.

III

The blackbird whirled in the autumn winds.
It was a small part of the pantomime.

IV

A man and a woman
Are one.   10
A man and a woman and a blackbird
Are one.

V

I do not know which to prefer,
The beauty of inflections
Or the beauty of innuendoes,   15
The blackbird whistling
Or just after.

VI

Icicles filled the long window
With barbaric glass.
The shadow of the blackbird   20
Crossed it, to and fro.
The mood
Traced in the shadow
An indecipherable cause.

VII

O thin men of Haddam,   25
Why do you imagine golden birds?
Do you not see how the blackbird
Walks around the feet
Of the women about you?

VIII

I know noble accents
And lucid, inescapable rhythms;   30

But I know, too,
That the blackbird is involved
In what I know.

IX

When the blackbird flew out of sight,   35
It marked the edge
Of one of many circles.

X

At the sight of blackbirds
Flying in a green light,
Even the bawds of euphony   40
Would cry out sharply.

XI

He rode over Connecticut
In a glass coach.
Once, a fear pierced him,
In that he mistook   45
The shadow of his equipage
For blackbirds.

XII

The river is moving.
The blackbird must be flying.

XIII

It was evening all afternoon.   50
It was snowing
And it was going to snow.
The blackbird sat
In the cedar-limbs.

THE HOUSE WAS QUIET AND THE WORLD WAS CALM

The house was quiet and the world was calm.
The reader became the book; and summer night

Was like the conscious being of the book.
The house was quiet and the world was calm.

The words were spoken as if there was no book,   5
Except that the reader leaned above the page,

Wanted to lean, wanted much most to be
The scholar to whom his book is true, to whom

The summer night is like a perfection of thought.
The house was quiet because it had to be.   10

The quiet was part of the meaning, part of the mind:
The access of perfection to the page.

And the world was calm. The truth in a calm world,
In which there is no other meaning, itself

Is calm, itself is summer and night, itself   15
Is the reader leaning late and reading there.

("So-and-So Reclining on Her Couch," p. 33.)

D. H. LAWRENCE   (1885–1930)

SNAKE

A snake came to my water-trough
On a hot, hot day, and I in pyjamas for the heat,
To drink there.

In the deep, strange-scented shade of the great dark carobtree
I came down the steps with my pitcher   5
And must wait, must stand and wait, for there he was at the trough
    before me.

He reached down from a fissure in the earth-wall in the gloom
And trailed his yellow-brown slackness soft-bellied down, over the
    edge of the stone trough
And rested his throat upon the stone bottom,
And where the water had dripped from the tap, in a small clearness,   10
He sipped with his straight mouth,
Softly drank through his straight gums, into his slack long body,
Silently.

Someone was before me at my water-trough,
And I, like a second comer, waiting.   15

He lifted his head from his drinking, as cattle do,
And looked at me vaguely, as drinking cattle do,
And flickered his two-forked tongue from his lips, and mused a
    moment,
And stooped and drank a little more,
Being earth-brown, earth-golden from the burning bowels of the
    earth   20
On the day of Sicilian July, with Etna smoking.

The voice of my education said to me
He must be killed,
For in Sicily the black, black snakes are innocent, the gold are ven-
    omous.

And voices in me said, If you were a man   25
You would take a stick and break him now, and finish him off.

But must I confess how I liked him,
How glad I was he had come like a guest in quiet, to drink at my
    water-trough
And depart peaceful, pacified, and thankless,
Into the burning bowels of this earth?   30

Was it cowardice that I dared not kill him?
Was it perversity, that I longed to talk to him?
Was it humility to feel so honored?
I felt so honored.

And yet those voices: 35
If you were not afraid, you would kill him!

And truly I was afraid, I was most afraid,
But even so, honored still more
That he should seek my hospitality
From out the dark door of the secret earth.   40

He drank enough
And lifted his head, dreamily, as one who has drunken,
And flickered his tongue like a forked night on the air, so black;
Seeming to lick his lips,
And looked around like a god, unseeing, into the air,   45
And slowly turned his head,
And slowly, very slowly, as if thrice adream,
Proceeded to draw his slow length curving round
And climb again the broken bank of my wall-face.

And as he put his head into that dreadful hole,   50
And as he slowly drew up, snake-easing his shoulders, and entered
    farther,
A sort of horror, a sort of protest against his withdrawing into that
    horrid black hole,
Deliberately going into the blackness, and slowly drawing himself
    after,
Overcame me now his back was turned.

I looked round, I put down my pitcher,   55
I picked up a clumsy log
And threw it at the water-trough with a clatter.

I think it did not hit him,
But suddenly that part of him that was left behind convulsed in un-
    dignified haste,
Writhed like lightning, and was gone   60
Into the black hole, the earth-lipped fissure in the wall-front,
At which, in the intense still noon, I stared with fascination.

And immediately I regretted it.
I thought how paltry, how vulgar, what a mean act!
I despised myself and the voices of my accursed human education.   65

And I thought of the albatross,
And wished he would come back, my snake.

For he seemed to me again like a king,
Like a king in exile, uncrowned in the underworld,
Now due to be crowned again.   70

And so, I missed my chance with one of the lords
Of life.
And I have something to expiate;
A pettiness.

("The Song of a Man Who Has Come Through," p. 120; "To Be Superior," p. 120; "What Ails Thee?—," p. 31; "Puss-Puss," p. 135; "The English Are So Nice!," p. 39; "Glory of Darkness," p. 157; "Bavarian Gentians," p. 158.)

EZRA POUND (1885–   )

THE TOMB AT AKR ÇAAR

"I am thy soul, Nikoptis. I have watched
These five millennia, and thy dead eyes
Moved not, nor ever answer my desire,
And thy light limbs, wherethrough I leapt aflame,
Burn not with me nor any saffron thing.   5

See, the light grass sprang up to pillow thee,
And kissed thee with a myriad grassy tongues;
But not thou me.
I have read out the gold upon the wall,
And wearied out my thought upon the signs.   10
And there is no new thing in all this place.

I have been kind. See, I have left the jars sealed,
Lest thou shouldst wake and whimper for thy wine.
And all thy robes I have kept smooth on thee.

O thou unmindful! How should I forget!   15
—Even the river many days ago,
The river? thou wast over young.
And three souls came upon Thee—
And I came.
And I flowed in upon thee, beat them off;   20
I have been intimate with thee, known thy ways.
Have I not touched thy palms and finger-tips,
Flowed in, and through thee and about thy heels?
How 'came I in'? Was I not thee and Thee?

And no sun comes to rest me in this place,   25
And I am torn against the jagged dark,
And no light beats upon me, and you say
No word, day after day.

Oh! I could get me out, despite the marks
And all their crafty work upon the door,   30
Out through the glass-green fields. . . .

*   *   *   *

Yet it is quiet here:
I do not go."

A VIRGINAL

No, no! Go from me. I have left her lately.
I will not spoil my sheath with lesser brightness,
For my surrounding air hath a new lightness;
Slight are her arms, yet they have bound me straitly
And left me cloaked as with a gauze of ether;   5
As with sweet leaves; as with subtle clearness.
Oh, I have picked up magic in her nearness
To sheathe me half in half the things that sheathe her.
No, no! Go from me. I have still the flavor,
Soft as spring wind that's come from birchen bowers.   10
Green come the shoots, aye April in the branches,
As winter's wound with her sleight hand she staunches,
Hath of the trees a likeness of the savor:
As white their bark, so white this lady's hours.

T. S. ELIOT (1888–1965)

THE LOVE SONG OF
J. ALFRED PRUFROCK

S'io credesse che mia risposta fosse
A persona che mai tornasse al mondo,
Questa fiamma staria senza piu scosse.
Ma perciocche giammai di questo fondo
Non torno vivo alcun, s'i'odo il vero,
Senza tema d'infamia ti rispondo.*

* *S'io credesse:* in Dante's *Inferno,* words addressed to Dante by a soul in Hell:

> *If I suspected I were speaking to one*
>   *Who someday might return to see the world,*
>   *Certainly this flame would cease to flicker.*
> *But since no one, if I have heard the truth,*
>   *Ever returns alive from this deep pit,*
>   *Without fear of dishonor I answer you.*

Let us go then, you and I,
When the evening is spread out against the sky
Like a patient etherized upon a table;
Let us go, through certain half-deserted streets,
The muttering retreats   5
Of restless nights in one-night cheap hotels
And sawdust restaurants with oyster-shells:
Streets that follow like a tedious argument
Of insidious intent
To lead you to an overwhelming question. . .   10
Oh, do not ask, "What is it?"
Let us go and make our visit.

In the room the women come and go
Talking of Michelangelo.

The yellow fog that rubs its back upon the window-panes,   15
The yellow smoke that rubs its muzzle on the window-panes
Licked its tongue into the corners of the evening,
Lingered upon the pools that stand in drains,
Let fall upon its back the soot that falls from chimneys,
Slipped by the terrace, made a sudden leap,   20
And seeing that it was a soft October night,
Curled once about the house, and fell asleep.

And indeed there will be time
For the yellow smoke that slides along the street,
Rubbing its back upon the window-panes;   25
There will be time, there will be time
To prepare a face to meet the faces that you meet;
There will be time to murder and create,
And time for all the works and days of hands
That lift and drop a question on your plate;   30
Time for you and time for me,
And time yet for a hundred indecisions,
And for a hundred visions and revisions,
Before the taking of a toast and tea.

In the room the women come and go   35
Talking of Michelangelo.

And indeed there will be time
To wonder, "Do I dare?" and, "Do I dare?"
Time to turn back and descend the stair,
With a bald spot in the middle of my hair—   40
[They will say: "How his hair is growing thin!"]
My morning coat, my collar mounting firmly to the chin,
My necktie rich and modest, but asserted by a simple pin—
[They will say: "But how his arms and legs are thin!"]

Do I dare   45
Disturb the universe?
In a minute there is time
For decisions and revisions which a minute will reverse.

For I have known them all already, known them all:—
Have known the evenings, mornings, afternoons,   50
I have measured out my life with coffee spoons;
I know the voices dying with a dying fall
Beneath the music from a farther room.
   So how should I presume?

And I have known the eyes already, known them all—   55
The eyes that fix you in a formulated phrase,
And when I am formulated, sprawling on a pin,
When I am pinned and wriggling on the wall,
Then how should I begin
To spit out all the butt-ends of my days and ways?   60
   And how should I presume?

And I have known the arms already, known them all—
Arms that are braceleted and white and bare
[But in the lamplight, downed with light brown hair!]
Is it perfume from a dress   65
That makes me so digress?
Arms that lie along a table, or wrap about a shawl.
   And should I then presume?
   And how should I begin?

       .   .   .   .

Shall I say, I have gone at dusk through narrow streets   70
And watched the smoke that rises from the pipes
Of lonely men in shirt-sleeves, leaning out of windows? . . .

I should have been a pair of ragged claws
Scuttling across the floors of silent seas.

       .   .   .   .

And the afternoon, the evening, sleeps so peacefully!   75
Smoothed by long fingers,
Asleep . . . tired . . . or it malingers,
Stretched on the floor, here beside you and me.
Should I, after tea and cakes and ices,
Have the strength to force the moment to its crisis?   80
But though I have wept and fasted, wept and prayed,
Though I have seen my head [grown slightly bald] brought in
    upon a platter,
I am no prophet—and here's no great matter;
I have seen the moment of my greatness flicker,

And I have seen the eternal Footman hold my coat, and snicker,   85
And in short, I was afraid.

And would it have been worth it, after all,
After the cups, the marmalade, the tea,
Among the porcelain, among some talk of you and me,
Would it have been worth while,   90
To have bitten off the matter with a smile,
To have squeezed the universe into a ball
To roll it toward some overwhelming question,
To say: "I am Lazarus, come from the dead,
Come back to tell you all, I shall tell you all"—   95
If one, settling a pillow by her head,
   Should say: "That is not what I meant at all.
   That is not it, at all."

And would it have been worth it, after all,
Would it have been worth while,   100
After the sunsets and the dooryards and the sprinkled streets,
After the novels, after the teacups, after the skirts that trail along
   the floor—
And this, and so much more?—
It is impossible to say just what I mean!
But as if a magic lantern threw the nerves in patterns on a screen: 105
Would it have been worth while
If one, settling a pillow or throwing off a shawl,
And turning toward the window, should say:
   "That is not it at all,
   That is not what I meant, at all."   110

        .   .   .   .   .   .

No! I am not Prince Hamlet, nor was meant to be;
Am an attendant lord, one that will do
To swell a progress, start a scene or two,
Advise the prince; no doubt, an easy tool,
Deferential, glad to be of use,   115
Politic, cautious, and meticulous;
Full of high sentence, but a bit obtuse;
At times, indeed, almost ridiculous—
Almost, at times, the Fool.

I grow old . . . I grow old . . .   120
I shall wear the bottoms of my trousers rolled.

Shall I part my hair behind? Do I dare to eat a peach?
I shall wear white flannel trousers, and walk upon the beach.
I have heard the mermaids singing, each to each.

I do not think that they will sing to me.   125

I have seen them riding seaward on the waves
Combing the white hair of the waves blown back
When the wind blows the water white and black.

We have lingered in the chambers of the sea
By sea-girls wreathed with seaweed red and brown   130
Till human voices wake us, and we drown.

RHAPSODY ON A WINDY NIGHT

Twelve o'clock.
Along the reaches of the street
Held in a lunar synthesis,
Whispering lunar incantations
Dissolve the floors of memory   5
And all its clear relations
Its divisions and precisions,
Every street-lamp that I pass
Beats like a fatalistic drum,
And through the spaces of the dark   10
Midnight shakes the memory
As a madman shakes a dead geranium.

Half-past one,
The street-lamp sputtered,
The street-lamp muttered,   15
The street-lamp said, "Regard that woman
Who hesitates toward you in the light of the door
Which opens on her like a grin.
You see the border of her dress
Is torn and stained with sand,   20
And you see the corner of her eye
Twists like a crooked pin."

The memory throws up high and dry
A crowd of twisted things;
A twisted branch upon the beach   25
Eaten smooth, and polished
As if the world gave up
The secret of its skeleton,
Stiff and white.
A broken spring in a factory yard,   30
Rust that clings to the form that the strength has left
Hard and curled and ready to snap.

Half-past two,
The street-lamp said,

"Remark the cat which flattens itself in the gutter,   35
Slips out its tongue
And devours a morsel of rancid butter."
So the hand of the child, automatic,
Slipped out and pocketed a toy that was running along the quay.
I could see nothing behind that child's eye.   40
I have seen eyes in the street
Trying to peer through lighted shutters,
And a crab one afternoon in a pool,
An old crab with barnacles on his back,
Gripped the end of a stick which I held him.   45

Half-past three,
The lamp sputtered,
The lamp muttered in the dark.
The lamp hummed:
"Regard the moon,   50
La lune ne garde aucune rancune,
She winks with a feeble eye,
She smiles into corners.
She smooths the hair of the grass.
The moon has lost her memory.   55
A washed-out smallpox cracks her face,
Her hand twists a paper rose,
That smells of dust and eau de Cologne,
She is alone
With all the old nocturnal smells   60
That cross and cross her brain."
The reminiscence comes
Of sunless dry geraniums
And dust in crevices,
Smells of chestnuts in the streets,   65
And female smells in shuttered rooms,
And cigarettes in corridors
And cocktail smells in bars.

The lamp said,
"Four o'clock,   70
Here is the number on the door.
Memory!
You have the key,
The little lamp spreads a ring on the stair.
Mount.   75
The bed is open; the tooth-brush hangs on the wall,
Put your shoes at the door, sleep, prepare for life."
The last twist of the knife.

THE HOLLOW MEN

A penny for the Old Guy

I

We are the hollow men
We are the stuffed men
Leaning together
Headpiece filled with straw. Alas!
Our dried voices, when   5
We whisper together
Are quiet and meaningless
As wind in dry grass
Or rat's feet over broken glass
In our dry cellar   10

Shape without form, shade without color,
Paralyzed force, gesture without motion;

Those who have crossed
With direct eyes, to death's other Kingdom
Remember us—if at all—not as lost   15
Violent souls, but only
As the hollow men
The stuffed men.

II

Eyes I dare not meet in dreams
In death's dream kingdom   20
These do not appear:
There, the eyes are
Sunlight on a broken column
There, is a tree swinging
And voices are   25
In the wind's singing
More distant and more solemn
Than a fading star.

Let me be no nearer
In death's dream kingdom   30
Let me also wear
Such deliberate disguises
Rat's skin, crowskin, crossed staves
In a field
Behaving as the wind behaves   35
No nearer—

Not that final meeting
In the twilight kingdom

III

This is the dead land
This is cactus land   40
Here the stone images
Are raised, here they receive
The supplication of a dead man's hand
Under the twinkle of a fading star.
Is it like this   45
In death's other kingdom
Waking alone
At the hour when we are
Trembling with tenderness
Lips that would kiss   50
Form prayers to broken stone.

IV

The eyes are not here
There are no eyes here
In this valley of dying stars
In this hollow valley   55
This broken jaw of our lost kingdoms
In this last of meeting places
We grope together
And avoid speech
Gathered on this beach of the tumid river   60
Sightless, unless
The eyes reappear
As the perpetual star
Multifoliate rose
Of death's twilight kingdom   65
The hope only
Of empty men.

V

Here we go round the prickly pear
Prickly pear prickly pear
Here we go round the prickly pear   70
At five o'clock in the morning.
Between the idea
And the reality
Between the motion
And the act   75
Falls the Shadow
          For Thine is the Kingdom

Between the conception
And the creation
Between the emotion   80
And the response
Falls the Shadow
                Life is very long

Between the desire
And the spasm   85
Between the potency
And the existence
Between the essence
And the descent
Falls the Shadow   90
           For Thine is the Kingdom

For Thine is
Life is
For Thine is the

This is the way the world ends   95
This is the way the world ends
This is the way the world ends
Not with a bang but a whimper.

CONRAD AIKEN (1889–   )

DEAD LEAF IN MAY

One skeleton-leaf, white-ribbed, a last year's leaf,
Skipped in a paltry gust, whizzed from the dust,
Leapt the small dusty puddle; and sailing then
Merrily in the sunlight, lodged itself
Between two blossoms in a hawthorn tree.   5
That was the moment: and the world was changed.
With that insane gay skeleton of a leaf
A world of dead worlds flew to hawthorn trees,
Lodged in the green forks, rattled, rattled their ribs
(As loudly as a dead leaf's ribs can rattle)   10
Blithely, among beds and blossoms. I cursed,
I shook my stick, dislodged it. To what end?
Its ribs, and all the ribs of all dead worlds,
Would house them now forever as death should:
Cheek by jowl with May.   15

That was the moment: and my brain flew open
Like a ripe bursting pod. The seed sprang out,

And I was withered, and had given all.
Ripeness at top means rottenness beneath:
The brain divulging seed, the heart is empty: 20
The little blood goes through it like quicksilver:
The hand is leather, and the world is lost.

Human, who trudge the road from Here to There:
Lock the dry oak-leaf's flimsy skeleton
In auricle or ventricle; sail it   25
Like a gay ship down red Aorta's flood.
Be the paired blossoms with dead ribs between.
Thirst in the There, that you may drink the Here.

WILFRED OWEN (1893–1918)

HAS YOUR SOUL SIPPED?

Has your soul sipped
    Of the sweetness of all sweets?
Has it well supped
    But yet hungers and sweats?

I have been witness   5
    Of a strange sweetness,
All fancy surpassing
    Past all supposing.

Passing the rays
    Of the rubies of morning,   10
Or the soft rise
    Of the moon; or the meaning
Known to the rose
    Of her mystery and mourning.

Sweeter than nocturnes   15
    Of the wild nightingale
Or than love's nectar
    After life's gall.

Sweeter than odors
    Of living leaves,   20
Sweeter than ardors
    Of dying loves.

Sweeter than death
    And dreams hereafter
To one in dearth   25
    Of life and its laughter.

Or the proud wound
    The victor wears
Or the last end
    Of all wars.   30

Or the sweet murder
    After long guard
Unto the martyr
    Smiling at God;

To me was that Smile,   35
    Faint as a wan, worn myth,
Faint and exceeding small,
    On a boy's murdered mouth.

Though from his throat
    The life-tide leapt   40
There was no threat
    On his lips.

But with the bitter blood
    And the death-smell
All his life's sweetness bled   45
    Into a smile.

GREATER LOVE

Red lips are not so red
    As the stained stones kissed by the English dead.
Kindness of wooed and wooer
Seems shame to their love pure.
O Love, your eyes lose lure   5
    When I behold eyes blinded in my stead!

Your slender attitude
    Trembles not exquisite like limbs knife-skewed,
Rolling and rolling there
Where God seems not to care;   10
Till the fierce love they bear
    Cramps them in death's extreme decrepitude.

Your voice sings not so soft,—
    Though even as wind murmuring through raftered loft,—
Your dear voice is not dear,   15
Gentle, and evening clear,
As theirs whom none now hear,
    Now earth has stopped their piteous mouths that coughed.

Heart, you were never hot
    Nor large, nor full like hearts made great with shot;   20

And though your hand be pale,
Paler are all which trail
Your cross through flame and hail;
 Weep, you may weep, for you may touch them not.

A TERRE

(Being the philosophy of many soldiers)

Sit on the bed. I'm blind, and three parts shell.
Be careful; can't shake hands now; never shall.
Both arms have mutinied against me,—brutes.
My fingers fidget like ten idle brats.

I tried to peg out soldierly,—no use!   5
One dies of war like any old disease.
This bandage feels like pennies on my eyes.
I have my medals?—Discs to make eyes close.
My glorious ribbons?—Ripped from my own back
In scarlet shreds. (That's for your poetry book.)   10

A short life and a merry one, my buck!
We used to say we'd hate to live dead-old,—
Yet now. . . . I'd willingly be puffy, bald,
And patriotic. Buffers catch from boys
At least the jokes hurled at them. I suppose   15
Little I'd ever teach a son, but hitting,
Shooting, war, hunting, all the arts of hurting.
Well, that's what I learnt,—that, and making money.

Your fifty years ahead seem none too many?
Tell me how long I've got? God! For one year   20
To help myself to nothing more than air!
One spring! Is one too good to spare, too long?
Spring wind would work its own way to my lung,
And grow me legs as quick as lilac-shoots.

My servant's lamed, but listen how he shouts!   25
When I'm lugged out, he'll still be good for that.
Here in this mummy-case, you know, I've thought
How well I might have swept his floors for ever.
I'd ask no nights off when the bustle's over,
Enjoying so the dirt. Who's prejudiced   30
Against a grimed hand when his own's quite dust,
Less live than specks that in the sun-shafts turn,
Less warm than dust that mixes with arms' tan?
I'd love to be a sweep, now, black as Town,
Yes, or a muckman. Must I be his load?   35

O Life, Life, let me breathe,—a dug-out rat!
Not worse than ours the existences rats lead—
Nosing along at night down some safe rut,
They find a shell-proof home before they rot.
Dead men may envy living mites in cheese,   40
Or good germs even. Microbes have their joys,
And subdivide, and never come to death.
Certainly flowers have the easiest time on earth.
"I shall be one with nature, herb, and stone,"
Shelley would tell me. Shelley would be stunned: 45
The dullest Tommy hugs that fancy now.
"Pushing up daisies" is their creed, you know.
To grain, then, go my fat, to buds my sap,
For all the usefulness there is in soap.
D'you think the Boche will ever stew man-soup?   50
Some day, no doubt, if . . .

                           Friend, be very sure
I shall be better off with plants that share
More peaceably the meadow and the shower.
Soft rains will touch me,—as they could touch once,
And nothing but the sun shall make me ware.   55
Your guns may crash around me. I'll not hear;
Or, if I wince, I shall not know I wince.
Don't take my soul's poor comfort for your jest.
Soldiers may grow a soul when turned to fronds,
But here the thing's best left at home with friends.   60

My soul's a little grief, grappling your chest,
To climb your throat on sobs; easily chased
On other sighs and wiped by fresher winds.

Carry my crying spirit till it's weaned
To do without what blood remained these wounds.   65

("Shadwell Stair," p. 32; "Insensibility," p. 24; "Anthem for Doomed Youth,"
p. 159.)

E. E. CUMMINGS   (1894–1962)

ALL IN GREEN WENT MY LOVE RIDING

    All in green went my love riding
    on a great horse of gold
    into the silver dawn.

    four lean hounds crouched low and smiling
    the merry deer ran before.   5

Fleeter be they than dappled dreams
the swift sweet deer
the red rare deer.

Four red roebuck at a white water
the cruel bugle sang before.   10

Horn at hip went my love riding
riding the echo down
into the silver dawn.

four lean hounds crouched low and smiling
the level meadows ran before.   15

Softer be they than slippered sleep
the lean lithe deer
the fleet flown deer.

Four fleet does at a gold valley
the famished arrow sang before.   20

Bow at belt went my love riding
riding the mountain down
into the silver dawn.

four lean hounds crouched low and smiling
the sheer peaks ran before.   25

Paler be they than daunting death
the sleek slim deer
the tall tense deer.

Four tall stags at a green mountain
the lucky hunter sang before.   30

All in green went my love riding
on a great horse of gold
into the silver dawn.

four lean hounds crouched low and smiling
my heart fell dead before.   35

("Humanity i love you," p. 126.)

ROBERT GRAVES (1895–   )

THE THIEVES

Lovers in the act dispense
With such meum-teum sense

As might warningly reveal
What they must not pick or steal,
And their nostrum is to say: 5
"I and you are both away."

After, when they disentwine
Your from me and yours from mine,
Neither can be certain who
Was that I whose mine was you.   10
To the act again they go
More completely not to know.

Theft is theft and raid is raid
Though reciprocally made.
Lovers, the conclusion is   15
Doubled sighs and jealousies
In a single heart that grieves
For lost honor among thieves.

("Hell," p. 21; "The Philosopher," p. 16.)

HART CRANE   (1899–1932)

GARDEN ABSTRACT

The apple on its bough is her desire,—
Shining suspension, mimic of the sun.
The bough has caught her breath up, and her voice,
Dumbly articulate in the slant and rise
Of branch on branch above her, blurs her eyes.   5
She is a prisoner of the tree and its green fingers.

And so she comes to dream herself the tree,
The wind possessing her, weaving her young veins,
Holding her to the sky and its quick blue,
Drowning the fever of her hands in sunlight.   10
She has no memory, nor fear, nor hope
Beyond the grass and shadows at her feet.

MOMENT FUGUE

The syphilitic selling violets calmly
        and daisies
By the subway news-stand knows
                how hyacinths

This April morning offers 5
  hurriedly
In bunches sorted freshly—
  and bestows
On every purchaser
  (of heaven perhaps) 10

His eyes—
  like crutches hurtled against glass
Fall mute and sudden (dealing change
  for lilies)
Beyond the roses that the flesh can pass. 15

W. H. AUDEN   (1907–   )

SEXT

I

You need not see what someone is doing
to know if it is his vocation,

you have only to watch his eyes:
a cook mixing a sauce, a surgeon

making a primary incision, 5
a clerk completing a bill of lading,

wear the same rapt expression,
forgetting themselves in a function.

How beautiful it is,
that eye-on-the-object look. 10

To ignore the appetitive goddesses,
to desert the formidable shrines

of Rhea, Aphrodite, Demeter, Diana,
to pray instead to St. Phocas,

St. Barbara, San Saturnino, 15
or whoever one's patron is,

that one may be worthy of their mystery,
what a prodigious step to have taken.

There should be monuments, there should be odes,
to the nameless heroes who took it first, 20

to the first flaker of flints
who forgot his dinner,

the first collector of sea-shells
to remain celibate.

Where should we be but for them?   25
Feral still, un-housetrained, still

wandering through forests without
a consonant to our names,

slaves of Dame Kind, lacking
all notions of a city   30

and, at this noon, for this death,
there would be no agents.

II

You need not hear what orders he is giving
to know if someone has authority,

you have only to watch his mouth: 35
when a besieging general sees

a city wall breached by his troops,
when a bacteriologist

realizes in a flash what was wrong
with his hypothesis when,   40

from a glance at the jury, the prosecutor
knows the defendant will hang,

their lips and the lines around them
relax, assuming an expression

not of simple pleasure at getting   45
their own sweet way but of satisfaction

at being right, an incarnation
of *Fortitude, Justica, Nous.*

You may not like them much
(Who does?) but we owe them   50

basilicas, divas,
dictionaries, pastoral verse,

the courtesies of the city:
without these judicial mouths

(which belong for the most part   55
to very great scoundrels)

how squalid existence would be,
tethered for life to some hut village,

afraid of the local snake
or the local ford demon,   60

speaking the local patois
of some three hundred words

(think of the family squabbles and the
poison-pens, think of the inbreeding)

and, at this noon, there would be no authority   65
to command this death.

III

Anywhere you like, somewhere
on broad-chested life-giving Earth

anywhere between her thirstlands
and undrinkable Ocean,   70

the crowd stands perfectly still,
its eyes (which seem one) and its mouths

(which seem infinitely many)
expressionless, perfectly blank.

The crowd does not see (what everyone sees)   75
a boxing match, a train wreck,

a battleship being launched,
does not wonder (as everyone wonders)

who will win, what flag she will fly,
how many will be burned alive,   80

is never distracted
(as everyone is always distracted)

by a barking dog, a smell of fish,
a mosquito on a bald head:

the crowd sees only one thing   85
(which only the crowd can see)

an epiphany of that
which does whatever is done.

Whatever god a person believes in,
in whatever way he believes,   90

(no two are exactly alike)
as one of the crowd he believes

and only believes in that
in which there is only one way of believing.

Few people accept each other and most   95
will never do anything properly,

but the crowd rejects no one, joining the crowd
is the only thing all men can do.

Only because of that can we say
all men are our brothers,   100

superior, because of that,
to the social exoskeletons: When

have they ever ignored their queens,
for one second stopped work

on their provincial cities, to worship   105
The Prince of this world like us,

at this noon, on this hill,
in the occasion of this dying.

STEPHEN SPENDER (1909–   )

WEEP, GIRL, WEEP

Weep, girl, weep, for you have cause to weep.
His face is uprooted from your sleep,
His eyes torn from your eyes, dream from your dream.
Where you were by the window all one night
A million stars wore too faint a light   5
To show his machine
Plunge dark through dark out of sight.

The wet tears on your face gleam
Down spires of the cathedral,
And in the crowded squares your lament   10
Makes a great angel whose instrument
Is strung on the heart behind the face of all.

LAWRENCE DURRELL   (1912–   )

NEMEA

A song in the valley of Nemea:
Sing quiet, quite quiet here.

Song for the brides of Argos
Combing the swarms of golden hair:
Quite quiet, quiet there.   5

Under the rolling comb of grass,
The sword outrusts the golden helm.

Agamemnon under tumulus serene
Outsmiles the jury of skeletons:
Cool under cumulus the lion queen: 10

Only the drum can celebrate,
Only the adjective outlive them.

A song in the valley of Nemea:
Sing quiet, quiet, quiet here.

Tone of the frog in the empty well,   15
Drone of the bald bee on the cold skull,

Quiet, Quiet, Quiet.

DYLAN THOMAS   (1914–1953)

THE FORCE THAT THROUGH THE GREEN FUSE
DRIVES THE FLOWER

The force that through the green fuse drives the flower
Drives my green age; that blasts the roots of trees
Is my destroyer.
And I am dumb to tell the crooked rose
My youth is bent by the same wintry fever.   5

The force that drives the water through the rocks
Drives my red blood; that dries the mouthing streams
Turns mine to wax.
And I am dumb to mouth unto my veins
How at the mountain spring the same mouth sucks.   10

The hand that whirls the water in the pool
Stirs the quicksand; that ropes the blowing wind
Hauls my shroud sail.
And I am dumb to tell the hanging man
How of my clay is made the hangman's lime.   15

The lips of time leech to the fountain head;
Love drips and gathers, but the fallen blood
Shall calm her sores.
And I am dumb to tell a weather's wind
How time has ticked a heaven round the stars.   20

And I am dumb to tell the lover's tomb
How at my sheet goes the same crooked worm.

IN MY CRAFT OR SULLEN ART

In my craft or sullen art
Exercised in the still night
When only the moon rages
And the lovers lie abed
With all their griefs in their arms,   5
I labor by singing light
Not for ambition or bread
Or the strut and trade of charms
On the ivory stages
But for the common wages   10
Of their most secret heart.
Not for the proud man apart
From the raging moon I write
On these spindrift pages
Not for the towering dead   15
With their nightingales and psalms
But for the lovers, their arms
Round the griefs of the ages,
Who pay no praise or wages
Nor heed my craft or art.   20

("A Refusal to Mourn the Death, by Fire, of a Child in London," p. 18.)

ROBERT LOWELL   (1917–   )

COMMANDER LOWELL
1888–1949

There were no undesirables or girls in my set,
when I was a boy at Mattapoisett—

only Mother, still her Father's daughter.
Her voice was still electric
with a hysterical, unmarried panic,   5
when she read to me from the Napoleon book.
Long-nosed Marie Louise
Hapsburg in the frontispiece
had a downright Boston bashfulness,
where she grovelled to Bonaparte, who scratched his navel,   10
and bolted his food—just my seven years tall!
And I, bristling and manic,
skulked in the attic,
and got two hundred French generals by name,
from *A* to *V*—from Augereau to Vandamme.   15
I used to dope myself asleep,
naming those unpronounceables like sheep.

Having a naval officer
for my Father was nothing to shout
about to the summer colony at "Matt."   20
He wasn't at all "serious,"
when he showed up on the golf course,
wearing a blue serge jacket and numbly cut
white ducks he'd bought
at a Pearl Harbor commissariat . . .   25
and took four shots with his putter to sink his putt.
"Bob," they said, "golf's a game you really ought to know how to play,
if you play at all."

They wrote him off as "naval,"
naturally supposed his sport was sailing.   30
Poor Father, his training was engineering!
Cheerful and cowed
among the seadogs at the Sunday yacht club,
he was never one of the crowd.

"Anchors aweigh," Daddy boomed in his bathtub,   35
"Anchors aweigh,"
when Lever Brothers offered to pay
him double what the Navy paid.
I nagged for his dress sword with gold braid,
and cringed because Mother, new   40
caps on all her teeth, was born anew
at forty. With seamanlike celerity,
Father left the Navy,
and deeded Mother his property.

He was soon fired. Year after year,   45
he still hummed "Anchors aweigh" in the tub—

whenever he left a job,
he bought a smarter car.
Father's last employer
was Scudder, Stevens and Clark, Investment Advisors,   50
himself his only client.
While Mother dragged to bed alone,
read Menninger,
and grew more and more suspicious,
he grew defiant.   55
Night after night,
à la clarté déserte de sa lampe,
he slid his ivory Annapolis slide rule
across a pad of graphs—
piker speculations! In three years   60
he squandered sixty thousand dollars.

Smiling on all,
Father was once successful enough to be lost
in the mob of ruling-class Bostonians.
As early as 1928,   65
he owned a house converted to oil,
and redecorated by the architect
of St. Mark's School. . . . Its main effect
was a drawing room, "longitudinal as Versailles,"
its ceiling, roughened with oatmeal, was blue as the sea.   70
And once
nineteen, the youngest ensign in his class,
he was "the old man" of a gunboat on the Yangtze.

THOM GUNN   (1929–   )

THE UNSETTLED MOTORCYCLIST'S VISION
OF HIS DEATH

Across the open countryside,
Into the walls of rain I ride.
It beats my cheek, drenches my knees,
But I am being what I please.

The firm heath stops, and marsh begins.   5
Now we're at war: whichever wins
My human will cannot submit
To nature, though brought out of it.
The wheels sink deep; the clear sound blurs:
Still, bent on the handle-bars,   10
I urge my chosen instrument

Against the mere embodiment.
The front wheel wedges fast between
Two shrubs of glazed insensate green
—Gigantic order in the rim   15
Of each flat leaf. Black eddies brim
Around my heel which, pressing deep,
Accelerates the waiting sleep.

I used to live in sound, and lacked
Knowledge of still or creeping fact.   20
But now the stagnant strips my breath,
Leant on my cheek in weight of death.
Though so oppressed I find I may
Through substance move. I pick my way,
Where death and life in one combine,   25
Through the dark earth that is not mine,
Crowded with fragments, blunt, unformed;
While past my ear where noises swarmed
The marsh plant's white extremities,
Slow without patience, spread at ease   30
Invulnerable and soft, extend
With a quiet grasping toward their end.

And though the tubers, once I rot,
Reflesh my bones with pallid knot,
Till swelling out my clothes they feign   35
This dummy is a man again,
It is as servants they insist,
Without volition that they twist;
And habit does not leave them tired,
By men laboriously acquired.   40
Cell after cell the plants convert
My special richness in the dirt:
All that they get, they get by chance.

And multiply in ignorance.

GEORGE STARBUCK   (1931–   )

FABLE FOR FLIPPED LID

There was a rat
who, whatever
he did, never
stopped getting fat-
ter and fatter fast-   5
er and faster till at last . . .

but I mustn't get
ahead of my story.
The laboratory
had to keep set-   10

ting him tougher and tougher problems . . . ENOUGH!

I must be chron-
ological.
One. They all   15
had to run

mazes. Two.
When they got through

a maze the prize
was food. Thirdly,   20
the more hurriedly,
the more size-

able. Fourthly, the more
. . . What was four?

Listen, I ran   25
this lab, and it wasn't
so very pleasant
having him an-

swer the questions quick
as the staff could pick   30
them out of the dic-
tionary IT MAKES ME SICK

all this bother about who
ate up the Grant.
I asked him "Well can't   35
you stop?" "Dunno how to,"

he said, "I hate
being overweight,

but in the heat
of competition   40
I've no volition:
I just compete.

I get carried away.
I'd eat Cape May

if I won it." I would-   45
n't put it past him.

One day I asked him
if he was so good

why didn't he
go on TV   50

and make a hundred
and sixty-four
grand, and what's more,
he did. I wondered

where it would lead to,   55
but I didn't need to:

he choked on a room-
ful of non-retur-
nable furniture
from "Bride and Groom."   60

INDEX

Italicized numbers indicate pages on which the full text of a poem first appears. If a poem appears more than once, subsequent page numbers are not italicized.

347

7 200